INTERNATIONAL RAILWAY ECONOMICS

To Duncan and Pod

International Railway Economics

Studies in Management and Efficiency

Edited by
K. J. BUTTON
and
D. E. PITFIELD

Gower

Published by

Gower Publishing Company Limited,
Gower House,
Croft Road,
Aldershot,
Hants, GU11 3HR
England

Gower Publishing ⸝
Old Post Road,
Brookfield,
Vermont 05036,
U.S.A.

British Library Cataloguing in Publication Data

International railway economics: studies in
    management and efficiency
    1. Railroads
    I. Button, K.J.   II. Pitfield, D.E.
    385'.1   HE1031

Library of Congress Cataloguing in Publication Data

International railway economics
    Includes bibliographies
    1. Railroads—Management—Addresses,
        essays, lectures
    I. Button, Kenneth John
    II. Pitfield, D.E., 1949—
    HE1621.I57   1985   385'.068   85—5509

Printed in Great Britain by
Blackmore Press, Shaftesbury, Dorset

ISBN 0 566 00854 8

Contents

Figures

Tables

Contributors

D. Allen, Section Evaluation Group, British Railways Board

K.J. Button, Department of Economics, Loughborough University

J.S. Dodgson, Department of Economics, Liverpool University

B. Fullerton, Department of Geography, Newcastle University

P. Gordon, School of Urban and Regional Planning, University of Southern California

C. Grimm, College of Business and Management, University of Maryland

R.G. Harris, School of Business Administration, University of California at Berkeley

R. Kilvington, Transport Studies Unit, Oxford University

C.A. Nash, Institute for Transport Studies, University of Leeds

K.W. Ogden, Department of Civil Engineering, Monash University

S. Openshaw, Department of Geography, Newcastle University

D.E. Pitfield, Department of Transport Technology, Loughborough University

T.V.S. Ramamohan Rao, Indian Institute of Technology, Kampur

S. Sriraman, Gokhale Institute of Politics and Economics, Pune

W.G. Waters II, Faculty of Commerce and Business Administration, University of British Columbia

A.E. Whiteing, Institute of Transport Studies, University of Leeds

G. Williams, Planning Group, British Railways Board

R. Willson, School of Urban and Regional Planning, University of Southern California

Preface

Preface

This volume grew out of our concern about the lack of accessible studies dealing with railway economics. Despite the immense popular interest in the railways there seemed to be few readily available and up-to-date detailed analyses of rail performance. Most of the existing work also tends to look at the experience of a single country or system, so there is limited scope for comparative analysis.

In this book is a collection of original papers, authored by internationally recognised experts in the field of railway economics, covering what we consider to be the main economic issues confronting the railways in the 1980s. While we have exercised some editorial control and provided direction, the authors were given a free hand to present their views and findings in their own styles.

Obviously, as we are also aware, some reviewers will comment that the book does not offer a comprehensive examination of railway economics; however, that was never the intention — it is not a text-book. Neither is the method of analysis employed consistent throughout the papers — a variety of approaches were welcomed. Nevertheless, we feel the various papers do present both a clear picture of the state-of-the-art in those aspects of railway operations that are of current concern and a set of research findings which will stimulate further consideration about the way in which thinking in these areas may develop.

K.J. Button
D.E. Pitfield

1 Introduction

K. J. BUTTON AND D. E. PITFIELD

1.1 Economics and rail transport

Railways have long attracted the attention of economists. Indeed,
John Maynard Keynes during his early years showed some interest for
running one: 'I find economics increasingly satisfactory, and I think I
am rather good at it. I want to manage a railway, or organise a trust or
at least swindle the investing public' (see Skidelsky 1983: 165). Individuals' interests develop for a variety of quite personal and, frequently,
unexpressionable reasons but the particular concern of economists
with the railways may well have been stimulated by two characteristics
of the industry.

Firstly, railways are large undertakings which have in the past and,
indeed, still do play an important role in the transport systems of
most countries. While there are some (such as Fogel 1964) who have
argued that this has often been overemphasised, it is nevertheless true
that vast quantities of goods and substantial numbers of people move
over the world's various railway networks every day. Equally, while
there may be debate about the role railways played in the past in stim-
ulating economic development, it seems beyond dispute that their
immediate withdrawal would result in serious economic disruption.
Maintaining the efficiency of the railway network, therefore, has
important practical importance. Moreover there are immense amounts
of capital tied up in the industry which means there could be substantial waste without efficient management. The very importance of rail-

1

ways to the economy, therefore, is itself likely to stimulate the interests of the economic profession.

Secondly, by its nature, the railway industry poses intriguing problems for more theoretically inclined economists. It is not by accident that Alfred Marshall sharpened his ideas on social investment criteria in the context of rail activities (see Whitaker 1975) nor that seminal works on pricing policy by Harold Hotelling (1938) stemmed from the study of contemporary problems associated with defining appropriate railway tariffs. Railways are characterised by substantial sunk costs, extremely low short-run marginal costs and the joint production of a multiplicity of separate outputs. (The multi-product nature of the industry extends beyond the crude, aggregate division between passenger and freight services to the jointness of outward and return journeys at the micro level.) Recent theoretical advances in cost theory also suggest that the greatest efficiency may be attained by the monopoly provision of services with all the associated difficulties of potential exploitation of monopoly power. At the same time, and seemingly perversely, potential inter-modal competition from road transport in some sectors of the transport market, and from sea and air transport in other sectors, has meant that in modern times many railway systems have not been able to devise sustainable pricing regimes and, thus, questions of appropriate government intervention have come to the fore. Further, railways share with most other modes of transport certain characteristics (e.g. the non-storability of output; the requirement of substantial consumer inputs, such as travel time, in the overall production function; the use of mobile, externality generating plant, etc.) which themselves have proved of considerable interest to the economics fraternity in recent years.

While one can point to the stimuli which seem to have precipitated research efforts on the part of economists the actual focus of their attention on the railways sector has exhibited little stability. Economists are essentially practical people concerned very much with the specific issues of the day. Grand designs are certainly developed but work at the margin tends to be reactive in the face of prevailing problems. Consequently, as specific problems confronting an industry or regulating bodies have changed over time, so has the direction of economic research. Certainly, this would, from a historical perspective, seem to be true of economists' interest in rail transport.

Differing domestic circumstances have meant that the specific interests of economists have not at any one time always been the same across countries, although there have been remarkable similarities in approaches towards issues such as regulation and deregulation. Further, the success or otherwise of economists in convincing both governments and railway managements to adopt their ideas has been varied both

2

over time and between countries. It would prove a Herculean task to attempt a global summary of the shifts in emphasis which have occurred but a broad brush approach drawing mainly on the experiences of the United Kingdom and, to a lesser extent, the United States as case study material to provide a point of context, is enlightening.

The main concern of economists in the nineteenth century was the regulation of railway companies so that their ability to develop monopoly powers could not be extensively exploited. (See for example, Savage (1966) for an account of early UK policy and MacGill (1917) for a study of US experience.) Coupled with this, and often stemming directly from the methods of regulation adopted, was a concern that a comprehensive system of rail services would be supplied embracing often quite disparate communities. Economists spent time in examining the appropriate pricing structures to be employed to meet these ends. A succession of parliamentary acts was passed in the United Kingdom to regulate fares and, as early as 1844, the Government took powers to purchase newly formed railway companies after a period of operation. (There were also proposals — advanced, for example, by the Duke of Wellington — for the development of a National Transport Plan.) The Railroad Act of 1856 introduced the first major set of rate regulations in the United States — once again designed to prevent exploitation of customers. The contribution of economists at this time is difficult to evaluate, but they did provide improved analytical frameworks for the assessment of the effects of different regulating packages and, also, enhanced understanding of exactly how the railway industry functions.

The policies of the nineteenth century continued up until the First World War. The need for high levels of coordination plus direction of resources on a non-commercial basis led, in the United Kingdom, to the Government assuming direct control of railways and their being placed under the operational control of a single Railway Executive Committee. The rundown of the system during this period was inevitable and was to pose subsequent problems in the post-war period when private sector status was reintroduced (albeit in much larger companies under the Railway Act 1921).

The inter-war period saw a continued emphasis on treating railways within the context of mainstream industrial economics but there were also some new elements. Railways all over the world came under increased pressure during the period of international depression in the 1930s (Aldcroft 1968). The changing nature of industrial production (i.e. the decline of the traditional, bulk industries such as coal-mining and steel which made extensive use of rail transport coupled with the rise of manufacturing industry with somewhat different transport needs and often located away from the main railway arteries) combined

3

with increased competition from road transport meant that the railways were hit rather more than many other sectors during this period. Attention now turned from containing the monopoly powers of railways to developing policies for their protection in the new environment. Economic arguments were developed for restricting competition rather than freeing the railways to compete more rigorously; these were couched in terms of the potential excesses, especially market instability, which could accompany high levels of competition and the need to contain the undesirable external costs (especially relating to safety) associated with road transport. The inception of the Interstate Commerce Commission in the United States in 1935 under the Motor Carrier Act (Farris 1983) and the passing of the Road and Rail Act (1933) in the United Kingdom were both designed to restrict entry into the road freight sector. The passage of the Road Traffic Act (1930) in the United Kingdom to regulate public road passenger transport was also essentially justified on these grounds.

The immediate period after the Second World War in the United Kingdom witnessed an experimental coordination of transport activities through common ownership. Transport coordination at both the national and international level (witness the establishment of United Nations bodies to assist in the latter) attracted particular attention during this period and the particularly difficult position of the railways in the United Kingdom (stemming from road competition and disinvestment in the industry throughout the 1930s and during the war) added practical weight to political arguments for nationalisation (see Thompson and Hunter 1973). Economists' concern now shifted from treating railways as an industry and to developing appropriate policies to pursue in a public enterprise context.

The 1950s saw disillusionment in the United Kingdom with the notion of central coordination of transport, partly on philosophical grounds but also stemming from the specific experiences associated with the 1947 Act. Efforts were concentrated on the development of appropriate rules which would ensure fair competition between modes (irrespective of whether they were publicly owned or not) in a less restricted market environment (i.e coordination was to be achieved through competition). In the case of the railways questions about the recovery of fixed costs and defining appropriate methods of appraising reinvestment programmes concerned economists. As it became appreciated in the early 1960s that the railway network was excessive for the prevailing demand conditions so interest moved to developing appraisal methodologies to handle disinvestment decisions with a particular interest being shown in the way joint costs and contributory revenues should be handled. Demand analysis also began to assume the role of an increasingly important field of study after the passing of the 1962

Transport Act which gave the railways considerably more freedom to practise price discrimination.

Changing social conditions and higher real incomes altered public attitudes towards transport in the United Kingdom in the late 1960s (see Joy 1973). An increasing awareness of the environmental damage done by transport coupled with public concern to provide a social transport system led to a reduced emphasis on the purely commercial aspects of transport provision. While competition offered high levels of efficiency it needed harnessing to achieve these wider goals. Economists became involved in the development of appropriate techniques to help management meet the new demands placed upon them. Social investment criteria and marginal cost pricing were made operational through the refinement of cost-benefit analysis and social evaluation procedures. Welfare economics had assumed a central role in the making of transport policy and where social efficiency deviated significantly from financial efficiency so the market mechanism had to be 'corrected'. In the railways case this meant the introduction, on a service by service basis to stimulate managerial efficiency, of social service subsidies under the 1968 Transport Act with a restructuring of its finances to separate commercial activities from social ones.

More recently, the emphasis has once more changed. Financial payments by governments to most nationalised railway systems have risen substantially (see Pryke and Dodgson 1975), while the private companies in the United States were confronted by mounting losses in the 1970s. The reaction in the United Kingdom has been to privatise parts of British Rail activities (e.g. hotels) and to seek greater efficiency both by improving productivity of the existing system and by examining ways of changing that system (embracing both technical change — such as greater electrification — and cut-backs in the network). Strategic planning and management, together with the appropriate economic principles to apply, have been given more emphasis. The approach in the United States has been that of restructuring the industry, mainly achieved under the Revitalisation and Regulatory Reform Act of 1970, (Hilton 1983) and, following the much earlier British example, easing many of the regulations relating to inter-state transport (under the Staggers Rail Act of 1980). Strangely, while the railways were the first US transport industry to be subject to regulatory reform in the 1970s, mainly because of the financial collapse of the Northeastern system, transport economists at the time were putting more effort into analysing the effects of regulation on the road and air transport sectors.

This extremely brief and general outline of how economists have involved themselves with the problems of the railways at different times reveals the responsive nature of applied economics as well as the changing nature of the problems confronting the rail sector. We are concerned here with focusing on the contemporary problems being encountered by the world's railway systems. Thus the papers in this volume do not represent a comprehensive treatment of the application of economics to railway operations and policy but rather home in on selected contemporary issues. Railway economics is a vast topic but our understanding of the way the railway market operates is gradually being enchanced by those actively researching in the field.

1.2 The rationale for this book

Although economists have continually been interested in the workings of the railway industry the number of books looking specifically at railway economics is remarkably small. Retrospective, historical studies appear with surprising regularity but books looking at, what might be termed, 'the state-of-the-art' are somewhat rarer. This collection of papers is an attempt to partially remedy this situation. It does not completely fill the gap — a much larger work would be required to achieve this — but it does cover most of the more important issues which are currently being debated. It also reflects the differing attitudes and approaches which various groups of economists — often with primary skills in planning, management or engineering — have developed with regard to the efficient provision of railway services.

The book is divided into four broad sections covering, in turn, the nature of management and performance indicators for railways; the question of costing; forecasting, evaluation and investment; and finally, studies of efficiency. Other divisions would have been possible but this breakdown conforms both with the general types of issue with which transport economists are currently concerned with and also the areas of rail activity which are at present causing the biggest problems.

In the first chapter in the management section, Dodgson provides a detailed assessment of recent developments in the measurement of railway productivity drawing upon a range of international experiences to illustrate and examine the practicality of theoretical advances in this field. As he points out in his introductory comments, considerable interest is currently being shown worldwide in the measurement of productivity in the context of the rising level of government subsidies to national railways systems. There is one notable exception, however, to this trend. Whereas most railway systems in Western Europe are receiving increasing levels of subsidies to retain their networks, the authorities in the United States have responded to changing patterns of demand by restructuring their rail industry. In Chapter 3, Harris and Grimm look at the managerial and organisational changes which have resulted from the American approach and the impact of these on railway performance. British Rail, being a unitary, nationalised industry, has not been subjected to the types of major structural reforms experienced by its American counterparts. Nevertheless, in Chapter 4 Allen and Williams demonstrate how British Rail are responding to changing circumstances and how changes ('a radical new look') are taking place to ensure improved information flows for a restructured management.

One of the major problems encountered by railway management (and, indeed, by those responsible for regulating or subsidising rail systems) is that of allocating costs. Railways have traditionally been thought of in terms of being decreasing cost industries, providing a range of services exhibiting a variety of joint cost allocation problems and generating numerous external costs. In Chapter 5 Waters offers a systematic examination of the difficulties associated with cost allocation in these circumstances and highlights the way the problems created have been handled (with differing levels of success) in North America. A much more detailed, case study approach, drawing on Australian experiences, is provided by Ogden in Chapter 6. His contribution focuses on the very topical question of truck cost allocation and, in particular, on ensuing equity in treatment between the road and rail transport industries. Given recent advances in economic theory, especially those policy implications which would seem to emanate from the development of ideas relating to contestable markets, the consistent treatment of track costs across modes is a subject of immediate concern.

Demand analysis and evaluation in the rail context have advanced considerably in recent years. Nevertheless there is a long way to go, especially as these are areas which tended, for often quite sensible reasons, to have been neglected in the past. Urban railway systems are currently enjoying a revival as a consequence of both the expansion of urbanisation and the realisation that many of the alternative approaches which have been examined in a bid to alleviate the so-called 'urban transport problem' have not proved as effective as initially hoped. (Indeed, there are now indications that even the World Bank is reforming its position with regard to fixed track urban public transport systems in Third World countries.) Two of the contributions in Part III look specifically at demand and evaluation and their relationship to urban railway issues. In Chapter 7 Gordon and Willson focus on the question of demand and provide a detailed econometric examination of the determinants of urban rail transit demand. In Chapter 8 Fullerton and Openshaw concentrate on the problems of investment appraisal and draw upon the example of the Tyneside Metro system in the United Kingdom to highlight the difficulties of applying social and cost-benefit techniques in the urban light-railway context. The third paper in this section looks at a different dimension of the forecasting, evaluation and investment aspect of railway economics and considers methods of forecasting freight demand in the United Kingdom. Freight is central to the viability of most railway operations, but until comparatively recently demand forecasting in this area has tended to be fragmentary and simplistic. Good forecasts are required if infrastructure evaluation is to be properly informed.

In Part IV the final set of papers look at economic efficiency. While the 1960s had, almost universally, been a period of economic expansion and, as a concomitant of this, concern with pure efficiency issues had tended to be given less attention than those relating to equity and social matters — a trend reflected in the railway sectors of many countries by higher real levels of subsidy — the situation has now changed. There are several ways in which efficiency in the provision of rail services may be considered. In Chapter 11 Kilvington considers the efficient provision of social services — and specifically those provided in sparsely populated areas — and looks at British and continental experiences for guidelines. The other two chapters in this section look at efficiency at a more technical level, albeit in relation to railways at opposite ends of the globe. Nash concerns himself with developing comparative measures of efficiency in the context of European railways while in Chapter 12 Rao and Sririman develop an econometric framework to look at the Indian experience. Interestingly, all these studies highlight the problems of data inadequacies for the respective tasks they have set themselves.

As can be seen from this brief examination of the contents, the book does not offer a comprehensive text on railway economics — that is not the intention. Areas such as pricing, for example, are only dealt with within the context of individual contributions. This, however, is due to the fact that major theoretical advances in pricing have taken place in the past and implementation and practical assimilation can only follow once questions concerning management systems, costing and efficiency measure have been resolved. Without adequate knowledge of appropriate costs and demand and with no clear idea of appropriate management structures and efficiency criteria, assessment of actual pricing regimes is impossible (or, at least, unlikely to produce more than crude, perhaps subjective, generalisations). Similarly, the papers offer limited coverage of the possible wider role of rail transport in economic development and (in such cases as the EEC) in economic integration. The problem here is the scale of the issues involved. The importance of rail transport in affecting spatial economic development is a topic deserving attention in the wider context of the impact of transport *per se* on economic growth rather than one focusing mainly on the internal workings of the railway industry. For practical reasons we have limited ourselves to issues concerning the internal functioning of the rail sector and leave questions of a broader, development nature to other writers.

Despite these noted omissions in the coverage of this volume, the more limited contents offered does enable the reader to appreciate some of the central contemporary problems which have received the attention of economists in world railways. Hopefully, such a codification will be of some value to those interested in the current state of the art of rail economics.

References

Aldcroft, D.N. (1968), *Railways in Transition* (Macmillan, London).

Farris, M.T. (1983), 'Evolution of the transportation regulatory structure of the US', *International Journal of Transport Economics*, Vol.10, pp.173—93.

Fogel, R.W. (1964), *Railroads and American Economic Growth* (Johns Hopkins University Press, Baltimore).

Hilton, G.W. (1983), 'The American railroad deregulation of 1980', *International Journal of Transport Economics*, Vol.10, pp.357—71.

Hotelling, H. (1938), 'The general welfare in relation to problems of taxation and of railway and utility rates', *Econometrica*, Vol.6, pp.242—69.

Joy, S. (1973), *The Train that Ran Away* (Ian Allen, London).

MacGill, C.E. (1917), *History of Transportation in the United States Before 1860* (Carnegie Institute, Washington).

Pryke, R. and Dodgson, J. (1975), *The Rail Problem* (Martin Robertson, London).

Savage, C. (1966), *An Economic History of Transport* (Hutchinson, London).

Skidelsky, R. (1983), *John Maynard Keynes: Hopes Betrayed 1883—1920* (Macmillan, London).

Thompson, A.W.J. and Hunter, L.C. (1973), *The Nationalised Transport Industries* (Heinemann, London).

Whitaker, J.K. (1975), *The Early Economic Writings of Alfred Marshall 1867—1890*, 2 Vols. (MacMillan, London).

Part I
Management and Performance Indicators

2 A survey of recent developments in the measurement of rail total factor productivity*

J. S. DODGSON

2.1 Introduction

Productivity can be viewed as a ratio between an organisation's output and its input. A good rate of productivity growth (in relation to previous rates of growth, or to the rates of growth achieved by other organisations) is then often taken as one measure of an organisation's success. There is considerable interest in measurement of the productivity performance of rail networks as an indicator of their efficiency, both over time and in comparison with other systems. In part this stems from the close interest that governments in many countries take in rail service operation because of the subsidies they provide, and their consequent desire to see whether services are being provided as effectively as possible (Lazarus 1982).

In considering measures of productivity, an important distinction to be made is between those which attempt to measure total factor productivity, so that an organisation's total output is expressed as a ratio of its total input, and those which are partial measures, either in the sense that they measure only labour productivity, so that output is expressed as a ratio of labour input, or in the sense that they are a form of performance indicator in which one particular component of output is expressed as a ratio of one particular component of input. Examples of the latter include train-miles per employee, train-miles per locomot-

*The author would like to thank R. Millward for helpful comments.

ive, passenger-miles per train-mile (average passenger train load), ton-miles per train-mile (average freight train load), tons hauled per freight car/wagon operated, ton-miles per train hour, ton-miles per gallon of fuel, and passenger-miles per gallon of fuel. Such measures may provide useful information, but by their very nature they present only a partial picture, and it is usually dangerous to infer conclusions from them directly without further information.

In Britain Deakin and Seward (1969) estimated both labour and total factor productivity growth in six transport sectors, including railways, for the period from 1952 to 1965. Pryke computed labour productivity growth and total factor productivity growth in British Rail, the publicly-owned national rail system, from 1948 to 1968 (1971), and labour productivity growth, in terms of output per equivalent worker, for the period from 1968 to 1978 (1981). A joint study by the British Railways Board and the University of Leeds (1979) has compared BR's labour productivity with that of nine other European rail systems by means of extensive comparisons of a wide range of different performance indicators. British Rail (1982) has since produced an analysis of its own productivity performance since 1977.

In the United States considerable work on total factor productivity measurement for rail services has recently been carried out by Caves, Christensen and their associates. This work considerably advances the methodology of total factor productivity measurement. The purpose of this chapter is to provide a survey of these recent developments. The aim is to stress both the economic foundations of the evaluation of productivity growth and productivity comparisons, and the policy implications of the results of studies of rail system productivity.

In section 2.2 we outline the theory of productivity measurement, the relationship of the concept of productivity and its growth to the economic theory of production and cost, and the possible sources of productivity increase within such a framework. Section 2.3 offers a survey of econometric studies of the structure of production and cost in the rail industry; it is the results of such studies which provide the essential link between the theory of cost and production and the empirical measurement of productivity growth. Section 2.4 provides a survey of the two related approaches to productivity growth measurement developed by Caves, Christensen and Swanson, and of the studies which have resulted from their work. The final section presents conclusions on the relevance of these recent developments and their implications regarding the value of attempts to measure productivity growth and to make inter-system productivity comparison.

2.2 The theory of productivity growth measurement

In this section we consider the issues involved in the measurement of productivity using the economic theory of production and cost. To begin with we assume that the railway firm produces a single homogeneous output q using n factors of production $x_1, ..., x_n$. The technological relation between inputs and outputs is given by the production function

$$q = f(x_1, ..., x_n, t) \qquad (2.1)$$

This shows the maximum output obtainable from any given combination of the inputs given the state of technological knowledge at time t.

Usually inputs will be substitutible and, assuming perfect substitutibility, the production function will yield a series of smooth isoquants showing alternative combinations of inputs which would produce particular levels of output. Figure 2.1 shows one such isoquant, for output level q^1, in the case where there are only two inputs x_1, labour, and x_2, capital. The ease of substitution is measured by the elasticity of substitution, σ, which is defined in this two-input case as the percentage change in the capital-to-labour ratio divided by the percentage change in the slope of the isoquant (the rate of technical substitution).

Let us suppose that q^1 is the output level which is to be produced. In effect, the isoquant shows the boundary, or frontier, of technically efficient points, since output q^1 could be produced by a combination of inputs lying above the isoquant, but this would be technically inefficient in the sense that the same output could be produced using less of both inputs. Hence, if the firm produced q^1 at point c it could reduce costs by, for example, reducing both inputs in equal proportion until it reached point a, at the same time ensuring that this combination of inputs was utilised in the most technically efficient manner possible. One measure of such technical inefficiency is the distance function measure, $0a/0c$, suggested by Farrell (1957). This measure lies between 0 and 1, and would be equal to 1 if point c lay on the isoquant so that the firm was technically efficient.

Point b also lies on the isoquant q^1 and is therefore also a technically efficient point. However, we are also interested in allocative efficiency in input use. Still assuming that q^1 is the output level to be produced, allocative efficiency will be achieved when the cost of producing that output is minimised, provided that the relative input prices are themselves allocatively efficient. Assume that the firm is a price-taker in the markets where it purchases its inputs. In the long run when all the inputs can be varied, and purchased at these given prices,

15

different levels of total costs will be shown by isocost curves, the slopes of which are determined by relative input prices. Costs will be minimised where one of the isocost curves is tangential to the isoquant; in Figure 2.1 relative factor prices are such that this occurs at point a on isocost rs. Hence although point b is technically efficient, it is allocatively inefficient, since the isocost curve tv passing through point b represents a higher level of total costs than does rs. In fact, the figure is deliberately drawn so that the technically inefficient point, point c, also lies on tv so that total costs at points b and c are equal to each other; technical inefficiency may or may not, in general, be worse than allocative inefficiency in terms of its effects in increasing costs over the minimum amount that they need to be.

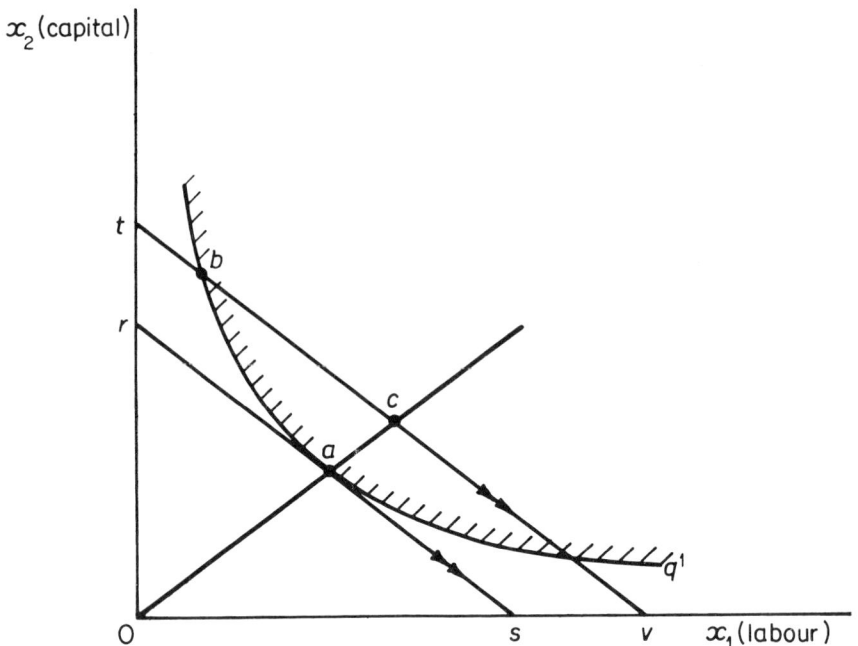

Point c represents production of output q^1 with a technically inefficient combination of inputs.

Figure 2.1   Technical and allocative inefficiency

16

The approach of minimising the cost of producing a specified level of output is referred to in the economics literature as the dual approach to the theory of production. The resulting (single product) cost function

$$c = g(q, p_1, ..., p_n, t) \tag{2.2}$$

shows the minimum cost of producing a specified output level q given values of input prices $p_1, ..., p_n$ and the state of technological knowledge at time t. The dual approach contrasts with the primal approach, where output is maximised subject to a cost constraint. As has been shown (see, for example, Varian 1978), an important property of duality is that production technology can be represented equally well either by a production function or by the associated cost function. Cost functions have a number of properties; in particular an equal proportionate increase in all input prices will lead to the same proportionate increase in costs, that is, the cost function is said to be linearly homogeneous in input prices. Furthermore, by Shephard's lemma, differentiation of the cost function with respect to input price yields the demand equation for that input given constant output;

$$\partial c / \partial p_i = x_i \tag{2.3}$$

In logarithmic terms

$$\partial \ln c / \partial \ln p_i = (\partial c / c) / (\partial p_i / p_i) = (\partial c / \partial p_i)...(p_i / c)$$

$$= (p_i x_i) / c \qquad = s_i \tag{2.4}$$

where s_i is equal to the input's cost share. That is, the elasticity of cost with respect to input price is equal to the input's share of total cost, provided that the firm engages in cost-minimising behaviour.

A common approach in the measurement of rail productivity is to use labour productivity, a ratio of output to labour input. With our simple two inputs and one output example the appropriate measure is q/x_1. Such measures can be seriously misleading because they ignore other inputs such as capital. Suppose we are comparing two railways which both happen to produce output q^1. If these railways face different relative factor prices, then allocative efficiency implies that they should operate with different capital-to-labour ratios. If firm 1 faces lower labour costs than firm 2, Figure 2.2 shows that it should operate at point d on isocost ru while firm 2 should operate at point e on isocost st. Clearly output per man is lower on railway 1 than on railway 2, but both are technically and allocatively efficient. Indeed firm 2 might have a higher output per man than firm 1 but still be neither allocatively nor technically efficient in its use of inputs; points

f and g illustrate such positions.

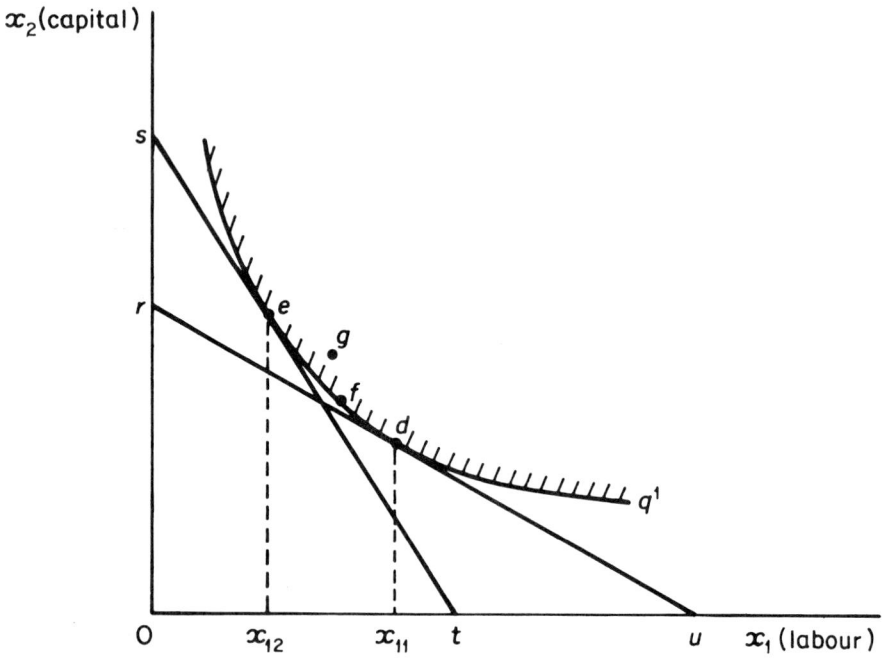

Point d represents point of production of output q^1 by firm 1.
Points e, f and g represent alternative points of production of output q^1 by firm 2.

Figure 2.2   Output per unit of labour

Similar problems arise with time-series comparisons of a single railway; output per head might fall because of changes in relative input prices which made it allocatively efficient for the enterprise to reduce its capital-to-labour ratio. The extent to which such problems will arise even when labour costs represent a high proportion of total costs, as they do for most railways, will depend upon the value of the elasticity of substitution between labour and capital.

The alternative to use of an unsatisfactory partial measure of productivity is to develop a measure of total factor productivity, where output is expressed as a ratio to some measure of total inputs, $q/(\sum_1^n a_i x_i)$, where the a_i are the weights given to the inputs. Index number problems may arise as to the appropriate weights to use where data are available only for discrete as opposed to continuous changes in input use.

Consider the measurement of changes in input use for a single firm over two time periods, 1 and 2. This is illustrated for the two input, x_1 and x_2, case in Figure 2.3. The initial position is at point a, with the firm minimising the cost of producing output q^1 and employing x_{11} and x_{21} units of the two inputs. Suppose in period 2 the firm employs inputs x_{12} and x_{22} and produces q^2. How do we measure the proportionate change in input use in the case of this discrete change? One approach is to value the inputs at their initial prices, p_{11} and p_{21}. Generalising to the n input case, the proportionate change in input use can be written as

$$\frac{\sum\limits_i^n p_{i1}x_{i2}}{\sum\limits_i^n p_{i1}x_{i1}} - 1 = \frac{\sum\limits_i^n p_{i1}x_{i2}}{\sum\limits_i^n p_{i1}x_{i1}} - \frac{\sum\limits_i^n p_{i1}x_{i1}}{\sum\limits_i^n p_{i1}x_{i1}}$$

$$= \frac{\sum\limits_i^n p_{i1}(x_{i2} - x_{i1})}{\sum\limits_i^n p_{i1}x_{i1}} \qquad (2.5)$$

where $(\sum\limits_i^n p_{i1}x_{i2})/(\sum\limits_i^n p_{i1}x_{i1})$ is a base-weighted quantity index. The term $\sum\limits_i^n p_{i1}x_{i2}$ is the post-change expenditure on inputs valued at their initial prices; in the two-input case shown in Figure 2.3 it is represented by the isocost line tu. The above approach is exactly equivalent to calculating the proportionate change in input use by weighting the proportionate change in each input by that input's initial cost share, since such an approach yields;

$$\sum\limits_i^n \left[\frac{p_{i1}x_{i1}}{\sum\limits_i^n p_{i1}x_{i1}} \left(\frac{x_{i2} - x_{i1}}{x_{i1}} \right) \right] = \frac{\sum\limits_i^n p_{i1}(x_{i2} - x_{i1})}{\sum\limits_i^n p_{i1}x_{i1}} \qquad (2.6)$$

19

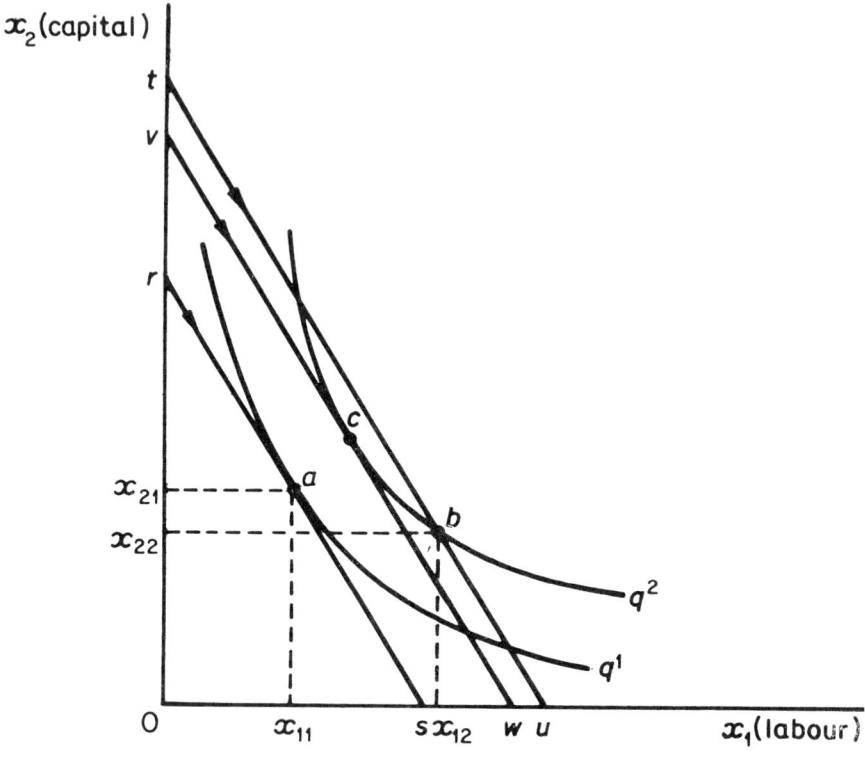

Figure 2.3 Index number measures of increased input use based on initial relative input prices

Two separate index number problems now arise. The first is the well-known problem of choice of the appropriate price weights. In the above analysis we have weighted input quantities by initial input prices or cost shares, but we might well alternatively choose final input prices or cost shares; generally this will result in a different estimate of the proportionate change in input use. The second problem is that if we do choose initial price weights, and estimate the proportionate change in input costs by (2.5), we will have overestimated the increase in input costs necessary to produce the second period level of output q^2. This can best be illustrated by reference to Figure 2.3. Use of equation (2.5) would yield an estimate of the proportionate change in input use equal to the ratio rt/Or, or su/Os. However, faced with such input prices the firm could actually produce output q^2 at minimum costs at point c, thereby incurring total costs represented by the isocost line vw. The proportionate change in input use could then be measured by the ratios rv/Or or sw/Os. This can be done by substituting a term for the true, or economic, base-weighted index of output for the base-weighted fixed input quantity index in equation (2.5). The true, economic, base-weighted quantity index is defined as

$$\frac{g(q^2, p_{11}, ..., p_{n1}, t)}{g(q^1, p_{11}, ..., p_{n1}, t)} \tag{2.7}$$

where $g(q^1, p_{11}, ..., p_{n1}, t)$ is defined as the minimum cost of producing quantity q^1 with input prices $p_{11}, ... p_{n1}$, and $g(q^2, p_{11}, ..., p_{n1}, t)$ is the minimum cost of producing output q^2 with the same initial input price vector. Use of such true, or exact, economic indices requires information on the structure of production (or, what is equivalent, on the structure of the cost function); that is, with regard to Figure 2.3, it requires information on the shape of the isoquant q^2 passing through point b on the diagram. Diewert (1976, 1981) and Samuelson and Swamy (1974) outline the form which such indices take for different types of production or cost function. True, or economic, indices can also be used where the input quantity indices are based on final rather than initial input prices. An alternative approach to quantity indices based on the economic theory of production is to use distance-function-based measures; Caves, Christensen and Diewert (1982) have investigated the use of such economic index numbers to measure growth in input, output and productivity.

We can now consider sources of productivity change. To do this we consider the reasons why productivity for a single enterprise might change through time. To abstract from index number problems we assume optimal and actual capital-to-labour ratios do not change because relative input prices are unchanged and the production function is homogeneous or homothetic, and exhibits Hicks-neutral technological progress,[1] so that the level of labour input can serve equally well as a measure of total inputs. This means that in Figure 2.4 the firm operates along the ray OA, and the productivity measure q/x_1 is a simple multiple of $q/\sum_i^n a_i x_i)$. There are three reasons why productivity defined as a ratio between output and input may rise:

(1) technical inefficiency may be reduced or removed with output unchanged; e.g. a move from point c to point a
(2) technological progress may occur with output unchanged; e.g. move from point a to point k

(3) there may be economies of scale in production, and output
   may rise; e.g. a move from point a to point j.

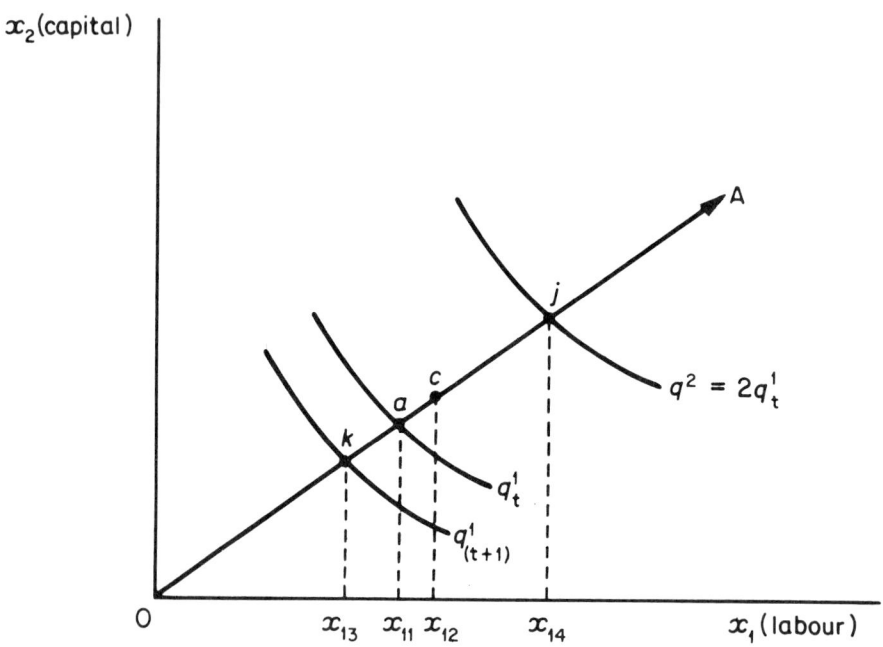

Point a represents production of output q^1 with level of technological
   knowledge at time t
Point c represents technically inefficient production of output q^1
   with level of technological knowledge at time t
Point k represents production of output q^1 with level of technological
   knowledge at time $(t + 1)$
Point j represents production of output q^2 (where $q^2 = 2q^1$ but x_{14}
   $< 2x_{11}$) with level of technological knowledge at time t

Figure 2.4   Alternative sources of productivity growth

Of course actual productivity change may be a mixture of all three
factors. Such sources of productivity growth are not equally due to

management success. Reductions in technical inefficiency might very well be due to management action; for example, in removing restrictive labour practices or in changing methods of working. But technological progress may occur because of developments outside the firm, although some might also be due to technological innovation within the organisation itself. Benefits from economies of scale depend on traffic levels, which in part depend on pricing and marketing but perhaps in greater part on changes in external factors, such as car ownership and income levels, and the structure and location of industry.

The literature on the measurement of productivity growth has tended to identify productivity change primarily with technological progress in the form of shifts in the production or cost function. In practice, though, actual measures of productivity growth have not distinguished between the three sources of change discussed, or have simply assumed the existence of constant returns to scale (see Griliches and Jorgenson 1967) and/or cost-minimising behaviour. More recently Caves, Christensen and Swanson (1980) developed a methodology, applied to the rail sector, for correcting for non-constant returns to scale. In a further recent important paper Nishimizu and Page (1982) developed a method to decompose productivity growth into the part due to technological progress and the part due to increased technical efficiency. This they did by estimating a frontier production function as the boundary of technically efficient points.

There is also a further possible source of productivity growth. The assumption made so far is that firms are free to vary all inputs. In the short run this will not be so and in consequence firms that have not been able to adjust optimally all their inputs in order to minimise long-run costs will appear to suffer from lower productivity than would be the case when optimally adjusted. In Figure 2.5 the firm is initially at point a producing output q^1. Suppose demand now rises so that q^2 becomes the optimal output (but that relative input prices do not change so that we can ignore index number problems that would arise with such changes). In the short run labour is variable, but suppose capital is fixed. Then in the short run the firm must move to point b and incur a level of total costs represented by the isocost vw. In effect the firm is minimising a variable cost function, where it seeks to minimise the cost of producing a given output level, q^2, given relative input prices and a constraint on the amount of fixed factors it must employ. In the long run output q^2 could be produced at point c with total costs represented by the isocost tu. Hence, output per unit of input at point b is the proportion $uw/0u (= tv/0t = ed/0e)$ less than it would be at point c.

Thus productivity comparisons over time might be distorted because a rail system was in the process of adjusting output, and cross-system comparisons might be distorted because different systems were at different stages of adjustment. In addition, there may often be institutional, government-imposed, reasons why rail systems are not free to vary all their inputs, particularly the route-miles over which the systems operate, even in a longer time period when such inputs might technically be varied. Again, Caves, Christensen and Swanson (1981a) have developed a methodology to deal with this problem, and have applied it to the rail sector.

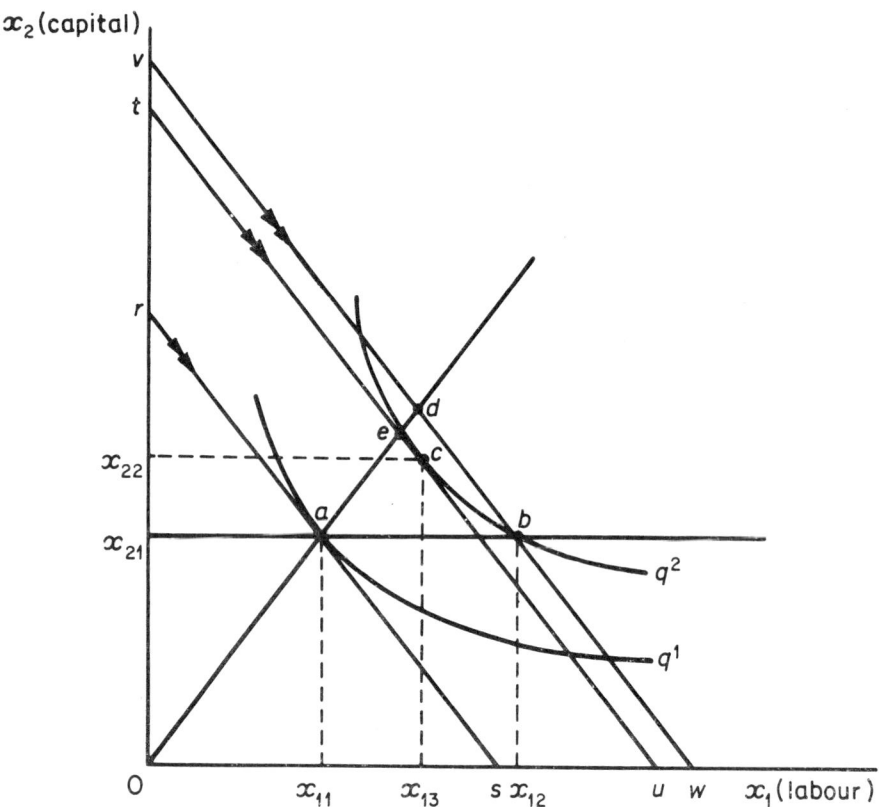

Figure 2.5 Productivity change in the short and the long run

A further difficulty related to speed of adjustment concerns technological progress itself. Much technological progress is embodied in the capital equipment used; for example, a steam locomotive is fundamentally different from a diesel, and mechanical semaphore signalling from modern electric colour-light power signalling. This means that, particularly in view of the long physical lives of many railway assets, when technological progress occurs it is not necessarily technically or allocatively efficient for an existing system to adopt best-practice technology immediately if it already has a stock of existing older-technology capital equipment which is not life-expired. Instead the replacement decision should be based on discounted cash flow comparisons of the future net earnings of the two types of equipment given that one type is already installed.

The final problem to note is that railways do not in practice produce a homogeneous output. Many railway companies provide both passenger and freight services, and these outputs are not themselves homogeneous. Hence there are problems in defining the appropriate measure of each type of output, since a failure to distinguish different types of output with different production/cost characteristics can lead to bias in productivity comparisons when output mix changes. For railways, these problems are compounded because the unit of production, the train-mile or the car-mile, differs from the unit of sale, the ton-mile or passenger-mile. Although passenger-miles and ton-miles are the most commonly-used measures of output, there is a need to distinguish different types of passenger and freight traffic.[2] On the freight side one ton-mile of freight may differ from another because of differences in the commodity carried, the length of haul involved, and the density and regularity of the flow. On the passenger side a passenger-mile on a long-distance high-speed service will involve different costs from a passenger-mile on an urban commuter or local stopping service. Unless allowance is made for such factors, comparisons through time may be misleading if product mix or quality of service changes, and cross-system comparisons may be misleading if product mix or quality of service varies between systems.[3]

The optimal disaggregation of output for a rail system with a wide mix of traffics is in practice likely to be a compromise between an ideal detailed breakdown and a much narrower one permitted by the data available. Once the disaggregation level is chosen, index number problems arise in aggregating different types of output to provide the overall output index. These issues have been extensively covered in the literature on the valuation of real output, recently surveyed by Sen (1979). In a perfectly competitive economy, in which constant returns to scale must prevail in equilibrium, the appropriate output weights should be based on the relative prices at which the different outputs are sold since (as long as there are no externalities) these prices reflect the relative valuation the economy places on the outputs produced. Obviously problems arise if, as in the case of railways, certain types of output are sold at subsidised or cross-subsidised prices. The standard index number problem of whether to use initial or final prices also applies. In addition, as for inputs, the question of the appropriate measure of the proportionate increase in the outputs can be answered by use of the economic theory of index numbers.

2.3 Measurement of production and cost in the rail sector

As we have seen, productivity growth measurement is intimately related to the structure of production and cost in the industry where growth of productivity is to be evaluated. Consequently, we next summarise the economic work on the measurement of production technology and costs in the rail industry. This work relates exclusively to North America since it is only in the United States (and Canada) that there exists a large enough sample of rail systems to provide the data required to undertake cross-section studies using econometric techniques. All US railroads are required to file detailed information on their operations and costs with the Interstate Commerce Commission, using specified standard procedures, and detailed data are also available for the Canadian systems.

Railroads in North America are distinguished by class. In the USA class I railroads were defined in 1981 as those generating an annual revenue in excess of $50 million. There were 38 such railroads and together they handled 98 per cent of total railroad traffic in that year.[4] The number of class I railroads has declined over the post-war period, partly because of upward revisions in the annual revenue figure (the main effect of such revisions was to re-classify 14 railroads, accounting for 1.3 per cent of 1977 traffic, in 1978) and partly because of mergers and bankruptcies.

Freight is by far the most important traffic handled. The tonnage hauled by class I railroads in the post-war period has shown no discernible long-term trend; 1477 million tons were originated in 1951 and 1453 million tons in 1981, and year-to-year traffic levels have generally fluctuated in line with economic conditions. Revenue ton-miles have however increased because of a steady increase in average length of haul, from 438 miles in 1951 to 627 miles in 1981. Rail's percentage share of intercity freight has been declining, though latterly at a fairly slow rate; rail mode share (compared with trucks, waterways, and pipelines) was 56 per cent in 1950, 44 per cent in 1960, 40 per cent in 1970, and 37 per cent in 1980. Route-miles owned have also declined over the same 30-year period, by some 20 per cent to a 1980 total of 179,000 miles. The post-war decline in inter-city (that is non-commuter) traffic was stabilised after 1971 when such services were taken over by Amtrak, which operates long-distance passenger services, partly over its own route in the Northeast Corridor, and partly over other systems.

Rail systems in Canada operate with similar technology and methods of working to those in the US. The two main systems, classified as class I, are Canadian National and Canadian Pacific. In 1981 these two systems hauled a combined tonnage of freight of 205 million tons with an average length of haul of 696 miles. The resulting 142,000 million ton-miles accounted for 89 per cent of rail ton-miles hauled in Canada in that year. Responsibility for passenger services has been transferred to VIA Rail, a Crown Corporation set up in 1977 which contracts with CN and CP for the operation of passenger trains over their tracks.

2.3-1 *Functional forms for production and cost functions*

Econometric studies of the structure of production and cost in the railroad industry (and indeed in other industries) have employed three main functional forms for the production or cost function. The first, and simplest, of these is the Cobb-Douglas production function. In the single output case this takes the form

$$q = A \prod_{i}^{n} x_i a_i \tag{2.8}$$

where A and the a_is are parameters to be estimated. This production function is homogeneous and separable,[5] and permits constant, increasing, or decreasing returns to scale depending on whether $\sum_{i}^{n} a_i$, the sum of parameters is equal to, greater than, or less than unity. Linear multiple regression can be used to estimate these parameters since, in logs,

$$\ln q = \ln A + \sum_{i}^{n} a_i \ln x_i \tag{2.9}$$

A major restriction of this functional form is that the elasticity of substitution between any pair of inputs must equal unity.

An alternative form for the production function which permits the elasticity of substitution to differ from one is the constant elasticity of substitution (CES) production function proposed by Arrow, Chenery, Minhas and Solow (1961). In the two-input case this takes the form

$$q = B \left[\delta x_1^\rho + (1 - \delta) x_2^\rho \right]^{r/\rho} \tag{2.10}$$

where $1/(\rho - 1)$ is equal to the constant elasticity of substitution between the two inputs x_1 and x_2.

More recently econometricians have developed functional forms to represent the structure of production which do not impose restrictions of homogeneity or homotheticity, separability, constant returns to scale, or constant elasticity of substitution. Two major developments have been involved. The first, already noted in section 2.2, is the use of duality theory and the realisation that the structure of production can be represented equally well by a cost function, provided that the cost function is well-behaved in the sense that it satisfies the general properties of cost functions which are derived by minimising the cost of producing a given level of output. Straightforward econometric estimation of such cost functions requires that output levels be exogenous.[6] The second development has been a search for what are termed flexible functional forms; these are functional forms which can provide a second-order differentiable approximation to any arbitrary, twice continuously-differentiable, production or cost function. This permits additional restrictions, such as homogeneity or homotheticity, separability, constant returns to scale, or constant elasticity of substitution to be tested rather than imposed.

The most commonly-used flexible functional form in the study of production is the translog, or transcendental logarithmic, cost function.[7] In the single output, n input case, this takes the form

$$\ln c = a_0 + a_1 \ln q + \tfrac{1}{2}\delta_{11}(\ln q)^2$$

$$+ \sum_{i}^{n} \beta_i \ln p_i + \tfrac{1}{2} \sum_{i}^{n} \sum_{j}^{n} \gamma_{ij} \ln p_i \ln p_j$$

$$+ \sum_{i}^{n} \rho_{1i} \ln q \ln p_i \qquad (2.11)$$

where $\gamma_{ij} = \gamma_{ji}$. Thus the log of total cost is a linear function of the logs of output and of input prices. To satisfy the linear homogeneity with respect to input prices property of a cost function, the restrictions

$$\sum_{i}^{n} \beta_i = 1, \ \sum_{i}^{n} \rho_{1i} = 0, \text{ and } \sum_{i}^{n} \gamma_{ij} = \sum_{j}^{n} \gamma_{ji} = \sum_{i}^{n}\sum_{j}^{n} \gamma_{ij} = 0$$

must also hold. In addition, the input cost share equations are linear functions of the logs of output and of input prices since, from equation (2.4) above,

$$s_i = \partial \ln c / \partial \ln p_i = \beta_i + \sum_{j}^{n} \gamma_{ij} \ln p_j + \rho_{1i} \ln q \qquad (2.12)$$

These cost share equations prove extremely valuable in improving econometric estimation, since the cost function equation (2.11) and the n input share equations (2.12) can be estimated jointly, considerably increasing the degrees of freedom.

2.3-2 Studies of the production and cost function in the railroad industry

An early econometric study based on the theory of production was that by Klein (partly reported in Klein, 1953). Klein used 1936 data for a sample of some 80 US class I railroads to estimate a Cobb-Douglas production function for railroad services. Two types of output (freight ton-miles, and passenger-miles) were distinguished, combined as a Cobb-Douglas output function, and estimated as a Cobb-Douglas function of three inputs (man-hours, tons of fuel, and train-hours — a measure of capital input). The sum of input parameters estimated was significantly greater than unity, indicating apparent economies of scale. Hasenkamp (1976) has since used the same data set to re-estimate the railroad production function with alternative forms for the output function, together with both Cobb-Douglas and CES forms for the input function. This was done by deriving and estimating the cost function and input demand equations appropriate to each of the alternative specifications. Again, the results appear to show economies of scale.[8]

In the 1950s and 1960s studies of costs in the US railroad industry were not directly based on the economic theory of production in the sense that functional forms for the cost functions to be estimated were derived from cost minimising behaviour. Instead they generally consisted of attempts to relate average or total costs directly to some measure of output by means of simple linear regression in order to determine whether economies of scale did indeed exist as Klein's study of pre-war evidence had suggested. Existence of economies of scale was usually measured in terms of the figure of 'per cent variable', which is equal to the ratio of marginal cost to average cost, that is the elasticity of total cost with respect to output), multiplied by 100.[9] This measure is equal to 100 per cent if there are constant returns to scale, less than 100 per cent with economies of scale, and over 100 per cent with diseconomies of scale. The Interstate Commerce Commission had estimated 'average' per cent variable at 80 per cent, but these results were criticised by Griliches (1972), both on the grounds that the ICC had taken the 'average' per cent variable as an average across all railroads, hence weighting very small and very large railroads equally, and on the grounds of use of an inappropriate method of deflating total costs and total output to improve the efficiency of the estimated parameters in their linear regression estimates of the relation between total costs and ton-miles, their chosen measure of output.

Griliches presented results for his own simple linear regression analysis of railroad total costs as a function of output, measured in gross ton-miles, for a cross-section of US railroads with five-year average data (to correct for the effect of any short-run variations in cost and output) for the period 1957 to 1961. Smaller railroads appeared to have higher average costs per ton-mile than larger ones, and the sample was arbitrarily divided into two roughly equal sizes by separating out companies with less than 500 miles of track from those with more than 500 miles. Assuming a linear total cost function, Griliches discovered economies of scale for the smaller railroads (with an average value of per cent variable per ton hauled in this group of 70 per cent). But these railroads only accounted for about 5 per cent of total traffic. For the larger railroads, the hypothesis of constant returns to scale could not be rejected, with an estimate of average per cent variable per ton hauled for this group of 99 per cent.

As Griliches acknowledged, his conclusions were based on very questionable definitions of cost and output, and on a very gross aggregation of all types of traffic, dimensions of output, regions of the country, and sizes of railroad. He argued that the constant returns to scale result might be expected because what, in effect, his cost function estimates do is to consider the effect on average costs if all traffic were to be expanded on average in the same proportions and with exactly the same distribution over the various commodities, types, routes and seasons as the previous traffic. In practice this is not how traffic does change, and of more interest is the question of what happens to average costs when only certain types of traffic change. But, as Griliches noted, this cannot be discovered from his broad analysis of total railroad costs and aggregated gross ton-miles of traffic.

Keeler (1974) developed a methodology to distinguish between economies of scale, that is of firm size, which occur when all types of traffic increase in the same proportion, and economies of density, which occur when traffic on a particular route infrastructure rises. Cobb-Douglas production functions were specified for two types of railroad output, freight gross ton-miles and passenger train gross ton-miles, which were assumed to depend on three variable inputs (labour, fuel, and rolling stock investment) and one fixed input (railroad trackage) which is difficult to vary both because of regulatory constraints on abandonments and because of technical factors. With output levels exogenous, railroads will minimise variable costs. Keeler derived the (non-linear) form of the resulting short-run total cost function using the Lagrangean approach of minimising costs subject to a desired output level and then solving for the resulting cost function.[10] The short-run cost function was then estimated using non-linear estimation techniques and pooled data for 1968, 1969 and 1971 for a sample of 51 of the railroads with more than 500 track-miles.

Once the short-run total cost function had been estimated, Keeler derived the long-run envelope cost function by determining the optimal track for any given output level from the short-run function. For each firm the optimal track for the traffic level they produced could be compared with their actual track to determine the overall amount of excess track capacity in the industry. For 1969 Keeler estimated this mileage at 200,000 miles, or nearly 60 per cent of all railroad trackage in that year; but indivisibilities would certainly prevent all of it being abandoned with all services maintained. Because of the excess capacity there are substantial economies of density to be reaped; short-run marginal cost estimates yield per cent variable values for most firms of below 70 per cent. But Keeler also found that if excess capacity were to be removed, so that the industry was operating on its long-run total cost curve, there would be constant long-run returns to scale.

Although Harris (1977) related density to route miles rather than track miles, his study confirmed Keeler's view of the existence of economies of traffic density. Harris used data for 1972 and 1973 on class I railroads deriving less than 1 per cent of their revenue from passenger traffic. Revenue (rather than gross) freight ton-miles were defined as the appropriate output variable, and railroad costs were adjusted to include capital rental costs as well as depreciation charges. The basic model assumed total costs were a linear combination of revenue freight ton-miles, revenue freight tons hauled, and miles of route operated. When deflated by ton miles this yields average cost per ton-mile as a linear function of the inverse of average length of haul (tons/ton-miles) and the inverse of traffic density (route-miles/ton-miles, or 1/tons hauled per mile of route). Results show a significant inverse relation across the sample of companies between average cost per ton-mile and tons handled per mile of route. These economies of traffic density were due more to higher operating costs per ton-mile on the systems with more lightly-used route networks than simply to higher capital costs per ton-mile on such systems.

The studies discussed so far either used a restrictive form of prod-uction technology in the railroad industry (Klein, Hasenkamp, Keeler) or were not based directly on the theory of production (Griliches, Harris). All faced problems in incorporating different types of output, particularly in allowing for the effects of both freight and passenger traffic on railroad costs. Brown, Caves, Christensen, and Tretheway (Brown, Caves and Christensen 1979; Caves, Christensen and Tretheway 1980) have attempted to deal with these problems by using the translog form of the cost function to analyse railroad costs. These studies are particularly important for the present paper since the cost estimates derived from such an approach form a crucial input into the productivity growth estimates carried out by the same researchers.

In order to analyse railroad costs the translog cost function has to be extended to incorporate multiple outputs. This extension is straightforward; with m outputs $q_1, ..., q_m$ the single output translog cost function (see equation 2.11) becomes

$$\ln c = a_0 + \sum_i^m a_i \ln q_i + \tfrac{1}{2} \sum_i^m \sum_j^m \delta_{ij} \ln q_i \ln q_j$$

$$+ \sum_i^n \beta_i \ln p_i + \tfrac{1}{2} \sum_i^n \sum_j^n \gamma_{ij} \ln p_i \ln p_j$$

$$+ \sum_i^m \sum_j^n p_{ij} \ln q_i \ln p_j \qquad (2.13)$$

where $\delta_{ij} = \delta_{ji}$ and $\gamma_{ij} = \gamma_{ji}$. For linear homogeneity in input prices we require the additional restrictions

$$\sum_i^n \beta_i = 1, \ \sum_j^n p_{ij} = 0, \ \text{and} \ \sum_i^n \gamma_{ij} = \sum_j^n \gamma_{ji} = \sum_i^n \sum_j^n \gamma_{ij} = 0$$

Brown, Caves and Christensen (1979) estimated this multiproduct cost function using Klein's 1936 railroad data set and output and input variables. Additional restrictions of homogeneity were then tested, but rejected. The results for the different specifications of the cost function were used to estimate marginal costs of freight and passenger services at different output levels, and to estimate scale economies. For the latter, the authors used the index

$$SCE = 1 - \sum_i^m (\partial \ln c / \partial \ln q_i) \qquad (2.14)$$

where $\sum_i^m (\partial \ln c / \partial \ln q_i)$, the sum of cost elasticities with respect to outputs, is equivalent to the single output per cent variable divided by 100. Brown, Caves and Christensen found all but 1 out of 67 railroads operating in the region of economies of scale in 1936, but of course Klein's data definitions do not permit any distinction to be made between economies of scale and economies of density.

The multi-product translog cost function suffers from the limitation that it cannot be used if some firms in the sample do not produce the full range of outputs, since there is no finite representation of the log of zero. This is a particular problem for railroads with the abandonment of passenger traffics. Caves, Christensen and Tretheway (1980) modified the translog function by substituting the Box-Cox transformation of output, which is equal to $Q_i = (q_i\lambda - 1)/\lambda$, $\lambda > 0$, for $\ln q_i$ in equation (2.13). The resulting cost function is referred to as the generalised multi-product translog cost function. The function was initially estimated with 1963 data for a sample of 56 railroads, 15 of which produced no passenger service, with two outputs (freight ton-miles, and passenger-miles) and three inputs (labour, fuel and capital).

In subsequent work the sample was extended to include data for 1956 and 1974, with additional binary variables included to allow for differences in the structure of production between years. Two additional output variables, average length of freight haul and average length of passenger trip, were distinguished and input definitions changed to include materials, equipment, and way and structures capital in addition to labour and fuel. A variable cost function, holding constant way and structures capital in order to allow for the difficulties in adjusting infrastructure, was also developed.[11] Caves, Christensen and Swanson (1981a) summarised the results for both total and variable cost functions with regard to the existence of economies of scale; the results appear to show that, apart from at low levels of output, there are only slight economies of scale if railroad output is increased with length of haul and trip fixed, but there are fairly strong economies if the output increases take the form of increased haul and trip lengths.

The fairly consistent post-war evidence with regard to broadly constant returns to scale to firm size for all but the smallest railroads (Griliches 1972; Keeler 1974; Caves, Christensen and Swanson 1981a) does not mean there will be no advantages of mergers between firms. In some cases a merging firm might bring more effective management to deal with the problems of its new partner. The main potential source of cost savings would appear to be those that could be achieved by parallel mergers, when abandonments or re-routing would permit the merged firms to gain greater economies of density by concentrating their traffics on fewer routes; in practice, such abandonments have often not been possible in the past because of regulation. Some recent empirical work (Levin and Weinberg 1979; Harris and Winston 1983) has concentrated on analysing the benefits of mergers in terms of their effects in improving service quality rather than in reducing costs. This work concluded that end-to-end mergers are likely to be more effective than the merging of parallel railroads in improving the quality of service provided to shippers.

All the cost studies discussed in this section had difficulty in defining appropriate measures of output, in order to deal with the problem that cost differences might be due to differences in the type or quality of rail service provided. Spady and Friedlaender (1978), and Friedlaender and Spady (1981) have estimated translog cost functions for truck and rail which incorporate quality-of-service variables. In addition, using monthly time-series data, Braeutigam, Daughety and Turnquist (1982) estimated a translog variable cost function for a single, freight-carrying, railroad incorporating a quality-of-service variable — speed of transit — in addition to the usual output, variable input price, and fixed input quantity variables. The speed variable data was derived using engineering process information to predict expected average speed of transit in each time period; the resulting quality variable was found to be statistically significant.

2.4 Rail productivity growth measurement in North America

Two approaches to the measurement of productivity growth or to inter-firm (or inter-country) comparisons of productivity may be distinguished. The first, the index number approach, is the traditional approach used in most studies of total factor productivity. The second, the econometric approach, is more recent. Both have been used to measure North American rail productivity growth by Caves, Christensen and Swanson. The current state of the art in productivity change measurement using index number techniques is outlined in Caves and Christensen (1978) and Caves, Christensen and Swanson (1980). Their approach uses the dual, cost function, approach to production theory, together with the economic theory of index numbers, and is much less restrictive with respect to the assumed structure of production technology than were earlier studies.

Since rail systems produce more than one type of output it is necessary to employ a multi-product cost function

$$c = g(q_1, ..., q_m, p_1, ..., p_n, t) \qquad (2.15)$$

where c is the minimum cost of producing specified levels of output $q_1, ..., q_m$ of the m types of output, given n input prices $p_1, ..., p_n$ and the state of technological knowledge at time t. The rate of change of costs through time, $(dc/c)/dt$, can be found by differentiating the log of c with respect to time

$$\frac{d\ln c}{dt} = \sum_i^m \left[\frac{\partial \ln g}{\partial \ln q_i} \cdot \frac{d\ln q_i}{dt} \right] + \sum_i^n \left[\frac{\partial \ln g}{\partial \ln p_i} \cdot \frac{d\ln p_i}{dt} \right] + \frac{\partial \ln g}{\partial t} \qquad (2.16)$$

Hence changes in cost are decomposed into the part due to changes in output levels, the part due to changes in input prices, and the residual part, $\partial \ln g / \partial t$, due to productivity growth, i.e. due to shifts in the cost function. With cost-minimising behaviour we can, from the logarithmic form of Shephard's lemma (equation 2.4), substitute input cost shares for cost elasticities with respect to input prices, so that (2.16) becomes

$$\frac{d\ln c}{dt} = \sum_{i}^{m} \left[\frac{\partial \ln g}{\partial \ln q_i} \cdot \frac{d\ln q_i}{dt} \right]_n + \sum_{i}^{n} \left[s_i \frac{d\ln p_i}{dt} \right] + \frac{\partial \ln g}{\partial t} \tag{2.17}$$

Since total cost, c, equals $\sum_{i} p_i x_i$, the term $d\ln c / dt$ can also be expressed as

$$\frac{d\ln c}{dt} = \sum_{i}^{n} \left[s_i \left(\frac{d\ln p_i}{dt} + \frac{d\ln x_i}{dt} \right) \right] \tag{2.18}$$

Substituting (2.18) into (2.17) we can derive productivity change as

$$-\frac{\partial \ln g}{\partial t} = \sum_{i}^{m} \left[\frac{\partial \ln g}{\partial \ln q_i} \cdot \frac{d\ln q_i}{dt} \right] - \sum_{i}^{n} \left[s_i \cdot \frac{d\ln x_i}{dt} \right] \tag{2.19}$$

Thus productivity growth (the negative of the decline in costs due to the shift of the production/cost function) is equal to the proportionate changes in outputs weighted by their respective elasticities of cost with respect to outputs, minus the proportionate changes in inputs weighted by the respective input cost shares.

If there were constant returns to scale and outputs were priced at marginal costs, Caves and Christensen note that the cost elasticity weights on outputs in equation (2.19) could be replaced by revenue share weights. In other words, the commonly used approach of using revenue shares as weights for output does not permit corrections to be made for the effects of economies or diseconomies of scale. It should also be noted that the productivity growth measure developed can only be used to provide separate measures of aggregate output growth and aggregate input growth if it is assumed that technological change is Hicks-neutral and that outputs and inputs are separable; in such circumstances the first term on the right-hand side of (2.19) can be interpreted as the proportionate change in aggregate output and the second term as the proportionate change in aggregate input.

In order to implement equation (2.19) empirically in discrete time Caves, Christensen and Swanson approximated the logarithmic derivatives of output levels and input levels by first differences in natural logs. The instantaneous weights were replaced by arithmetic averages of cost elasticities or input shares at the beginning and end of each period; this modification is justified in terms of the economic theory of index numbers, which was discussed in section 2.2, because the resulting index, known as the Tornqvist index, has been shown to the true, or exact, index corresponding to the homogeneous translog form of the production function (Diewert 1976).

These modifications to deal with discrete time yielded the productivity growth formula for productivity growth between periods t and t − 1:

$$
-\left[\ln g_t - \ln g_{(t-1)}\right] = \sum_i^m \left[\left(\frac{1}{2}\left(\frac{\partial \ln g}{\partial \ln q_i}\right)_t + \frac{1}{2}\left(\frac{\partial \ln g}{\partial \ln q_i}\right)_{(t-1)}\right)\left(\ln q_{it} - \ln q_{i(t-1)}\right)\right]
$$
$$
- \sum_i^n \left[\left(\frac{1}{2}(s_i)_t + \frac{1}{2}(s_i)_{(t-1)}\right)\left(\ln x_{it} - \ln x_{i(t-1)}\right)\right] \tag{2.2}
$$

To summarise, such an approach requires data on

(1) output levels of the different types of output to be distinguished;
(2) input levels for the different types of input to be distinguished;
(3) elasticities of cost with respect to output for each of the different types of output;
(4) input cost shares for each of the inputs.

Item (3) presents the most problems, since it requires information on the underlying cost structure.

Caves, Christensen and Swanson used this approach to measure the post-war productivity growth of both US (Caves, Christensen and Swanson 1980) and Canadian (Caves and Christensen 1978) class I railroads. For the US railroad industry they distinguished four categories of output (freight ton-miles, average length of freight haul, passenger-miles, and average length of passenger trip), five categories of input (labour, fuel, equipment, way and structures, and materials), and used them to estimate productivity growth in the industry between 1951 and 1974. Data on average length of haul and trip permit allowance to be made for the effect of reduced terminal or other costs per ton-mile or per passenger-mile when average haul or trip length increases. The five-input data series were constructed from a finer classification of inputs (for example, from data on hours worked by different groups of workers) using economic index number procedures, and extensive work was carried out on the economic measurement of capital inputs, always a serious problem in total factor productivity studies using the perpetual inventory method.[12]

To determine the elasticities of cost with respect to the four types of output distinguished Caves, Christensen and Swanson used cross-sectional data from a sample of railroads to estimate the generalised translog multi-product cost function developed by Caves, Christensen and Tretheway (1980) and discussed in section 2.3-2. This cost function and the related cost share equations were estimated with data for three years, 1955, 1963 and 1974. The industry cost elasticities for each of these three years were derived as cost-weighted averages over the individual railroads in each year's sample, and cost elasticities for other years between 1951 and 1974 extrapolated or interpolated. These cost elasticity estimates, together with input weights equal to input cost shares in each year, could then be combined with the output and input indices to derive productivity growth estimates between each pair of years from 1951 through to 1974.

Caves, Christensen and Swanson estimated that productivity in US railroads grew by an average of 1.5 per cent per annum over the whole period from 1951 to 1974. These results were discovered not to be sensitive to the inclusion of average haul and average trip length in addition to the ton-mile and passenger-mile output indices, nor to the effect of (slight) non-constant returns to scale. However they did yield much lower productivity growth estimates than had earlier studies which used traditional productivity measurement methods with revenue as output weights and/or 'national income originating in the railroad industry' as input weights. In addition, Caves, Christensen and Swanson also showed how use of fixed weights throughout the study period could yield results different from their more satisfactory method of permitting output and input weights to vary from year to year.

These same methods were also used to estimate productivity growth between 1956 and 1975 for the two class I Canadian railroads, Canadian National and Canadian Pacific (Caves and Christensen 1978). The same five input indices were used as in the US study. For output, the study used passenger-miles and freight ton-miles, with two alternative series for the latter; one of these was unweighted ton-miles, and the other ton-miles cross-classified by commodity and length of haul and weighted by revenue weights which, except for export grain haulage where an estimate of marginal costs was used, could be regarded as reflecting marginal costs because of the competitive pricing policies of the Canadian systems. Addition of average haul and trip length to the output indices, as done in the US study, was later found not to affect the overall results.

A major problem in the Canadian study was the lack of a sufficient sample of systems to estimate a cross-sectional cost function for Canadian rail systems in order to derive the cost elasticities of outputs to be used as output weights; there are only two class I Canadian railroads and fewer than 10 class II railroads. Instead the American cost function estimates used in the US study were employed, and cost elasticity of output values derived for railroads with the output and input price values set equal to those of CN and CP in each of the sample years. For rail systems of this size the hypothesis of constant returns to scale could not be rejected, and so the cost elasticity values used were normalised to yield constant returns.

With the unweighted ton-miles index of freight output, productivity was estimated to have grown at an average rate of 3.1 per cent per annum for CN, 2.7 per cent per annum for CP, and 2.8 per cent per annum for the two systems combined, over the period from 1956 to 1975. Estimated growth rates were slightly greater when weighted ton-miles were used. Caves and Christensen noted that these productivity growth rates are about twice the US rates over the same period.

In a further paper Caves and Christensen (1980) used these Canadian results to compare in detail the relative performance of the two Canadian systems. CN is a government-owned crown corporation while CP Rail is a private corporation, but both operate in a competitive environment and serve the whole country so, Caves and Christensen argued, their relative performance can be viewed as a case study of the advantages of private versus public ownership in circumstances where the public company is not protected by regulation or other means, with a view to determining whether public ownership per se leads to less efficient operation. Caves and Christensen argued that their study showed that it did not. Between 1956 and 1965, when competitive pressures were less great, CN's productivity was between 10 and 20 per cent lower than that of CP. Both roads' productivity was stagnant between 1956 and 1962 and grew rapidly in 1963 and 1964. But from 1964 to 1968 CN's productivity grew while CP's did not and, although CP productivity growth exceeded CN from 1968 to 1975, the overall productivity levels of the two systems were broadly equal to each other in 1975. These results hold whether unweighted, or revenue-weighted, ton-miles are used as the freight output index. The authors conclude that 'there is no evidence of a significant difference in levels of productivity in the mid-1970s', and that these results suggest that 'the off-noted inefficiency of government enterprises stems from their isolation from effective competition rather than their public ownership per se' (Caves and Christensen 1980: 973 and 974).

The studies discussed so far have used index number techniques to estimate productivity growth. They have also assumed that the rail systems under review have been free to vary all their inputs to their cost-minimising levels, and hence have never been in anything but a long run cost-minimising position. But rail systems are rarely in a position to adjust their capacity at will, and we have seen that the US systems are no exception to this situation. Even in Canada, despite the competitive pricing environment for all commodities except grain, there have been government restrictions on abandonments of unprofitable branch lines, particularly in the Prairie Provinces. In such circumstances, a long-run total cost function cannot exist, and instead railroads can be viewed as minimising a variable cost function, defined as a function showing the minimum variable cost given specific outputs to be produced, specified input prices for the variable inputs, and specific levels of the fixed factors which are difficult to adjust.

Caves, Christensen and Swanson (1981a, 1981b) used such a function to analyse productivity growth in both the USA and Canada. The data set employed was the same as in their earlier studies, but the approach to productivity growth measurement was different. Instead of the index number approach, in which productivity growth is derived by weighting input and output indices by weights derived from input cost shares and from econometric estimates of a cost function, the alternative approach uses the econometric estimation of a cost function over the whole period for which productivity growth estimates are required directly in the estimation of productivity growth. Since productivity growth can be viewed as a shift in the production or cost function, if the cost function can be estimated in such a way that it includes data on costs at different points of time, differentiation of this cost function with respect to time provides a direct estimate of productivity growth, albeit one that is more likely to be subject to the vagaries of econometric estimation than is the index number technique.

This econometric approach to productivity growth can be used either for a total or a variable cost function. Caves, Christensen and Swanson (1981a) provide two definitions of productivity growth in the multi-product case. PGY is the equiproportional rate at which all outputs can be increased with all inputs held constant, while PGX is the equiproportional rate at which all outputs could be reduced if all outputs were held constant. These two measures are equal with constant returns to scale and related to each other by the formula PGY = PGX·RTS, where RTS is the degree of returns to scale, defined here as the inverse of the sum of cost elasticities with respect to outputs. Defining the total cost function in logs:

$$\ln c = g(\ln q_1, ..., \ln q_m, \ln p_1 ..., \ln p_n, t) \tag{2.21}$$

Caves, Christensen and Swanson show that PGX and PGY can be defined in terms of derivatives of this cost function as

$$PGX = -\partial \ln g / \partial t \tag{2.22}$$
$$\text{and} \quad PGY = -(\partial \ln g / \partial t) \cdot RTS = -(\partial \ln g / \partial t) / \sum_i^m (\partial \ln g / \partial \ln q_i) \tag{2.23}$$

39

With r fixed factors whose quantities are given by $z_1,...,z_r$, the variable cost function can be defined as

$$\ln v = h(\ln q_1...,\ln q_m, \ln p_1,...,\ln p_{n-r}, z_1,...z_r,t) \tag{2.24}$$

Again differentiation of this yields estimates of productivity growth

$$PGX = -(\partial \ln h/\partial t)/\left[1 - \sum_i^r (\partial \ln h/\partial \ln z_i)\right] \tag{2.25}$$

$$\text{and} \quad PGY = -(\partial \ln h/\partial t)/\left[\sum_i^n (\partial \ln h/\partial \ln q_i)\right] \tag{2.26}$$

Hence estimation of the appropriate (total or variable) form of a cost function, together with use of either equations (2.22) and (2.23), or (2.25) and (2.26), can yield direct estimates of productivity growth.

Caves, Christensen and Swanson (1981a) estimated both variable and total cost functions for comparison using their data set for US railroads and the generalised translog multi-product form of the cost function. As in the earlier study the data were combined to yield an overall cost function in which the different years were represented by additional variables which represent differences in the structure of production in the three years, 1955, 1963 and 1974. For the variable cost function the familiar output measures of ton-miles, average length of freight haul, passenger-miles, and average trip length were combined with data on input prices for three variable inputs (labour, fuel, equipment and materials) and quantities of one fixed input (way and structures capital). To estimate the instantaneous derivative of the log of variable cost with respect to time all variables except the binary variables representing the period to which the data relates were held constant at the mean of their values for the representative firm and the difference between the resulting estimates of the log of variable cost in the two years divided by the number of intervening years to provide an average annual rate of decline in costs between the periods. In such a way equations (2.25) and (2.26) could then be used to derive average annual growth rates in productivity between 1955 and 1963, and between 1963 and 1974.

This procedure yielded estimates for PGX of 3.4 per cent per annum for the first period and 0.6 per cent per annum for the second, and for PGY of between 3.5 and 4.2 per cent for the first period and between 0.6 and 0.7 per cent for the second. (The estimates of PGY vary according to the definition of output used in the returns to scale index.) Estimation of a total cost function with the same data set and procedures for incorporating the effects of changes in the structure of production yielded lower productivity growth estimates: for PGX these are 1.0 per cent per annum for the first period and 0.4 per cent per annum for the second, and for PGY 1.0—1.2 per cent for the first period and 0.5 per cent for the second. As noted, if some inputs are fixed, then the variable cost function is the appropriate one to use.

Now, however, there is an apparent inconsistency between the total cost function results for US railroads using the index number and the econometric approaches to the estimation of productivity growth. For the period from 1955 to 1974 the earlier index number approach gave an average annual estimate of productivity growth of 1.5 per cent per annum, while the econometric approach gives an average annual growth rate of only 0.8—1.0 per cent. Caves, Christensen and Swanson argued that this can be explained by reference to the effect of scale economies with respect to increases in average haul and trip length; the econometric estimates of productivity growth consider changes in costs of a representative firm with fixed output. The index number approach uses industry totals, but although industry output levels have remained fairly stable, average firm output has increased because of mergers. The scale effects of these firm level economies are masked in the industry aggregate figures and appear as productivity growth. When similar comparisons were made for Canadian railways using both econometric and index number procedures, the results were similar to each other because CN and CP are of a size where scale economies have been exhausted.

Finally Caves, Christensen and Swanson (1981b) used the econometric methodology to compare Canadian and US productivity growth rates. In this paper the variable cost function estimation procedures were the same as in Caves, Christensen and Swanson (1981a), except that data for the two Canadian railroads was added to the sample, and additional binary variables to permit differences in the structure of production between American and Canadian railroads to be modelled were added to the estimating equation. Estimates of productivity growth for Canadian and US railroads could then be made using equations (2.25) and (2.26). These comparisons were made (i) for railroads having characteristics of the typical US system, and (ii) for railroads having characteristics of the typical Canadian system. They showed that the productivity growth rate of the Canadian systems exceeded that of the US systems, particularly in the 1963 to 1974 period.

As well as these comparisons using the econometric method, the performance of CN and CP was also compared by the index number method with that of two American systems, Atchison Topeka and Sante Fe, and Southern Pacific, which are broadly similar in size and other characteristics and, like CN and CP, also regarded as being well-managed. Between 1956 and 1963 CN and CP productivity growth rates lay between those of the ATSF and SP but exceeded them thereafter, even though these two US companies have a better productivity growth record than the typical US railroad.

Productivity level comparisons are more difficult to interpret because of differences in operating environment, but Caves, Christensen and Swanson argued that they too showed superior Canadian performance in the 1963–74 period, despite the severe climatic conditions in which CN and CP operate. In conclusion, Caves, Christensen and Swanson argued that the better performance of the Canadian systems was attributable to the absence of regulation. On the basis of the herioc assumption that without regulation the US industry would have performed as well in productivity growth terms as its Canadian counterpart, they made some estimates of the economic costs of railroad regulation in the States in terms of the extra costs incurred because such productivity growth could not be achieved

2.5 Conclusions

This chapter has surveyed recent work on the measurement of rail total factor productivity which has considerably extended the methodology for the measurement of productivity change in an organisation over time and for the making of productivity comparisons between organisations. As well as the derivation of the productivity indices themselves, this work has also been used to reach policy conclusions, particularly with regard to the relative efficiency of private versus public ownership in an unregulated environment, and with regard to the relative efficiency of firms in regulated and unregulated environments.

These recent developments, firmly based on the economic theory of production, represent a considerable improvement over previous measures of total factor productivity. However, many problems remain. One common to all total factor productivity measurement methods is the measurement of capital stock quantities and prices. Although this might be somewhat less of a problem in the rail sector than in other sectors such as manufacturing, since data exist for most rail systems on quantities, qualities and ages of locomotives and rolling stock, and on route and track facilities, the data problems are still likely to be formidable, especially if cross-country comparisons between systems with different accounting and other conventions are wanted.

In addition, both the index number and the econometric methods of measuring productivity developed by Caves, Christensen and Swanson require econometric estimates of cost functions; the former to estimate elasticities of costs with respect to outputs for use as an intermediate input into the productivity measurement process, and the latter for the direct measurement of productivity change as a shift in the cost function. Despite the advantages derived from the sample size required to estimate the cost function and its associated input demand equations jointly, this still requires a large enough sample of consistent cross-sectional and/or time-series data. This may preclude its use for cross-system comparisons in Europe, where each national rail system reports its cost, output, and other results in a different form, and will make a time-series comparison for a single rail system difficult because of the need to obtain a long enough consistent series of (usually annual) data for that system. Econometric problems also arise when rail output is not exogenous, though most national rail systems do operate with regulated prices.

As we have seen, a major difficulty with cost function estimation is that of the appropriate definition of outputs and of inputs, and the resultant problem that the estimated cost function may not properly capture those characteristics of output that actually cause costs to vary between systems or through time. Alternative specifications of the structure of the cost function, and alternative disaggregations of inputs and outputs, will yield different estimates of the cost function and cost elasticities, and it is not a straightforward matter to choose 'the best' (in an econometric sense) estimate. In addition, while there are considerable advantages in use of flexible functional forms, such forms, as Wales (1977) has clearly demonstrated, may not necessarily satisfactorily approximate the cost function over the whole range of cross-sectional and/or time-series data even though they yield a satisfactory approximation to the cost function at a single point. There was some evidence of this in the initial work on the estimation of the generalised translog multi-product cost function for the US railroad industry (Caves, Christensen and Tretheway 1980).

The cost-function-based approaches also assume cost-minimising behaviour.[13] If some inputs are fixed, a long-run cost function cannot be estimated from short-run data. Caves, Christensen and Swanson's (1981a) results show how econometric-approach productivity growth measures derived from an (incorrect) long-run cost function can differ from those derived from a short-run, variable, cost function. Satisfactory estimation of such a variable cost function requires correct identification of those inputs that are fixed in the short-run and those that can be assumed to be variable, while the data available must be able to permit the appropriate level of disaggregation. Moreover, if the long-run cost function does not exist, the index number approach of equation (2.19) cannot be used to measure productivity change because the input cost shares will not be the appropriate input weights since cost-minimising input levels are not employed.

Cost-minimising behaviour also implies the absence of technical inefficiency; cost-minimising firms must always be on the boundary of their production frontier, employing allocatively efficient input combinations given the constraints facing them. If technical inefficiency does exist, then the estimated cost function will not be the true cost function,[14] since actual costs will be higher than they need to be given the state of technological knowledge. Apparent shifts of the cost function might then be due wholly or partly to a reduction in technical inefficiency rather than to productivity growth in the sense of a shift in the function. Thus it may be misleading to interpret measured productivity growth as being purely due to changes in the underlying production technology, rather than to changes in the efficiency with which an existing technology is applied.

Finally, it should be noted that the work surveyed in this chapter has assumed that input prices are exogenous to the firm and are themselves allocatively efficient. This might not be so. For example, subsidised organisations might pay wages above those necessary to retain their workforce (an example of managerial slack or X-inefficiency), while governments might provide capital to rail systems at subsidised cost. Such distortions in factor prices will in turn distort the productivity measures used.

Despite all the difficulties, a correct methodology is an essential pre-requisite to the measurement of a meaningful concept of productivity. This, Caves, Christensen and Swanson have provided. Unfortunately in view of the data and other problems that remain, productivity measurement continues to be a hazardous procedure, and the consumer of productivity statistics must always tread cautiously in drawing conclusions from productivity estimates.

Notes

1   Hicks-neutral technological progress has the effect of leaving the rate of technical substitution between inputs (which is equal to the slope of the isoquant) unchanged provided that the proportions in which they are employed are unchanged.

2   The crudest method of all to measure output is to add unweighted passenger-miles and ton-miles to derive a measure known as 'traffic units', but this is clearly very unsatisfactory.

3   For example, a system with a high proportion of long-distance bulk traffic is likely to require fewer inputs per ton-mile than a system with a high proportion of short-distance general merchandise.

4   Statistics in this and the following paragraph are from Association

of American Railroads (1982).

5 Homogeneity of a production function implies that the slopes of isoquant surfaces are parallel along any ray that passes through the origin. Related functions, known as homothetic functions, also share this property. Separability, of which there are a number of types, imposes restrictions on the relationship between the rates of technical substitution between pairs of inputs and the quantities of other inputs employed.

6 When output cannot be assumed to be exogenous, instrumental variable techniques can be used to estimate the cost function. See Friedlaender, Winston and Wang (1983) for an example of this approach to cost function estimation with non-exogenous outputs.

7 An excellent outline of this cost function, together with an empirical application, is to be found in Christensen and Greene (1976).

8 A further finding was that the estimated form of the output function implied that cost-minimisation would be achieved by ceasing to produce one of the outputs. Even though the data relate to 1936 this may not be too surprising in view of the long history of attempts by US railroads to abandon passenger traffics (Hilton 1980); indeed using the same data set, Brown, Caves and Christensen (1979) have recently estimated that marginal costs of passenger services were below fares for all but 4 out of 67 of the railroads in 1936.

9 We can write

$$MC/AC = (\partial c/\partial q)/(c/q) = (\partial c/c)/(\partial q/q) = (\partial \ln c)/(\partial \ln q).$$

10 See Keeler (1974) for the derivation of the short-run cost function. The Lagrangean approach is generally messy and often intractable; this is one major reason why, as long as output is exogenous, it is usually more convenient to use the dual approach and specify either the total or the variable cost function directly.

11 Caves, Christensen and Swanson found the elasticity of variable costs with respect to way and structures capital was positive, indicating consistency with Keeler's findings of excess capacity and Harris's of increased operating costs per ton-mile with lower traffic density levels.

12 But see Miller (1983) for criticism of the perpetual inventory method of evaluating inputs of capital services.

13 See Millward and Parker (1983) for further discussion of the inefficiency that arises from firms' not minimising their costs of production, and the relationship between this type of inefficiency and productivity growth measures that are based on the assumption of cost-minimising behaviour.

14 Unless a frontier production or cost function is explicitly estimated.

See Nishimizu and Page (1982).

References

Arrow, K.J., Chenery, H.B., Minhas, B.S. and Solow, R.M. (1961), 'Capital-labour substitution and economic efficiency', *Review of Economics and Statistics*, Vol.4, pp.225–50.

Association of American Railroads (1982), *Yearbook of Railroad Facts 1982*, (AAR, Washington, DC).

Braeutigam, R.R., Daughety, A.F. and Turnquist, M.A. (1982), 'The estimation of a hybrid cost function for a railroad firm', *Review of Economics and Statistics*, Vol.64, pp.394–403.

British Railways Board (1982), *Productivity Performance: An Analysis by the British Railways Board of its Productivity Performance Since 1977*, (BRB, London).

British Railways Board and University of Leeds (1979), *A Comparative Study of European Rail Performance*, (BRB, London).

Brown, R.S., Caves, D.W. and Christensen, L.R. (1979), 'Modelling the structure of cost and production for multi-product firms', *Southern Economic Journal*, Vol.16, pp.256–73.

Caves, D.W. and Christensen, L.R. (1978), *Productivity in Canadian Railroads, 1956–1975*, (Canadian Transport Commission, Ottawa).

Caves, D.W. and Christensen, L.R. (1980), 'The relative efficiency of public and private firms in a competitive environment: the case of Canadian railroads', *Journal of Political Economy*, Vol.80, pp.958–76.

Caves, D.W., Christensen, L.R. and Diewert, W.E. (1982), 'The economic theory of index numbers and the measurement of input, output and productivity', *Econometrica*, Vol.50, pp.1393–414.

Caves, D.W., Christensen, L.R. and Swanson, J.A. (1980), 'Productivity in U.S. railroads, 1951–1974', *Bell Journal of Economics*, Vol.11, pp.166–81.

Caves, D.W., Christensen, L.R. and Swanson, J.A. (1981a), 'Productivity growth, scale economies, and capacity utilization in U.S. railroads, 1955–1974', *American Economic Review*, Vol.71, pp.994–1002.

Caves, D.W., Christensen, L.R. and Swanson, J.A. (1981b), 'Economic performance in regulated and unregulated environments; a comparison of U.S. and Canadian railroads', *Quarterly Journal of Economics*, Vol.26, pp.559–81.

Caves, D.W., Christensen, L.R. and Tretheway, M.W. (1980), 'Flexible cost functions for multiproduct firms', *Review of Economics and Statistics*, Vol.62, pp.477–81.

Christensen, L.R. and Greene, W.H. (1976), 'Economies of scale in U.S. electric power generation', *Journal of Political Economy*, Vol.84, pp.655–76.

Deakin, B.M. and Seward, T. (1969), *Productivity in Transport: A Study of Employment, Capital, Output, Productivity and Technical Change*, (Cambridge University Press, Cambridge).

Diewert, W.E. (1976), 'Exact and superlative index numbers', *Journal of Econometrics*, Vol.4, pp.115–45.

Diewert, W.E. (1981), 'The economic theory of index numbers: a survey', in A. Deaton (ed.), *Essays in the Theory and Measurement of Consumer Behaviour*, (Cambridge University Press, Cambridge).

Farrell, M.J. (1957), 'The measurement of productive efficiency', *Journal of the Royal Statistical Society A*, Vol.120, pp.253–81.

Friedlaender, A.F. and Spady, R.H. (1981), *Freight Transport Regulation*, (MIT Press, Cambridge, Mass.).

Friedlaender, A.F., Winston, C. and Wang, K. (1983), 'Costs, technology and productivity in the U.S. automobile industry', *Bell Journal of Economics*, Vol.14, pp.1–20.

Griliches, Z. (1972), 'Cost allocation in railroad regulation', *Bell Journal of Economics and Management Science*, Vol.3, pp.26–41.

Griliches, Z. and Jorgenson, D.W. (1967), 'The explanation of productivity change', *Review of Economic Studies*, Vol.34, pp.249–83.

Harris, R.G. (1977), 'Economies of traffic density in the rail freight industry', *Bell Journal of Economics*, Vol.8, pp.556–64.

Harris, R.G. and Winston, C. (1983), 'Potential benefits of rail mergers: an econometric analysis of network effects on service quality', *Review of Economics and Statistics*, Vol.65, pp.32–40.

Hasenkamp, G. (1976), 'A study of multiple-output production functions; Klein's railroad study revisited', *Journal of Econometrics*, Vol.4, pp.253–62.

Hilton, G.W. (1980), *Amtrak: The National Railroad Passenger Corporation*, (American Enterprise Institute for Public Policy Research, Washington, DC).

Keeler, T.E. (1974), 'Railroad costs, returns to scale and excess capacity', *Review of Economics and Statistics*, Vol.56, pp.201–8.

Klein, L.R. (1953), *A Textbook of Econometrics*, (Row Peterson & Co., Evanston, Ill.).

Lazarus, P.E. (1982), 'Productivity and the relationship between railway administrations and governments', *Rail International*, pp.51–7.

Levin, R.C. and Weinberg, D.H. (1979), 'Alternatives for restructuring the railroads: end-to-end or parallel mergers?', *Economic Inquiry*, Vol.17, pp.371–88.

Miller, E.M. (1983), 'A difficulty in measuring productivity with a perpetual inventory capital stock measure', *Oxford Bulletin of*

Economics and Statistics, Vol.45, pp.297–306.

Millward, R. and Parker, D.N. (1983), 'Public and private enterprise in comparative behaviour and relative efficiency', in R. Millward *et al* (ed.), *Public Sector Economics*, (Longman, London).

Nishimizu, M. and Page, J.M. (1982), 'Total factor productivity growth, technological progress and technical efficiency change: dimensions of productivity change in Yugoslavia, 1965–1978', *Economic Journal*, Vol.92, pp.920–36.

Pryke, R.W.S. (1971), *Public Enterprise in Practice: The British Experience of Nationalization Over Two Decades*, (MacGibbon and Kee, London).

Pryke, R.W.S. (1981), *The Nationalised Industries: Policies and Performance Since 1968*, (Martin Robertson, Oxford).

Samuelson, P.A. and Swamy, S. (1974), 'Invariant economic index numbers and canonical quality: survey and synthesis', *American Economic Review*, Vol.64, pp.566–93.

Sen, A. (1979), 'The welfare basis of real income comparisons: a survey', *Journal of Economic Literature*, Vol.17, pp.1–45.

Spady, R.H. and Friedlaender, A.F. (1978), 'Hedonic cost functions for the regulated trucking industry', *Bell Journal of Economics*, Vol.9, pp.159–179.

Varian, H.R. (1978), *Microeconomic Analysis*, (Norton & Co., New York).

Wales, T.J. (1977), 'On the flexibility of flexible functional forms', *Journal of Econometrics*, Vol.5, pp.183–93.

3 Revitalisation of the US freight industry: an organisational perspective

R. G. HARRIS AND C. GRIMM

3.1 Introduction and overview: organisational change and industry performance

3.1—1 Industry decline and policy changes

In 1980, US railroads hauled 1.5 billion tons of freight an average distance of 590 miles, with total freight revenues exceeding $26 billion. However, the rail industry has been steadily losing ground to other modes: water carriers for bulk commodities, pipelines for liquids and liquified commodities, and motor carriers for manufactured commodities. Thus, from 1940 to 1975, the rail industry's share of total freight revenues fell from 76 to 38 per cent, while motor carriers increased their market share from 17 to 53 per cent (US Department of Transportation 1979).

Not surprisingly, the industry did not fare well financially during this period. Throughout the post-war period, rail profits have been consistently below those earned in other industries and significantly below the long-run cost of capital to the industry. Since the 1970s, public policy-makers have acknowledged the industry's low and declining profitability, punctuated by bankruptcies and loss of service in the Northeast and Midwest.

During the past decade, US rail policy (culminating in the 1980 Staggers Rail Act) has steadily eased regulatory burdens and allowed competitive forces to operate in the rail industry. The common theme in recent legislation and regulatory implementation has been to give rail managers and shippers the opportunity to chart their own courses. Carriers, not regulatory bodies, are to decide which markets to serve, what rates to charge, what structural configuration to choose, and how (or even whether) to coordinate joint routes and rate divisions with connecting carriers. Carriers and shippers are free to negotiate contracts and are heartily encouraged to do so by the Interstate Commerce Commission (ICC). A growing number of commodities are now completely exempt from ICC control, and carriers may design service, pricing, and marketing as they choose with few regulatory constraints.

In conjunction with and in response to these changes, a merger wave is sweeping the industry. Since the public consolidation of the northeastern railroads into Consolidated Rail Corporation (ConRail), four major rail mergers have been approved by the Commission:

(1) Burlington Northern − Control and Merger − St. Louis−San Francisco Railroad (BN−Frisco);
(2) CSX Corporation − Control − Chessie System and Seaboard Coast Line (CSX);
(3) Union Pacific − Control − Missouri Pacific and Western Pacific (UP−MP−WP); and
(4) NS Enterprises − Control − Norfolk and Western and Southern Railroad (NS).

Students of the rail industry are engaged in interpreting these recent events and reviewing evidence of the effects of deregulation, primarily in terms of economic and financial measures; that is not our intention here. Instead, we will offer a perspective in this chapter based on the premise that organisational change is a key to industry revitalisation. In that sense the paper is intended to supplement the more traditional economic analyses of deregulation and industry performance.

3.1−2 Organisational nature of industry problems

The myriad studies of the effects of regulation upon the performance of the US railroad industry have given impetus to the deregulation movement. In these studies, analysts have concentrated almost exclusively upon economic effects: losses in technical efficiency, allocative efficiency and other measures of economic welfare which can be traced to regulatory policies and practices. The major classes of these economic effects are excess capacity, intermodal misallocation of traffic, continuance of uneconomic services, lower capital and labour productivity, and slower rates of technological innovation and adoption. Hence, proponents of deregulation cite these losses as potential benefits from deregulation.

There may be disagreement over the magnitude of these effects, but there is an astonishing degree of consensus that these effects have occurred, and that deregulation will bring substantial benefits by reducing or eliminating these inefficiencies. Even so, this preoccupation with essentially static measures of inefficiency obscures the effects of regulation and misdirects the debate over deregulation. It is our premise that the fundamental problems in the industry are not technological or economic, but organisational. The most important effects of railroad regulation have been upon the organisation of the industry (typically called corporate structure), upon relations among organisations in the industry, and upon the structure and performance of organisations in the industry.

The functions of human organisations are to seek out and exploit advantages and opportunities, to find better ways of utilising human and natural resources, to anticipate and respond to changing demands upon the organisation, and to manage interdependence with other organisations. By all these measures, the central failure of the US railroad industry is organisational, in that an industry which is by physical structure and extent of operations a system[1] is organised disjointly with suboptimisation by components (i.e. individual rail carriers). Relations among highly interdependent organisations are characterised by distrust, deceit and lack of cooperation. Individual organisations lack the vitality and adaptability to perform well, whether performance is measured by private profit or public interest. If these claims are true, changes in regulatory policy regarding rates, service requirements, physical abandonment and investment may not bring the anticipated benefits, at least not in the foreseeable future.

It is not argued that there are no good railroad managers, indeed given the obstacles and lack of incentives, there are a surprising number of highly competent managers in the industry. Nor is this characterisation of the industry intended to suggest that railroad management is primarily responsible for the current plight of the industry. Rather, the argument is that any public policy which fails to take account of these organisational failures will surely not succeed in revitalising the industry. The chief concern of this chapter, accordingly, is with the effects of deregulation upon the organisation of the industry and the organisations in the industry. The objective will be the delineation of public policy measures which will promote rationalisation of the industry structure, allow or induce cooperative relations among interdependent organisations, and provide incentives for improved organisational performance.

The traditional *industrial organisation* approach to industry structure, conduct, and performance is concerned mainly with the number of firms in a market, since the chief policy issue is the degree of competition. To the extent that firms are interdependent, it is because there are a small number of firms, so that the actions of any one company affect the market position of the other companies in the industry. In the railroad industry, all rail carriers are interdependent with at least some, if not all other rail carriers, for two reasons. Analagous to manufacturing industries, rail carriers are interdependent as competitors, i.e. in any given rail market, there are never more than a few railroads, hence the actions of any one carrier affect all of the others. If one carrier in a market corridor (which, for railroads, is the relevant market) expands capacity by adding a second track or installing centralised train control, there will almost certainly be important effects upon the other carriers in the corridor.

But US railroads are interdependent in quite another way, for which there are few analogies in manufacturing. Because rail services often extend beyond the boundaries of a single firm (according to the Association of American Railroads, 1980, 70 per cent of rail traffic is handled by more than one carrier), rail carriers are dependent on each other as suppliers of services. In no other industry are firms both competitively and cooperatively interdependent. In manufacturing, firms buy from suppliers, but do not compete with those suppliers for business (there are of course exceptions to this rule but in no case is it an important industry characteristic). In many public utility industries, companies must cooperate to provide services. But those utilities do not compete with each other in any important way.

In addition to the competitive/cooperative interdependence of rail carriers, there is yet one other reason why the organisation of the industry has such profound effects upon industry performance. Dependence upon other organisations is seldom critical for an organisation when there are large numbers of potential cooperators. A manufacturing firm, for example, may depend upon other companies for essential supplies to its own production process. But typically, there are a large number of potential suppliers (i.e. the firm faces a competitive market), so relations between the firm and its suppliers are seldom problematic. If one relationship breaks down (e.g. the supplier is found to be unreliable), the firm can exit that relationship easily, and begin purchasing those supplies from some other supplier.

It is very often the case that rail carriers do not have that option. Supply relations in the rail industry are almost always characterised by small numbers and highly imperfect information. In other words, the market between US railroads is not competitive, and a rail carrier may be forced to continue dealing with another carrier even though there are serious deficiencies in the supply relationship. If a shipper wants to move freight from A to C, the originating carrier serves only A to B and there is only one carrier serving B to C, then carrier AB must either cooperate with carrier BC or forgo the traffic. Though there are often alternative routings so that a carrier does not face a monopoly supplier, in few cases can these markets rightly be termed competitive.

An important consequence of this organisational dependence is that rail managers often perceive an incongruity between their performance and outcomes. If managers of carrier AB make every effort to provide the best service possible in order to satisfy the shipper, while carrier BC provides inferior service, then managers of AB may find it fruitless to continue making their best effort. In most situations such as these, it would be very difficult for the shipper to know where the source of the bad service lies, at AB, BC, or both. Thus, we should not be particularly surprised by the poor service quality typically provided by rail carriers, or even by the lack of concern with service quality by most rail managers. As discussed by Pfeffer and Salancik (1978), it is an axiom of organisational behaviour that organisations function well only when they have control over the resources required, or can easily obtain those resources in competitive markets. When shipments transcend the boundaries of a carrier, this axiom is violated.[2]

One strategy for dealing with organisational interdependence is, of course, to merge the organisations. To manage competitive interdependence, firms merge horizontally; for cooperative interdependence, they merge vertically. Horizontal implies mergers between two companies in different industries who have a buyer—seller relationship. However, because of the competitive/cooperative interdependence in the railroad industry, there is confusion between these terms. A railroad merger may be designed to manage competitive dependence, in which case it would be termed horizontal (i.e. a parallel merger). But railroads may also merge to reduce cooperative dependence. Such mergers would properly be called vertical, even though the merger involves two firms in the same industry (i.e. an end-to-end merger). The primary distinction between parallel and end-to-end mergers has been based upon their differential competitive effects. While most observers believe that parallel mergers have more serious anti-competitive effects than end-to-end mergers, the exclusive concern with competition obscures the motives for mergers from an organisational or behavioural perspective. Whether vertically or horizontally, organisations merge in order to reduce dependence on other organisations.

Mergers being as important as they are to organisational structure, relations, and performance in the industry, they will be a central concern in this chapter. In particular, we discern the potential effects of deregulation upon merger policies and practices, and, in turn, the potential effects of mergers (and the opposite of mergers, divestiture) upon the structure and performance of the industry.

In many cases, such as when consolidations significantly reduce competition, mergers are not the preferred strategy for dealing with organisational interdependence. Accordingly, we also consider alternatives to mergers as methods of improving organisation performance. These alternatives include joint cooperation by bilateral or multilateral agreements (e.g. joint trackage rights, car routing protocol); membership in and abeyance to industry organisations (e.g. Association of American Railroads, rate bureaux); market exchange relations (e.g. renting equipment from another railroad on a *per diem* basis); and externally imposed cooperation (e.g. an ICC order to provide cars to certain railroads).

In section 3.2, the effects of regulatory policy upon organisational structure and relations are summarised. It is seen that, because of the effects of regulation upon the evolution of the organisation of the industry, retrospective studies of mergers are of little benefit. Furthermore, a review of the negative effects of regulation upon past mergers and inter-organisational cooperation help in connecting potential gains from railroad reorganisation to specific regulatory policies. It is shown that, even without any regulatory authority over mergers or other forms of reorganisational cooperation, railroads would not be free to merge as they like, since anti-trust law would continue to apply.

After the review of regulatory policy and its effects, a natural way to proceed might be to itemise various types of organisational change and attempt to attribute specific costs and benefits. The problem with that approach is that many of the potential benefits of organisational change might be realised in whole or in part without organisational change. Here the goal is to understand the consequences directly attributable to organisational changes; thus care must be taken not to include benefits which could be obtained by some other means.

Various categories of changes in the structure and performance of the US railroad industry (and, to the extent it is related, the freight transport system) are defined together with an examination of the degree to which those changes are dependent upon some corresponding organisational change. For example, the elimination of redundant main lines in corridors of consolidation potential is totally dependent upon some form of organisational change, whether by exit of one carrier from the corridor through bankruptcy, joint trackage agreement between two carriers, or merger of two carriers. In some cases, dependence upon organisational change will turn out to be critical, in other cases, negligible.

Section 3.3, therefore, considers the dependence of physical restructuring upon organisational change. The basic types of physical restructuring to be examined include abandonment of rural branch lines and urban industrial sidings; main line rehabilitation and consolidation; rehabilitation, consolidation and relocation of classification yards and terminals; and capital-intensive investments in the physical infrastructure.

In section 3.4, the potential effects of organisational change upon railroad operations, productivity and service quality are examined. These effects are categorised as traffic flow consolidation, reduction in circuitous routings, information systems and service quality control, improved utilisation of physical plant that equipment, increased labour productivity and intermodal operational flexibility. The main difference between this account of potential benefits and previous studies lies in the emphasis upon service improvements. It is symptomatic of the commercial disorientation of the railroad industry that studies of potential improvements have concentrated almost exclusively on reducing the costs of production. For too long the industry has perceived its function as providing low cost transportation. Yet railroads have lost much of their traffic share precisely because they have been too concerned with costs and too little concerned with quality of service. As massive shifts of high-valued commodities to motor carriers indicate, many shippers willingly pay higher prices in exchange for better service. Hence, we show that the potential effects of organisational change upon service quality are substantial — perhaps even greater than potential cost reduction effects.

In the final section the potential effects of organisational change upon technological innovation and diffusion, organisational adaptability, and managerial incentives, domain and performance are explored. Care must be exercised here, given the lack of analytical clarity and empirical measurement. But unmeasured does not mean unimportant, so conclusions are ventured when they can be defended as reasonable speculation. In this section, concern turns from the industry environment of railroad organisations to the more general managerial environment of which relations with other railroads are only a part. This broader environmental orientation allows such questions as: under what circumstances are competent managers likely to be attracted to an industry? How do organisational design and structure affect managerial performance? How does lack of commercial incentives affect managerial attitudes? How can the domain of good managers be expanded; the domain of incompetent managers be contracted? These are exceedingly difficult questions, the answers to which must be considered speculative. But asking such questions is completely consistent with the basic premise: that organisational failure is the primary cause of the industry's current plight, and organisational change is essential to the industry's revitalisation.

The chief objective of the chapter is therefore, to examine the impact of regulatory policies, deregulation in particular, upon organisational structure, relations and performance in the rail freight industry.

In reaching that objective, an attempt is made to assess the relationship between organisational structure and industry performance in terms of financial viability, reliability and quality of services, amount of scarce human and natural resources employed to produce those services, and the contribution of the industry to achieving broader social, political and economic objectives.

The underlying methodology is welfare economics. As a heuristic standard, use is made of the optimal performance of the rail industry and, to some extent, the surface freight system in general. Since one is dealing with human institutions and policies one could not achieve that optimum even if it could be defined. Nevertheless, a normative standard services the useful function of indicating the directions in which policies ought to be leading us. Further, by stating explicitly the consequences of alternative industry structures and regulatory policies, a better sense of the trade-offs between competing objectives should be attained, since often it is only possible to have more of one thing at the expense of something else (e.g. more competition among railroads, less technical efficiency).

3.2 The effects of regulation upon organisational structure, relations and performance in the rail freight industry

3.2—1 Market competition versus regulation in the rail industry

Almost from its inception, the US railroad industry has been engaged in a process of corporate consolidation and reorganisation. While the rate of mergers and reorganisations has fluctuated widely over various periods, the number of rail carriers has constantly declined, and the average size of rail carriers increased. Despite this continuing change, many believe that the balkanisation of the industry has been a major cause of its failure. Indeed it is striking to compare the organisation of the US rail system with that of any other country in the world. In virtually every country, rail services are provided by a monopolist (or, in a few cases, two or three companies).

The rationale for a monopolistic structure is straightforward: given the nature of its physical structure and operations, the railroad industry is a system. By the definition of system, if decisions are made at the level of subsystems, outputs will be suboptimised. It is a basic axiom of decision theory that decisions must be made at that level which incorporates all effects of the decision. In a system, decisions that have systematic effects should be made at the system level, whether by a single authority (i.e. a monopolist) or by coordination authorities (e.g. through a complex protocol for decision-making). It should be noted, however, that coordination among subsystems implies either voluntary participation or being subject to external authority. If there is no external authority (e.g. central planner), and if subsystems are unwilling to coordinate voluntarily, suboptimisation will prevail. In a system, lack of coordination among actors leads to the tyranny of large numbers.

A classic example of systems planning and operations is the US telephone industry: the family of American Telephone and Telegraph and its subsidiary companies is a near monopolist, which until recently provided virtually the only means of long-distance telecommunications services. But there are also hundreds of other independent phone companies, all of which are connected to the Bell System, and in more than just an operational sense. It is widely appreciated (at least by subscribers of independent companies) that multiple actors must coordinate in order to provide a typical long-distance call. In addition to providing the central decisions for handling individual calls, though, the Bell System has also provided the central decisions for standardising technology (so that equipment is compatible), physical capacity (to maximise capacity utilisation), and rate-making processes (so that phone companies have not had to negotiate the division of proceeds from each single call).

The comparative efficiency, low cost and quality of service of the US telephone system is generally recognised. That does not mean that the telephone industry, which is itself undergoing reorganisation, is the appropriate analogue for reorganising the railroad industry, but it does point to a paradox in regulatory policy toward the industry. Before turning to that paradox, however, we first discuss the historic roles of regulation in the railroad industry.

Often people equate regulation of the US railroad industry with the Interstate Commerce Commission. The ICC is a prominent actor and it has primary regulatory responsibility for surface freight transportation, but it is a mistaken view that railroad regulation is an exclusive ICC preserve. The surface freight transportation system operates in a complex social, political, and legal environment, of which ICC regulation is only a part. If, in discussing the potential effects of deregulation, we limit ourselves to the authority, policies and practices of the Interstate Commerce Commission, we do ourselves a grave injustice.

Here the term regulation is used in its generic sense: the body of law and set of political institutions which control, constrain, induce or otherwise attempt to modify the behaviour of railroad companies. The main classes of these regulatory institutions are: transportation planning and funding agencies (e.g. Departments of Transportation at state and federal levels); state public utility commissions; labour relations and labour protection laws and agencies; bankruptcy laws and their implementation by courts and trustees; trade associations and rate bureaux (although private, voluntary agencies, one of their main functions is to regulate behaviour of members); securities laws and enforcement agencies; environmental protection laws and enforcement agencies; urban and regional development and industrial planning authorities; and anti-trust laws and enforcement agencies.

While all of these regulatory institutions have important effects upon the organisation and performance of the rail industry, the anti-trust laws are of central importance to this section. Further, anti-trust law is important because organisational change in the industry will depend in large part upon the extent to which the industry is subject to, or exempt from, anti-trust enforcement. Therefore, even a total elimination of the ICC's authority over rail or intermodal mergers would not necessarily lead to organisational restructuring, because both historically and conceptually, anti-trust and regulation are altern-ative mechanisms for achieving social control of private enterprises. The US has not, and probably will not, experience a sharp decrease in one without a sharp increase in the other.

In a predominantly market economy, traditional reliance has been upon market competition as the primary mechanism for promoting economic efficiency and distributional equity. Market competition forces producers to minimise costs and prevents them from charging prices above those costs, at least over the long run. The purpose of anti-trust law is to preserve and promote market competition. Anti-trust is a political institution intended to make markets work better. Historic-ally, anti-trust laws were applied mainly to the manufacturing sector of the economy, wherein the underlying economic characteristics suggested that competition would best promote efficiency and equity. However, (as discussed in Grimm, (1983)), anti-trust laws and proced-ures are now being applied to a greater extent in the railroad industry.

The rationale for regulation is quite different. In certain cases, the economic characteristics of an industry are such that competition (i.e. having many producers) would reduce technical efficiency: the cost of producing each unit of output would exceed the attainable minimum. In these cases (i.e. structural or natural monopolies) monopoly (or, perhaps, oligopoly) is the more efficient industry structure. But in the absence of market competition, the monopolist could exploit its inherent bargaining advantage to raise prices above the costs of product-ion, causing allocative inefficiencies and distributional inequities. Historically, anti-trust law has not been relied upon in these cases, since competition is not the desired outcome. Rather, it is common-place in the US to resort to social control by administrative regulation, which is intended to substitute for market competition. The function of administrative regulation is to prevent a structural monopolist from behaving like a monopolist, by keeping prices in line with costs and limiting profits to a normal level.

To be sure, administrative regulation has served other purposes as well. In particular, regulation has often served to cartelise what would otherwise be a competitive industry. Regulation has usually been used to prevent competition on the grounds of protecting infant industries (e.g. airlines) or stabilising destructive competition (e.g. motor carriers). Because regulation in such cases tends to protect producers rather than consumers, deregulation is sought as the appropriate remedy.

Still, in other infrastructure industries — telephone, electricity, natural gas and postal systems — reliance has been exclusively upon administrative regulation of structural monopolies.[3] The irony in the case of railroads is that there has never been a commitment to rely entirely upon regulation by administrative control. The Interstate Commerce Commission (ICC) was founded (and its authority enhanced by subsequent legislation) on the premise that railroads are natural monopolies and that, in the absence of market competition, rail users should be protected from exploitation by political intervention. Thus, the paradox of railroad regulation lies in the fact that virtually every piece of railroad regulation legislation has also directed the ICC to 'promote competition' in the industry. When competition has not been required in the supply of electricity or local telephone services, why has it in the railroad industry?

There are a number of answers to that question. First, there has always been disagreement over the extent to which railroads are structural monopolies. Measures of railroad costs, whether economies of scale, traffic density or traffic flow consolidation, are contradictory on this point (although for many shippers who consider themselves captive to a particular railroad, the answer is very clearly that railroads are monopolies). Second, given locational flexibility and alternative modes of transportation, there is considerable opinion that even when there is only one railroad in a market, geographic competition (i.e. shipping to a different market), locational adjustments (actual or potential), and intermodal competition will reduce or eliminate the railroad's monopoly power over shippers in that market. Third, there has always been considerable scepticism about the ability of a regulatory agency actually to protect shippers from monopoly power; accordingly, shippers often argue that only a combination of regulation and market competition will protect them from monopoly exploitation.

But for whatever reasons, the fact is that there has been no commitment to either form of social control, competition or regulation. In that paradoxical public policy lies the explanation of the organisational failures of the railroad industry. By applying both types of social control, railroads and society have been denied the benefits of either. Had there been a full commitment to competition, the railroads would have been allowed the commercial freedom allowed other competitive industries. Had there been regulation, as in the telephone or electricity industries, this may have achieved the technical efficiencies which accrue to monopoly organisation of system industries.

Ultimately, the issue of the trade-off between competition (as a mechanism of social control) and monopoly (as a means of achieving technical control) in the railroad industry is addressed. In the remainder of this section, though, there is an examination of the effects of this paradoxical public policy upon the organisational structure of the industry.

3.2—2 Effects of regulation

To reiterate, the nature of regulatory policy was not the product of the ICC, but was legislatively mandated by the US Congress. Virtually every piece of legislation affecting the ICC and railroads has contained directives to preserve prevailing patterns of service, or to promote competition. It may be true that the ICC was overly enthusiastic in its attempts to comply with those directives, but that does not change the essential fact that the policy was a legislative product.

One consequence of this regulatory policy has been to preserve economically obsolete rail capacity. Given dramatic shifts in the spatial location of economic activity and flows of commodities among those locations, the resemblance between the railroad route system of 1975 and 1900 is striking. When the enormous increases in the capacity of rail lines (due to dieselisation, longer trains, larger cars, automated signalling and centralised train control) are taken into account, it is also striking that so few main lines were abandoned during that period.

Because there is a near one-to-one correspondence between rail physical structure and organisational structure, the perpetuation of physical capacity by regulatory policy had the effect of protecting and preserving railroad companies. Not only did the ICC attempt to preserve railroad corporate and physical structures, but special provisions of the Bankruptcy Act mandate that 'the court shall take into consideration, in addition to the best interests of creditors and the debtor, the public interest in the preservation of the debtor's rail service'. The very economic forces which are signalling by financial failure, the lack of economic viability (and, very often, social utility), were prevented from operating. Both physical structure and corporate structure were preserved.

Moreover, attempts to rationalise the industry — both physically and organisationally — met with staunch resistance. The ICC often denied, and at the least delayed, efforts to consolidate the industry structurally. While the consequences of such policies are fairly obvious in terms of excess physical capacity, the less obvious effects upon organisational vitality are probably more important in the long run. One important purpose of mergers in a market economy is the expansion and contraction of managerial domains. As corporate managements succeed, their domains expand, both through internal growth and external acquisition. As managements fail, or are less successful, their domains are contracted, by internal decline or acquisition by another company. The lifeblood of organisational vitality is change: growth and expansion if successful, decline and contraction if not. The story of any large, highly successful American industry can be told in such terms, yet regulatory policies have prohibited such a mechanism from operating in the railroad industry.

In addition to these structural effects, regulatory policies tightly constrained efforts of rail carriers to cooperate in the provision of rail services. In some cases, the ICC prohibited cooperation, as in the case of joint trackage rights or market swaps. The more pervasive interference, though, was denying rail carriers the incentives necessary to induce organisational cooperation. An excellent example of the latter phenomenon was the restrictive rate-making policies for special services such as piggyback or through trains. To the extent that carriers were prevented from passing on cost reductions by lowering rates, or charging for higher service quality by raising the rates of specialised services, they had no incentive to adopt them.

These pervasive, largely negative, effects of regulation upon corporate structure and organisational relations make assessments difficult. The issue here is not whether mergers and other forms of reorganisation have been good or bad in the past, but whether, in a dramatically changed regulatory environment, organisational changes have private and/or public benefits which exceed their costs. That is, it is necessary to speculate about the potential effects of organisational change under deregulation.

Under the assumption of deregulation, then, retrospective studies of past railroad mergers are of little use, for several reasons. First, the sample of observations (i.e. previous railroad mergers) is terribly biased because mergers must be approved by the ICC before they can be consummated. Whether in response to legislative mandates or an expression of the tendency of regulating agencies to protect the firms they regulate, the ICC has seldom approved mergers which might have realised significant benefits, in either reducing costs or improving market performance. The apparent reason for this posture is that the greater the benefits of a particular merger, the greater the likelihood that some other railroad(s) would be harmed by the consolidated carrier. Under the 'do no harm' principle of regulation, such mergers are denied, delayed until the participants are exhausted, or are conditional upon acceptance by other railroads. Hence, measurement of benefits from past mergers in a regulated environment is badly biased with respect to the potential effects of merger in a deregulated environment.

Even where no sampling bias exists, however, there is another source of bias in retrospective measurements. As suggested, regulatory policies have often prevented consolidated carriers from realising the potential benefits of the consolidation of traffic on some lines and downgrading or discontinuing service on redundant lines. Regulatory barriers have prohibited, or at least inhibited, such benefits from being realised. Likewise, labour protection legislation often prevents the realisation of another class of potential benefits, improving the productivity of employees, by reducing redundancy and taking advantage of economies of scale and traffic density.

Yet a third class of regulatory effects distorts retrospective measurement of the benefits of reorganisation: the forced inclusion of weak carriers as a condition for approving mergers of strong carriers. In an industry with substantial excess capacity, a prime function of mergers should be to reduce capacity by forcing weak firms out of business. By requiring those firms, their management, employees and physical capacity to be included in a potential viable consolidated carrier, an anchor is tied around the stronger carrier's neck, then it's discovered they don't fly very well!

Finally, regulatory policies on mergers have often had the effect of preventing mergers from actually being mergers in the operational sense. Many of the so-called rail holding companies, or family lines, are purely financial artefacts, with little or no operational consequence. There may well be some benefits in common ownership of what were formerly independent carriers, but they are only a fraction of the total potential benefits of organisational restructuring.

None of these arguments suggest that there is nothing to learn from the lessons of history, but do support extreme caution when extrapolating into the future in light of dramatically changed circumstances. The primary value of retrospective studies of rail mergers and reorganisations lies in identifying those regulatory policies that have had the most deleterious effects upon railroad reorganisation. If the potential benefits of organisational change are to be realised, it is precisely those regulatory policies that must be changed.

3.3 The potential effects of organisational change upon the physical structure of the rail freight industry

3.3—1 The problem of excess capacity

The connection between organisational structure and physical structure is widely appreciated, so much so that the two problems are often
treated as synonymous. In fact, they are not. There are numerous
opportunities for rationalising the physical structure of the industry
that do not depend in any critical way upon some corresponding
organisational change. Still, one can only proceed so far in physical
rationalisation without concomitant organisational change. This section
assesses this dependence of physical restructuring upon organisational
change.

Though highly related, the main classes of physical restructuring
possibilities (rural branch lines, urban lines and classification yards,
and consolidation of main lines) are treated separately. In each
category, the potential benefits (and costs) of physical restructuring
are evaluated and the dependence of those benefits upon organisational
changes of specified types are estimated.

3.3—2 Rural branch lines

The problem of excess capacity in the form of light density branch
lines still exists today in spite of the abandonment of about 2000
miles of line annually over the past decade (Keeler 1983). In one
study (Harris 1977b), estimates of economically unviable branch line
mileage ranged from 20,000 to 45,000 miles in 1977; estimates of
total railroad losses on these lines ranged from $90 to $350 million
annually. Estimates of economic viability are typically based on
current operating conditions: traffic volume, revenue per unit of
traffic, and costs of service. Abandonment is, in fact, only one method
for reducing the losses now incurred in the provision of unprofitable
rail service. Other alternatives include increasing traffic volume, raising
rates, reducing costs or some combination of these.

Provisions of the 1980 Staggers Rail Act have allowed railroads to
raise rates on light density lines to cover the costs of service. A second
method of reducing losses from unviable branch lines depends in part
upon organisational restructuring. In many cases, there are duplicative
branch lines serving a geographic region, where, with current traffic
and rail mileage, all or most of the lines are economically unviable. If
some of the lines were abandoned, however, traffic on the remaining
lines might increase to the point where those lines became profitable.
Of course, abandonment of branch lines has occurred and will continue
to occur without changes in organisational structure. As systems
analysis shows, though, the rational way to eliminate (or add) links in
a transportation network is not by disjoint choices by disparate
decision-makers. There are too many interdependencies between links

in a network to expect that historical accident (e.g. the bankruptcy of one carrier) will lead to anything remotely resembling a rational system. The need for systemic planning is the underlying rationale for federal subsidies of state rail planning, though, and such planning may well be sufficient. If that is the case, then increasing traffic on some branch lines by eliminating redundant branch lines may not require corporate restructuring. To the extent state rail planning is inadequate in this respect, parallel rail mergers could greatly facilitate rational system investment and disinvestment decisions, including branch line abandonment, though possible anti-competitive harms from such mergers must also be weighed. The potential benefits of parallel mergers in eliminating excess branch line capacity are probably highest in the Midwest, where there is the greatest overlapping of rail carrier route systems.

Reducing costs of service is yet a third way to alleviate the financial burdens of unviable branch lines. The main regulatory barrier to reducing branch line costs is the set of work rules which require rail carriers to employ far more labour than is actually needed to produce services. Changes in those work rules would, accordingly, enable some branch lines to continue service without incurring losses. Since it is widely appreciated that substantive changes in work rules are not likely in the foreseeable future, so the increasing attractiveness of an organisational device for reducing the costs of branch line service (i.e. short-line operation). One of the chief advantages of this technique is that short-line carriers are often exempt from industry work rules, thereby improving labour productivity. Also, when operated by a shipper or group of shippers, short-line railroads have a direct stake in improving the quality of service.

Many of the hundreds of short-line railroads now in operation are very successful enterprises, either in the sense that they earn profits, or reduce the total distribution costs of the owning shipper(s). They are not, however, a panacea for the branch line problem. There are no practical conditions under which some branch lines would be viable; in an analysis of branch line viability that assumed crew costs to be zero, 30,000 miles of branch lines were still found to be economically unviable. (A survey of short-line railroad experiences is provided by John Due (1982).)

There remains one potential effect of organisational change upon the resolution of the branch line problem. Even in the historical regulatory environment, when abandoning unviable lines was often difficult, and always time consuming, some railroad companies did a much better job of pruning their systems in the light of changed operational and marketing circumstances. Correlation analysis of the percentage of unviable branch lines and carrier profitability discussed by Harris

(1977b) reveals a strong negative correlation. That is, the strong carriers have already eliminated many of their unviable branch lines when abandonment was difficult, while weak carriers, on average, had not. While it is difficult to attribute direction of causality based upon such correlations, there is the further evidence that some carriers did not abandon lines that had already been approved (sometimes years before) by the ICC.

That evidence illustrates a central point. Simply eliminating some regulatory barriers will not be sufficient to rationalise the physical structure or operations of the industry. Without wholesale organisational change, without introducing managers who know the difference between traffic volume and financial viability, without offering managers the incentives necessary to induce a high level of performance, deregulation is likely to have only minor effects.

3.3—3 Urban lines and classification yards

To a certain extent, the analysis of rural branch lines also applies to urban branch lines and industrial sidings. Many of these urban lines are not financially viable with current rates, costs and traffic levels. In some cases, increased rates (after deregulation), increased traffic (perhaps shifted from abandoned lines), and/or reduced costs (e.g. by short-line operation) may enable lines to attain viability. There will no doubt be cases where abandonment is the only feasible alternative.

The difference between rural and urban areas, so far as the rail structure is concerned, however, is that urban areas are typically served by several rail carriers, while rural areas are usually served by only one or, at most, two or three. In urban areas, consequently, the system independence among carriers is greatly accentuated. The location of most urban rail lines was determined by the spatial distribution of people and economic activities of at least a century ago; urban rail networks seldom make any sense in the light of present spatial characteristics of urban areas.

As in the case of urban lines and sidings, the number, size, and location of yards and terminals reflect urban forms of another era. While yards have been modified, abandoned or relocated in some cases, there has been strikingly little change in the light of dramatically evolved urban spatial forms. There have also been tremendous changes in the technology of rail classification, which, it would seem, would necessitate corresponding changes in the spatial distribution of rail yards. Since rail classification and sorting has become more capital and less land intensive, one potential improvement would be reducing the number of yards by consolidating classification services into a portion of existing yards. In virtually every case, though, yards are owned by different carriers and consolidation would have differential impacts on participating carriers (i.e. some would benefit far more than others). Thus, such physical consolidation is not likely to occur unless preceded by organisational consolidation, either by merger or joint venture.

Another potential source of benefits is the relocation of yards, which may be seen as part of the consolidation process. Relocation means abandoning some or all of the existing yards in an urban area and constructing a new yard elsewhere, perhaps even well outside the urban area itself. Despite numerous studies showing enormous benefits of such relocations (e.g. the Potomac yards case), major urban yard relocations have seldom occurred, for a number of reasons. First, relocation requires enormous net capital investment, even after the often substantial salvage value of the abandoned land is balanced against the gross investment. It has been difficult for all railroads to borrow or raise equity capital except for equipment trusts and leases, where the equipment can be offered as collateral.

A second reason for failing to exploit potential relocation benefits is that lines and yards are owned by individual carriers, and if potential benefits are to be achieved, relocation planning and implementation would require active cooperation by all parties. Such cooperation would be difficult in any situation, but in this case the problems are magnified by the differential impacts of relocation sites. Even though there may be net social gains of relocation, any particular carrier may not be better off, and usually some will benefit much more than others.

Hence, one can expect that carriers will act opportunely, and unless action is forced upon them by external control, will fail to act collectively. The function of a hierarchical organisation in these cases is to internalise the benefits to a single actor, thereby providing the necessary incentive to act. (According to Williamson (1975) hierarchy may succeed market relations in 'small numbers, impacted information situations', a fitting description of most railroad bargaining situations.)

For this reason, organisational consolidation is almost certainly a precondition for the physical consolidation and relocation of urban lines and terminals. Three types of organisational change might facilitate physical restructuring:

(1) merger of carriers which own lines and yards in an urban area (which might be either a parallel or end-to-end merger);
(2) acquisition of competing lines and/or yards by a single carrier, with consolidation, relocation, and sale of classification services to competing carriers (highly unlikely, for reasons of opportunistic behaviour); or
(3) creation of an urban firm, with consolidation of all lines, sidings, yards and terminals into one company. That firm

would either provide collection and distribution services or own the infrastructure and charge line-haul carriers for use of the facilities.

An important benefit of a centralised urban carrier would be the reduction of monopoly power among line-haul carriers. In spite of the 'shippers' right to route', carriers that originate traffic have tremendous power over shippers (e.g. in the supply of cars) and can exert that power to assure that the traffic moves as far as possible over their lines (i.e. long hauling). A consolidated urban carrier could choose among competing carriers for the line-haul part of the movement, and no line-haul carrier would have a competitive advantage over other carriers.

In closing, one should note that even consolidation of existing facilities into a private monopoly enterprise may not offer sufficient inducement for major modifications of urban rail structures. In some cases, a sizeable share of the total benefits of consolidation and relocation would be external even to a monopolist (i.e. benefits that could not be captured through the pricing system because they do not accrue to customers of the carrier). Improved land use, reduced air and noise pollution, and improved passenger transportation service are three examples of such potential benefits. Even if that is true, it is not a sufficient argument for public ownership, but it does suggest that public subsidisation of urban rail consolidation and relocation may be justified in some cases.

3.3—4 Main lines

While there has been measurable progress in eliminating excess rail capacity in the form of branch lines during the past several decades, somewhat less progress has been made when it comes to 'main lines'. The quotation marks are used advisedly: many so-called main lines should be abandoned (or downgraded to local branch line service) precisely because they are no longer main lines. In every single market where there are duplicative main lines now in service, they are owned by different carriers; hence, the problem of redundant railroad lines is essentially a problem of redundant railroad companies. The nature of railroad economics and operations indicate substantial benefits from the consolidation of traffic onto a true mainline system, combined with abandonment or downgrading of remaining lines.

In spite of these potential benefits, main line consolidation is problematic. One issue here is that even though many of these lines are economically obsolete and substantial savings could be realised by their abandonment, the owning companies, or, more precisely, the managers of the owning companies have a strong incentive to keep the lines in service as long as possible. The reason is very simple: in order to manage a railroad, you must have a railroad to manage. The owners of the firms (whether debt or equity) would very often be better off if the firm were liquidated, particularly if another carrier purchased potentially viable links in the bankrupt carrier's system.

A critical problem with main line consolidation is that the requisite organisational restructuring would result in reduction of rail competition. There are four possible forms of organisational change which would facilitate (or follow from) main line consolidation, and three of them reduce rail competition:

(1) Parallel mergers of carriers in a market would allow the merged carrier to consolidate traffic on one of the lines and either downgrade or discontinue service on the other line. Whether or not the merged carrier consolidates physical structure, competition is reduced because relocation costs and entry barriers are extraordinarily high.

(2) Exchange of markets (market swaps) by two carriers, whereby carrier A gives up service in one market in exchange for carrier B giving up service in another market, thereby leaving B as the sole carrier in the first market and A the single carrier in the second. While rail service in each market is preserved, rail competition in both markets is eliminated (or, if there is a third carrier serving the market which is not involved in the agreement, merely reduced).

(3) Joint trackage rights agreements enable one carrier to use another carrier's tracks, enabling the first carrier to abandon (or downgrade) its own line in a market. Very often these agreements involve exchange of trackage rights, i.e. carrier A agrees to allow carrier B to jointly use its tracks in one market, while carrier B allows carrier A to use its tracks in another market. Joint trackage agreements are the only form of organisational change which does not reduce or eliminate rail competition. That this form of organisational change facilitates physical rationalisation without reducing competition is very instructive, for it points to a critical characteristic of the railroad industry. Railroads are not like airlines, which have no physical infrastructure, nor are they like motor carriers, whose operations are separated from the ownership of its infrastructure. So long as railroad operations are integrated with the ownership of physical structure, we will confront a trade-off between physical rationalisation and efficiency on the one side and market competition on the other.

(4) The remaining form of organisational change is simply abandonment of a line in a market by the owning carrier, whereby the carrier no longer can provide service in that market. While some intermediate points may lose service by definition of there being redundant routes in the market, the endpoints will not lose rail service. Again, competit-

ion is reduced by the elimination of the carrier and its route. Whether mergers are allowed or not, main line consolidation will almost certainly occur after deregulation. As suggested at the outset, if there is excess capacity in an industry, rate competition will ultimately force some firms to reduce their capacity or force them into bankruptcy. So even if deregulation is accompanied by provisions restricting mergers which are anti-competitive, whether enforced by the ICC or the Antitrust Division, the number of competitors in many markets will generally be reduced.

If viewed from an experimental perspective, one may not be terribly concerned about such probabilities. After all, if markets are really allowed to work, it will certainly be found out, once and for all, whether or not railroads are natural monopolies. On the other hand, one might be concerned that in this process of creative destruction something less than optimal results will be obtained. The routes and carriers which are eliminated in that process will be determined largely by historical accident, i.e. the current status of one carrier (in terms of the condition of its facilities and the extent of its market power) *vis-à-vis* other carriers in the market. There are many cases where the best route in a corridor, as measured in terms of its natural characteristics (i.e. distance, grades, curves, river crossings, etc.) is presently in the worst condition because the owning carrier has not had sufficient funds to maintain it. Or perhaps the line is in fairly good condition, but the owning carrier has an inferior competitive position in originating or terminating traffic in the market (Grimm and Harris, 1983a and b, discuss this issue more fully). Whatever the reasons, best routes could be the first to go.

The critical issue involved in main line consolidation and the requisite organisational changes is the nature of railroad competition. Though discussed by Keeler (1983), Levin (1981), and others, knowledge of rail economics is insufficient to answer the critical questions: how much competition is enough? And how much competition is too much? Still, several points can be made.

The first thing one can say is that legislators and regulators have for too long equated competition with number of competitors. If there is sufficient traffic to support only two rail carriers in a market, then perpetuating three or more carriers does not promote competition, it diminishes it. In order to have competition, competitors must be allowed to compete and they must have the ability to compete. Deregulation of rates may allow carriers to compete, but if there is an attempt to preserve an uneconomically large number of railroads in each market, they may lack the ability to compete. If none of them can earn enough to maintain their facilities, invest in capital improvements, or better their quality of service, then shippers would not be served by competitors.

It can also be said with a degree of confidence that in many markets there are presently too many competitors. The physical condition of the lines, the poor quality of service, the lack of organisational vitality, and the poor financial performance of most firms in the industry are all evidence that we have too many railroad companies in many markets. In these cases, competition would be improved by mergers, line acquisitions or abandonments, which would reduce the number of competitors.

That is not to say that monopolists ought to be serving all rail markets. While it is not known precisely what the relationships among traffic volume, revenues, infrastructure capital and maintenance costs, and operations are, it seems that many major markets can support only two or three rail carriers. In those cases, two or three carriers may well provide more effective rail competition than the current larger number of carriers.

3.4 Potential effects of organisational change upon operational rationalisation

The operation of a system is usually a manifestation of the physical structure of the system. In the case of the railroads, the existence of excess physical capacity, redundant lines and terminals, combined with disjoint, suboptimising decisions by rail carriers, has contributed to the operational failures of the industry. Prior to rail deregulation, traffic often moved over every conceivable route between two points; many carriers utilised literally hundreds of junctions to connect traffic with other carriers; traffic was hauled over distances twice as long as the shortest route; and, not surprisingly, the quality of service which resulted ranged from bad to worse.

Studies of rail operations have often failed to separate the economies of traffic density from the economies of concentrating traffic flow over certain links and through certain junctions and terminals in the system. It is very difficult empirically to separate these effects, because one of the consequences of consolidating traffic flow is an increase in traffic density on some lines. Furthermore, our understanding of the economic relationships between line operations and classification operations is very limited. Even though difficult to measure empirically, there is an important conceptual difference between the two sources of improving rail performance. Still, structural reforms usually precede operational improvements; so long as there are too many routes or junctions in a market, traffic consolidation is not likely to occur.

Having dealt with structural consolidation issues in the previous section, we turn to traffic flow consolidation and its potential for reducing rail costs and improving rail service. First the major benefits of consolidating rail traffic are considered, then the extent to which these benefits are dependent upon facilitating organisational changes.

The main effect of traffic flow consolidation upon a system is to increase the throughput, i.e. to increase the number of units produced per link per unit of time. While railroad cars are discrete units of production physically, the operation of railroads can be seen as a continuous flow process, rather like a pipeline. As throughput increases, there are all sorts of potential economies which can be realised. Cars travelling from a common origin to a common destination can be blocked, which reduces switching and classification requirements (up to the ultimate form of blocking, the unit train). Reducing classifications reduces costs by improving equipment and crew utilisation rates, and, of course, expenditures on classification yards.

Another important benefit of traffic flow consolidation is reducing circuitry or length of haul, if traffic is shifted to a shorter routing. In the past, most rail traffic has moved unnecessarily long distances, due to long-hauling by carriers and the existence of innumerable junctions between connecting carriers. Circuitry increases car ownership and maintenance costs (by raising the number of ton miles per mile of track, a determinant of maintenance expense). The best estimate of total circuitry, a study by the AAR Staff Studies Group (1978), is 4.6 per cent, which is probably biased conservatively. Even so, reducing circuitry by 4.6 per cent would save the expenses associated with 1.3 billion car miles annually.

A third class of benefits from consolidating traffic, if done rationally, would be to concentrate traffic on the best routes, not only in terms of distance, but in terms of grades, junctions, yards, and condition of the roadway. A recent AAR staff study estimates on the order of 15 per cent savings in transit time, and a 40 per cent improvement in reliability (measured by the standard deviation of transit time) from moving traffic over the fastest route in 137 major markets. The corresponding cost savings, from improved equipment and crew utilisation, would be very considerable.

Sammon (1978) has estimated that the total savings from traffic flow consolidation are in the order of $575 million annually. As he notes, these are in addition to the cost savings which might be obtained from structural rationalisation. Even so, they grossly understate the benefits of operational rationalisation, since they measure only the static cost savings which accrue to the railroad industry.

Probably an even greater source of benefits is the improved service quality accruing to rail users. Take, for example, the car hour savings from concentrating traffic on the fastest routes. The estimated cost savings to the industry is $250 million annually, owing to a 15 per cent reduction in car ownership costs; this is obtained by using estimates of shippers' valuation of transportation service quality, and the Association of American Railroad's estimate of potential service quality improvements for shippers of produce and food products, which account for roughly 10 per cent of total rail traffic. According to Winston's (1978) estimates, produce shippers would value a 15 per cent reduction in mean transit time at $880 million (in 1976 dollars), and a 40 per cent reduction in the standard deviation of transit time at $550 million. This class of rail users, in other words, would receive over $1.4 billion annually in benefits from improved service quality. Further evidence on the value of service quality improvements to shippers is provided by Harris and Winston (1983).

Shippers of produce probably have a higher valuation of service quality than any other class of shippers, so one can not generalise from these results to all rail traffic. Even so, the results point to a very real problem in analysing the rail industry: altogether too often analysts measure benefits only in terms of rail cost savings when all evidence points to service quality as a major problem and potential benefit. As in the case of produce shippers, transportation users are often willing to pay more for transport service if it is timely and reliable. Indeed, the case of the produce shippers is so instructive because most of them have already shifted over to motor carriers, which means they are paying much higher rates, but receiving much better service. There is every reason to believe that if railroads were able to improve significantly their service, they could raise rates and win back traffic formerly lost to trucks.

The other bias in these estimates of potential benefits of operational rationalisation — even if we include service quality improvement — is that they are static in nature. The real benefits of rationalising rail operations will be realised over the longer run, as technology and organisations adapt to a changing environment. The potential economies of traffic flow consolidation would stimulate technological innovation which could capitalise on higher traffic density and classification throughputs. For example, the feasibility of intermodal operations is dramatically improved (as shown by the Banks (1974) study) when traffic flow is consolidated.

Deregulation of rates and physical abandonment should allow some of these benefits to be realised. Rate competition will in many cases drive traffic to best routings, and will reduce the incentives for circuitous long-hauling. The ability to differentiate services and their respective prices will provide strong incentives to improve service in general and design specific services to suit the needs of particular shippers. Usage-based pricing would also provide shippers with an incentive to avoid use of costly rail services, such as classification yards, perhaps by relying more on piggyback or containerised service from terminal to terminal.

An environment of commercial freedom and rate competition may well induce railroads to adopt a marketing orientation. Rather than merely solicit traffic from current users, rail managers will have incentives to seek out new users, to create new services, and to cooperate with other rail companies in the provision of those services. Hence, we could expect a significant improvement in the performance of organisations and in cooperation among organisations in a deregulated environment.

On the other hand, recent ICC decisions regarding intercarrier relationships, particularly those relating to through rates and interchange of traffic, will substantially affect interline rail services. In the absence of ICC governance, there may well be economic incentives for carriers to reduce or eliminate interline service in order to gain a larger share of the total revenues for a given trip. This would be particularly true in cases involving interline service by a large rail carrier in cooperation with a small carrier, since small carriers are unlikely to hold countervailing power in other markets. Where the interline routing is the more efficient, myopic behaviour by rail managers could lead to deterioration of rail service quality.

However, even in situations involving interline service between two or more large carriers, there may be a need for some continued regulation. If one assumes (as is done in this chapter) that rail managers are not always rational in a strict profit-maximising sense, it is not unrealistic to imagine a cycle of gateway closures, retaliatory actions in other markets and a general degradation of service quality in whole regions of the country. Indeed, there is evidence that this has already happened.[4] Again, the behaviour of rail organisations will largely determine whether continuing regulation will be needed.

So long as rail movements transcend organisational boundaries, as 70 per cent of rail traffic now does, operational rationalisation and its associated cost savings and service improvements will depend critically upon organisational change. Realisation of these potential benefits, it is argued, would be facilitated by the following types of changes in industry structure and organisational relations:

(1) Operational consolidation of yards and terminals, though intimately connected with structural consolidation, should be included here because of the organisational implications. Not only the structure of urban rail networks, but also their operation could be greatly improved

through organisational consolidation. The possibilities include merging of carriers serving the urban area (which might be either end-to-end or parallel); joint venture by the carriers; or creation of an independent company (either as carrier or as facilities provider to other carriers).

(2) Parallel mergers enable the consolidated carrier to rationally flow traffic through a corridor, whether or not accompanied by changes in physical structure. Parallel mergers would also reduce the connections with carriers at either end of the consolidated carrier, which would improve flows of traffic through the corridor. As just noted, parallel mergers would facilitate the consolidation of traffic through classification yards and, by increasing the volume of traffic for any origin-destination pair, would sometimes enable the carrier to bypass yards altogether. The competitive implications of parallel mergers have already been discussed; suffice it to add here that any calculation of the trade-off between corporate consolidation and competition should include operational as well as structural benefits.

(3) End-to-end mergers reduce the dependence of carriers on other carriers in the provision of services which must now be interlined. Not only would this reduce transactions costs and give the carrier physical control over the movement, but it would also assign accountability to the carrier. When multiple carriers handle a movement, the shipper has little information about the service quality each has to offer. Moreover, even if both carriers wanted to provide good service, they would have difficulty doing so within the limits of current railroad information systems. For the most part, rail information systems are historical: they report what happened after it has happened. In order to be useful for quality control, an information system must be contemporaneous or nearly so, i.e. it must provide information about what is happening as it is happening. When movements leave a system, carriers lose control over and knowledge of their whereabouts. We cannot expect rail managers to improve service quality significantly if rail managers do not have control over or responsibility for service quality.

Another important consequence of end-to-end mergers would be the reduction of junction points connecting formerly separate carriers and the concentration of traffic across best routes. To some extent, rate deregulation will promote this development, but an integrated operator would have strong incentives to maximise potential benefits; transactions costs would be reduced; and dependence upon uncooperative carriers would be eliminated.

Though the effects are less salient *vis-à-vis* parallel mergers, end-to-end mergers may also present anti-competitive concerns. As discussed in Grimm (1983) and Grimm and Harris (1983b), railroads may pursue end-to-end mergers primarily to increase their leverage *vis-à-vis* shippers and carriers. Vertical foreclosure and price squeezing can be facilitated through such mergers. Accordingly, as with parallel mergers, the ICC must carefully scrutinize such merger proposals and explore conditions which can be attached to merger approval which allow efficiencies to be realised but redress competitive problems.

3.5 Potential effects of organisational change upon managerial incentives and performance

Earlier sections have dealt, for the large part, with the organisational structure of the railroad industry and the relations among organisations in the industry. In this section attention is focused on the organisations themselves, to assess the potential benefits or organisational change upon managerial incentives and performance. In order to make that assessment, railroads must be seen for what they are: organic, human organisations. As organisms must adapt to their environment or face threats to their survival, so also must human organisations. There is one critical characterisation of human organisations which is central to the purpose of this section. Organisations can change in one of two ways: by modifying the behaviour of current members of the organisation or by modifying the membership of the organisation. In terms of the railroad industry, concern should be with organisational changes which will improve the performance of current railroad managers and induce new managers into the industry.

This dynamic element of organisational change, if critical, is often overlooked. No organisation can thrive, or even survive, without infusions of new blood. One natural process by which new people (and their new ideas and enthusiasm) are brought into an organisation is attrition. As some organisation members voluntarily leave an organisation (retirement, joining other organisations), they can be replaced by new members. The natural process of replacement, consequently, is an important source of organisational revitalisation.

There is a second natural process by which organisations revitalise themselves, namely through the process of growth. As the size of the organisation expands, it must add new people to assume the increasing tasks and responsibilities of the growing concern. The process of growth has another important effect: it attracts competent people to the organisation because people realise that growth is a sign of vitality and opportunities for personal development and advancement. Those opportunities are also an important incentive for people once they have joined the organisation, since those who perform well are likely to have increasing opportunities for personal growth and material rewards.

These two natural processes of organisational revitalisation — replacement and growth — are very limited in a declining environment like the railroad industry. Total employment in the industry has fallen dramatically over the past three decades, which means that more attrition than replacement has occurred (i.e. members have been leaving the organisations but have not been replaced in equal numbers). Needless to add, very few railroad organisations have been growing internally at a rate which would, by bringing in significant numbers of new people, provide a source of revitalisation.

As powerful as these effects have been in restricting the process of human revitalisation in the railroad industry, the static or declining environment of the industry has yet another profound effect upon organisational behaviour. Railroad organisations are not only static in terms of participants, they are also static in structure. Students of comparative organisation, such as Wyckoff (1976), have found railroad companies to be among the most rigid, hierarchical organisations in the American economy. That reputation is sufficiently well-known to prevent many competent people from joining railroad companies in the first place. But even when there are competent managers, they are often limited in their performance by a repressive organisational structure.

There are numerous indicators of the moribund nature of railroad organisations: the average age of railroad executives; the lack of experience of top railroad managers in industries other than railroading; the tendency of railroad managers to come from engineering, production backgrounds (as opposed to marketing, finance, etc.); the average length of time between promotions within organisations; the lack of participation of managers in organisational decisions (i.e. the concentration of decision-making authority at the top of the hierarchy); the infrequency of significant structural changes in railroad organisations (for the most part railroads are organised the same way they have been for a century); and, last but hardly least, the poor performance of railroad organisations.

These characteristics of railroad organisations, and the depth of their historical roots are facts to which one must pay heed. The single act of deregulation of rates and common carrier obligations does not mean one is starting with a clean slate. Commercial freedoms alone will not, consequently, revitalise the railroad industry. Given the present condition of many railroad organisations, deregulation must be accompanied by policies designed to facilitate organisational revitalisation.

To a certain extent, of course, eliminating or reducing environmental constraints should have positive effects on organisational health. Confronted with new opportunities for marketing and profit-making, many railroad managements will modify their structures and behaviour. One should expect, for example, that rate-making freedom will induce a quantum increase in the degree of marketing orientation in the firm. That, in turn, should lead to the promotion of existing rail managers, and the attraction of new managers, who have special marketing skills.

One should also expect a profound — if gradual — change in the industry's self image from that of an institution (rather like a church) to that of a commercial enterprise. US railroads are no longer in the business of running trains and perpetuating an important part of the American heritage. Railroads are in the business of providing transportation services to transportation users. Regulation, by its tendency to protect the *status quo*, has served to foster an institutional attitude; deregulation will force a modernising of managerial attitudes.

But there are still good reasons for believing that, short of deliberately induced organisational change, deregulation will be insufficient if industry revitalisation is the ultimate objective. The fact of the matter is that there are enormous qualitative differences among current railroad managements. Given the restrictive environment in which they must operate, some railroad companies are relatively well-managed. One might reasonably expect that these organisations will thrive in a deregulated environment; indeed, managers of these companies favour deregulation precisely because they see it as an opportunity for organisational and personal growth and development.

But there are railroad firms which are very badly managed, which lack even a modest degree of organisational vitality, which will fight deregulation because their managers recognise that commercial freedom is a threat to their continued cosy existence. If deregulation occurs, few of these firms will be able to cope, nor are they likely to attract, through any voluntary process, managers who could cope with a destabilised environment. Having lost the protection of administrative regulation, these firms are likely to seek protection from some alternative source: by public subsidy, by reorganisation in bankruptcy, or publicly-mandated inclusion in a merger of other carriers.

In the same way an organisation revitalises itself by replacement of organisational members, an industry revitalises itself by replacing one organisation with another. Typically, this does not happen voluntarily; organisations do not usually leave an industry because they choose to, but because they are forced to leave. Most industries are constantly revitalising themselves as firms go bankrupt, leave the industry, and are replaced by the entry of new firms or the growth of existing organisations. That does not mean that all the managers and employees of existing firms must leave the industry; the more competent, productive people are usually hired by remaining firms. Some managers are forced from the industry, though, and that is one revitalising effect of exit. Much more important in its impact upon industrial vitality is the elimination of an organisation, which by its financial failure has demonstrated that it could not cope with its environment.

This process of organisational Darwinism constantly revitalises an industry through survival of the fittest. It might be argued that the most profound effect of regulation upon the railroad industry has been the inhibition of this natural process of revitalisation. Virtually every major railroad organisation that has ever existed is extant today, if in slightly altered form. Some organisations have been allowed to merge, but seldom eliminated. Reorganisation in bankruptcy is simply a euphemism for perpetuating failing organisations and protecting the jobs of its current managers.

Such policies in a manufacturing industry would be bad enough; perpetuating incompetent managements and their physical capacity would certainly have negative effects upon the rest of the industry. But there is a fundamental difference between manufacturing and railroad industries: production in manufacturing is independent, production of rail services is interdependent. An organisation in a manufacturing industry does not depend upon incompetent organisations; in railroading, organisations are often forced to depend upon such. Hence, the effects of perpetuating moribund organisations in the railroad industry have been catastrophic: they have prevented the natural process of organisational replacement, and have forced competent organisations to depend upon the incompetent. Students of organisational behaviour could easily predict that in such an environment, organisational resource dependence will eventually drag the quality of all organisations down to the lowest common denominator.

Public policy must, therefore, include provisions for organisational replacement. A natural process must be facilitated by which organisations in the industry can revitalise themselves, and if they fail to do so, be replaced by competent organisations. Managers will perform well only if they have both positive incentives for success, and negative incentives for failure. While the following list is not exhaustive, it suggests strategies which would facilitate these processes of organisational change.

(1) Improved bankruptcy procedures would speed up the process of reorganisation and, more importantly, enable the physical assets of organisations to be liquidated (i.e. enable the organisation to be eliminated). There are cases when managers ought to be given the opportunity to reorganise, if the main causes of failure are extenuating. Allowing managers to perpetuate their organisations and protect their own jobs, however, is often a gross disservice to the public as well as

other companies dependent upon the bankrupt carrier.

(2) Another important class of benefits of railroad mergers, whether parallel or end-to-end, is revitalisation, as successful organisations expand through acquisition of less successful enterprises. That process expands the domain of competent managers, and either contracts or replaces that of incompetent managers.

(3) While intermodal mergers may have limited operational benefits and could in some instances be anti-competitive, most transportation analysts would argue that motor carrier organisations are far more vital than railroads. Intermodal mergers may well introduce motor carriers' marketing mentality to railroad organisations, whether by a railroad acquiring a motor carrier or vice versa. Intermodal mergers may also expose railroads to some very different organisational structures, which, it has been argued, are better suited to the provision of transportation services (e.g. profit-centred organisational forms). Finally, the threat of takeover by a motor carrier may stimulate organisational change, even without mergers. In a deregulated environment, there will be many new profitable opportunities. If current managers do not exploit these opportunities, their companies may be susceptible to acquisition by a more effective organisation which will.

(4) As noted above, takeover by conglomerate merger of acquisition of majority shareholder control, will present railroad companies with the chance to provide new services, abandon unprofitable services, charge rates which reflect costs, and develop new technologies. Good railroad management will exploit these opportunities and, in doing so, increase the profitability of the firm. If managers do not exploit profit-making opportunities, there will be a gap between realised and potential profit. That gap will be reflected in an under-valuation of the company's shares on the stock market (i.e. the present discounted value of the firm's potential profit stream will exceed the current market price of the firm). By allowing conglomerate or shareholder takeovers, we provide a negative incentive for managers to exploit such opportunities, for if they fail to do so, they may well be replaced by managers who will.

(5) In most growth industries, entrepreneurship provides a critical source of new ideas and talents. One can only be astounded by the dramatic organisational changes in the air freight industry in the past few years. Shippers now face an enormous range of price-service quality combinations; new companies offering new services appear almost daily; those who have something the market wants grow at incredible rates; and companies which had not made significant changes in their services for years have been forced to exit from the

industry or change their behaviour.

The structural characteristics and operational economies of the rail industry in many ways naturally inhibit such entrepreneurial activities (i.e. entry barriers are exceptionally high, due to capital and transactions costs). Still, it must be recognised that entrepreneurship has been inhibited by regulatory processes which preserve organisational status quo. Public policies towards organisational change, therefore, should not be limited to modifying the structure, relations, and performance of current organisations, but should attempt to facilitate entry of new organisations into the industry.

All signs now point toward basic change in railroad policies. However, the thrust here has been to demonstrate that rate-making and service discontinuance provisions alone will not induce industry revitalisation. The accumulation of decades of organisational preservation has resulted in an industry of moribund organisations whose very structure prevents revitalisation. Organisational change and adaptation to a new environment is a prerequisite to any railroad revitalisation.

Notes

1   The American College Dictionary defines *system* as '1. an assemblage or combination of things or parts forming a complex or *unitary whole*: a railroad system'. It is ironic that what lexicographers choose to illustrate as a 'system' is not operated as one!

2   It is very interesting to note that in the case where rail service is reputedly best   autos and auto parts — it is the shippers who provide the integrating function among 'cooperating' rail carriers. To be sure, the market power of large auto companies (*vis-à-vis* rail carriers) partially explains the superior rail service they receive. But perhaps even more important is the extent and sophistication of auto manufacturers' logistics systems. Compared to railroad operations and planning, auto companies utilise highly sophisticated logistics planning and analysis, and have elaborate information and quality control systems. Thus, they receive high quality rail service because their managers operate the distribution system as a system.

3   The postal system is, of course, a special case, in that it is operated as a public enterprise rather than a regulated private enterprise. Even though the form of 'regulation' is different, however, it is operated as a monopoly system. This institutional difference is instructive, since in virtually every other advanced country in the world, all of the infrastructure industries are public enterprises.

The rationale for public ownership of these industries is the same as the rationale for regulating them; if efficiency is grounds for not relying upon competition as the social control mechanism, then some substitute must be designed. In spite of the oft-cited arguments of public enterprise inefficiency, the argument for public enterprise (versus regulated private enterprise) is that it avoids duplicate management, i.e. management by employees of the private enterprise and by employees of the regulating agency. For a sophisticated discussion of public enterprise as a mechanism of social control, see Shepherd (1965).

4   The *Journal of Commerce* (16 February 1983) documents a route cancellation battle between Conrail and the Chessie System.

References

Association of American Railroads (1975), *A Preliminary Look at Cost Saving from Rationalizing Circuitous Rail Routes*, Staff Memorandum 75−12. Staff Studies Group (Washington, DC).

Association of American Railroads (1978), *Estimated Savings from Increased Traffic Flow Concentration*, Staff Memorandum 78−10. Staff Studies Group (Washington, DC).

Association of American Railroads (1980), *The Economic ABZ's of the Railroad Industry* (Washington, DC).

Banks, R.L. and Associates (1974), *Short Line Techniques to Improve Financial Viability of Light Density Lines* (Federal Railroad Administration, US Department of Transportation, Washington, DC).

Baumel, C.P., Miller, J.J. and Drinka, T.P. (1976), *A Summary of an Economic Analysis of Upgrading Branch Rail Lines: A Study of 71 Lines in Iowa* (Iowa State University, Ames, Iowa).

Conant, M. (1964), *Railroad Mergers and Abandonments* (University of California Press, Berkeley, California).

Davis, G.M., Sherwood, C.S. and Jones, R.W. (1975), 'An estimate of labor protection cost in selected railway consolidations', *ICC Practitioners Journal*, Vol.43, pp.56−71.

Due, John F. (1977), 'Alternative approaches to preserving branch line railroad service' paper presented to the Conference of National Association of Farm Cooperatives.

Due, J.F. (1977), 'Factors affecting the abandonment and survival of class II railroads', *Transportation Journal*.

Due, J.F. (1982), *The Experiences of Local Enterprises Formed to Take Over Railway Lines Abandoned by Major Systems — A Preliminary Study* (BEBR Working Paper, University of Illinois, Urbana-Champaign).

French, P.W. (1976), *A Framework for Evaluating the Impacts of Railroad Line Consolidation*, Vol.20, Studies in Railroad Operations and Economics (Massachusetts Institute of Technology, Cambridge, Mass.).

Friedlaender, A.F. (1969), *The Dilemma of Freight Transport Regulation* (The Brookings Institution, Washington, DC).

Gellman, A.J. (1971), 'Surface freight transportation', in W. Capron (ed.), *Technological Change in Regulated Industries* (The Brookings Institution, Washington, DC).

Grimm, C. (1983), *Strategic Motives and Competitive Effects in Railroad Mergers: A Public Policy Analysis*, doctoral dissertation, Institute of Transportation Studies dissertation series (University of California, Berkeley).

Grimm, C. and Harris, R.G. (1983), 'Structural economics of the rail freight industry: concepts, evidence, and merger policy implications', *Transportation Research*, Vol.17A, pp.271–81.

Grimm, C. and Harris, R.G. (1983), 'Vertical foreclosure in the rail freight industry: economic analysis and policy prescriptions', *ICC Practitioners Journal*, Vol.50, pp.508–31.

Harris, R.G. (1977), 'Economies of traffic density in the rail freight industry', *Bell Journal of Economics*, Vol.8, pp.556–64.

Harris, R.G. (1977b), 'Rationalizing the rail freight industry: a case study in institutional failure and proposals for reform', doctoral dissertation, Department of Economics (University of California, Berkeley).

Harris, R.G. (1978), 'Rationalizing the physical structure of the U.S. rail industry', prepared statement to Joint Economic Committee, Hearings on National Railroad Policy (Sioux Falls, South Dakota).

Harris, R.G. (1979), *The Potential Effects of Deregulation Upon Corporate Structure, Merger Behavior and Organizational Relations in the Rail Freight Industry*, report to the Federal Railroad Administration (Washington, DC).

Harris, R.G. and Keeler, T.E. (1981), 'Determinants of Railroad Profitability: an econometric study' in K.D. Boyer and W.G. Shepherd (eds.), *Economic Regulation: Essays in Honor of James R. Nelson* (Institute of Public Utilities, East Lansing, Michigan).

Harris, R.G. and Winston, C. (1983), 'Potential benefits of rail mergers: an econometric analysis of network effects on service quality', *Review of Economics and Statistics*, Vol.65, pp.32–40.

Johnson, J.C. and Whiteside, T.C. (1975), 'Professor Ripley revisited: a current analysis of railroad mergers', *ICC Practitioners Journal*, Vol.42, pp.419–52.

Keeler, T.E. (1976), *On the Economic Impact of Railroad Freight Regulation*, Center for the Study of American Business, Working

Paper No. 17 (Washington University, St. Louis, Missouri).

Keeler, T.E. (1974), 'Railroad costs, returns to scale, and excess capacity', *Review of Economics and Statistics*, Vol.56, pp.201–8.

Keeler, T.E. (1983), *Railroads, Freight, and Public Policy* (The Brookings Institution, Washington, DC).

Lang, S.A. and Burd, S.A. (1978), 'Railroad profit measurement and organisational structure', *Transportation Research Forum Proceedings*, Vol.19, pp.176–81.

Levin, R.C. (1981), 'Railroad rates, profitability, and welfare under deregulation', *Bell Journal of Economics*, Vol.12, pp.1–26.

MacAvoy, P.W. and Snow, J.W. (eds.) (1977), *Railroad Revitalization and Regulatory Reform* (American Enterprise Institute for Public Policy Research, Washington, DC).

Meyer, J.R., Peck, M.J., Stenason, J. and Zwick, C. (1959), *The Economics of Competition in the Transportation Industries* (Harvard University Press, Cambridge, Massachusetts).

Moon, A.E. (1975), *Urban Railroad Relocation: Nature and Magnitude of the Problem*, Vols.1–4 (Federal Railroad Administration and Federal Highway Administration, US Department of Transportation, Washington, DC).

Moore, T.G. (1975), 'Deregulating surface freight transportation', in Almarin Phillips (ed.), *Promoting Competition in Regulated Markets* (The Brookings Institution, Washington, DC).

Murray, T.J. (1972), 'A new look at rail employee merger protection, Norfolk and Western R.R. v. Nemitz: an assessment', *Case Western Reserve Law Review*, Vol.24, pp.103–43.

National Commission on Productivity and the Council of Economic Advisers (1973), *Improving Railroad Productivity*, final report of the Task Force on Railroad Productivity (Washington, DC).

Pfeffer, J. and Salancik, G.R. (1978), *The External Control of Organizations* (Harper and Row, New York).

Reebie Associates (1976), *National Intermodal network Feasibility Study*, Vols.1–4 (Office of Policy and Program Development, Federal Railroad Administration, US Department of Transportation, Washington, DC).

Sammon, John P. (1978), 'Returns to traffic flow concentration in the railroad industry', *Transportation Research Forum Proceedings*, Vol.19, pp.104–11.

Schroeder, Gilbert (1968), 'Antirust-railroad mergers – a matter of public interest', *De Paul Law Review*, Vol.18, pp.272–84.

Shepherd, W.G. (1965), *Economic Performance Under Public Ownership* (Yale University Press, New Haven, Connecticut).

Sidhu, N., Charney, A.H. and Due, J.F. (1977), 'Cost functions of class II railroads and the viability of light traffic density railway lines', *Quarterly Review of Economics and Business*, Vol.17.

Sloss, J., Humphrey, T.J. and Krutter, F.N. (1975), *An Analysis and Evaluation of Past Experience in Rationalizing Railroad Networks*, Vol.16, Studies in Railroad Operations and Economics (Massachusetts Institute of Technology, Cambridge, Mass.).

US Department of Transportation (1978), *A Prospectus for Change in the Freight Railroad Industry* (Office of the Secretary, Washington, DC).

US Department of Transportation (1979), *The Railroad Situation: A Perspective on the Past, Present and Future of the Railroad Industry* (Washington, DC).

US Interstate Commerce Commission (1978), *Rail Merger Study: Final Report* (Rail Services Planning Office, Washington, DC).

US Interstate Commerce Commission (1977), *Railroad Conglomerates and Other Corporate Structures* (Washington, DC).

US Interstate Commerce Commission (1977), *The Role of Government in Railroad Restructuring*, Issue Paper Number 5, Rail Merger Study (Rail Services Planning Office, Washington, DC).

Williams, J.H. (1970), *The Effects of Deregulation on Railroads* (Federal Railroad Administration, US Department of Transportation, Washington, DC).

Williams, J.H. (1978), prepared statement to Hearings before Federal Railroad Administration (US Department of Transportation, San Francisco).

Williamson, O.E. (1975), *Markets and Hierarchies: Analysis and Antitrust Implications* (The Free Press, New York).

Winston, C. (1978), *Mode Choice in Freight Transportation*, Sloan Working Paper 7802, Department of Economics (University of California, Berkeley).

Wyckoff, D.D. (1976), *Railroad Management* (Lexington Books, Lexington, Massachusetts).

4 The development of management information to meet the needs of a new management structure for British Rail

D. ALLEN AND G. WILLIAMS

4.1 The management problem

Since 1982 British Rail has taken a radical new look at the way in which it is organised to cope with its business, a business which for 'social reasons' is supported by government to the extent of about one-third of its income. These are the payments in compensation for meeting a public service obligation, i.e. to operate services which it would not do or do to the same extent if it were motivated solely by commercial considerations. But there is more than a social side to railways in Britain, it is in addition operating in commercial markets for inter-urban travel, freight movements and the movement of parcels, newspapers, etc. Each has different markets and faces different types of competition. Realistically, it might continue to be one railway, but managerially it demands a new approach — sectorisation to sharpen the business link with cost control.

Traditionally the railway has been organised on a geographical and functional basis. There are five railway regions (Eastern, London Midland, Scottish, Southern and Western) with day-to-day operating responsibilities. In addition there are functional departments (operating, civil, mechanical and electrical and signal engineering, finance, personnel, etc.). The essential emphasis has been on cost control — a cost-driven approach, with gross receipts as an overlay, rather than an essential part of a net result. There was, of course, a significant marketing presence but not in sector terms as we now know them.

The fundamental problems of such a system were that:

(1) Only one person — The Chief Executive (Railways) — bore major responsibility for both costs and revenue (i.e. had a 'bottom line' responsibility). This was of course at total railway level.

(2) To have had regional profit and loss accounts would have presented too many difficulties: commonality and jointness of costs and problems regarding contributory revenue (both discussed later) would have been greater than under a sector approach; there would also have been much poorer identification of the separate markets.

(3) Below the Chief Executive there was no adequate focus on net revenue results and this meant management accountabilities were unclear: the railway was too much cost-led. With over 4000 cost centres there was no doubt that costs could indeed be controlled but the new initiative was to secure that control in a net revenue arena. This could pose different questions and promote different solutions in a whole range of decisions, not least in terms of marketing, resource use and capital investment.

(4) In managerial terms the distinction between the 'commercial' and 'social' sectors of the railway business was not adequately reflected.

On this last point, government has required since 1975 that the Freight and Parcels Businesses should become commercially self-standing. In other words these businesses should earn sufficient receipts to cover those costs which would not be incurred were there no Freight and Parcels Businesses and, ultimately, generate a required rate of return against assets employed (5 per cent after current cost depreciation). Increasingly government has looked to the Inter-City Passenger Business to meet a similar commercial requirement. The present government's view is that no mode of inter-urban transport should be subsidised and, therefore, only the Provincial and London & South East Passenger Businesses convey a social dimension which should be supported by the taxpayer.

The pressures towards sector management and away from the traditional management structure have, therefore, been twofold. In the first instance is the need to better identify bottom line responsibilities at levels considerably below the total railway, so that receipts and expenses can be better related one to the other and the appropriate trade-offs perceived and acted upon. Secondly, there has been the pressure from government to distinguish between the 'commercial' and 'socially necessary' sectors of the railway.

Thus sector management has emerged with five business sectors each with its own sector director who holds full delegated responsibility from the chief executive for his own bottom line result:

Social

(i)   London & South East
The services primarily designed to meet the needs of commuters
in and out of London in a radius of some 100 km
(ii) Provincial
Cross-country and local passenger services including commuting
to and from conurbations outside London

Commercial

(i)   Inter-City
A network of inter-urban services over relatively long distances;
essentially high quality services between major population centres
(ii) Freight
The movement of freight in trainloads and through a dedicated
network of wagonload services; a considerable dependence on
bulk movements and needs a lot of specialised handling equipment
(iii) Parcels
High speed movements of small packages, letter mails, newspapers,
etc. — about 50 per cent of which is in special parcels trains

4.2 Management information needs and accounting philosophies

Having decided to go for a management structure based primarily on
sectors, each with a bottom line responsibility, it might seem a simple
matter to divide up the relevant costs, revenues and physical indicators
between the five sectors. Unfortunately because the railway has
relatively high levels of common and joint costs and because receipts
sometimes flow across sector boundaries the matter is not at all simple.
There is no point producing statistics, whether financial or physical, if
they are going to be widely misinterpreted. It is always important to
understand how the numbers are put together.
    A short excursion into financial and economic technicalities is
worthwhile at this juncture to explain: the distinction between specific,
common and joint costs; and the distinction between attributed earnings and contributory revenue.
    Firstly, there is the distinction between the various categories of
cost.

(1) Specific costs are those which are wholly attributable to a unit of
operation (in this case a sector). They are not shared with other units

of operation and would be wholly removed were the sector to cease operation. An example of a specific cost would be the provision costs of certain classes of electric multiple unit used exclusively for London & SE purposes on Southern Region.

(2) Common costs are those costs which are shared between units of production but are capable of being changed in quantum if one or other of the units of production were removed. The classic case of a common cost is a locomotive fleet shared between the passenger and freight businesses: remove one of the sectors and the demand for locomotives will reduce, though not necessarily pro rata.

(3) Joint costs are those costs shared between two or more units of production but which are largely invariant on the removal of any one of those units. Certain types of track and signalling assets are cases of joint costs in the railway context. These joint costs are the most difficult to handle and, unfortunately, the railway is blessed or cursed with a higher proportion of joint costs than most other industries.

Secondly, there is the distinction between attributed earnings and contributory revenue. This is usually illustrated in the context of passenger traffic.

(1) Attributed earnings takes a journey which may involve more than one sector and attributes the total fare between the sectors involved normally pro rata to mileage within each sector, but sometimes on a more complex basis.

(2) Contributory revenue looks at cross-sectoral flows of revenue from a different standpoint. In looking at contributory revenue at risk this concept assesses the revenue to be gained or lost both within a sector and beyond that sector were the one sector's services to be enhanced or reduced.

Commonality and jointness of costs and revenues and, beyond those of physical indicators, are therefore, very real problems in attempting to sub-divide the railway, whether that sub-division is the traditional regional one or the new sector one. However, these difficulties are very much worth facing as the price to be paid for the benefits in terms of cost control, revenue enhancement and basic trade-offs between receipts and expenses which will flow from the bottom line responsibilities inherent in sector management.

4.3 The new sector evaluation system

The new management information approach is concerned with building a control system around the five sector directors as the prime movers. This requires the establishment of budgets and plans in sector terms, which have management commitment. However, the system recognises that sector management (the businesses) can achieve little without the production/resource management, represented by the regions and functions. Further, sector directors have delegated bottom line responsibility for certain of their sub-sectors (e.g. the East Coast Main Line Inter-City Service is a sub-sector of the Inter-City Sector) to the existing regional general managers.

Sector management information has, therefore, been designed to provide data within a complex management structure. Any cost information can be provided for a sector by region and by function within region, right down to the level of a cost centre within a function within a region. The interrelations of sectors with functions and regions is well illustrated in the Swiss roll where Figure 4.1 shows how one sector cuts across all five regions and involves a number of functions. The diagram has been intentionally simplified. It is not to scale, nor indeed does it show the full pattern of relationships which in practice are far more extensive. Nevertheless, it demonstrates the potential interraction between managers and the consequent need for information.

In order to achieve such a data base it has been necessary to develop a new computerised Sector Performance, Accounting and Monitoring System (SPAMS). This is due for introduction in 1985 and will provide for:

(1) Information on all areas of costs for which sectors are managerially responsible and not just the direct costs;
(2) A direct link wherever possible between the physical management of assets and financial consequences;
(3) A system which as far as possible simply and directly traces costs back to their point of origin;
(4) A system which permits sector directors and the spending functions to talk the same financial language;
(5) A regime capable of forecasting, monitoring and reporting expeditiously and at intervals appropriate for management to meaningfully react to evolving circumstances;
(6) A system which reflects specific use of resources by sector where possible; reflects common use of resources through reasonable methods of attribution where necessary; and still reflects joint costs where relevant, particularly in infrastructure provision, but without sacrificing the principle that all erstwhile indirect costs should be the managerial responsibility of one or other of the sector directors.

The SPAMS system, therefore, emphasises clear management responsibilities and the identification of whole numbers of committed resources wherever possible to a sector. This often involves a 'top down' approach rather than the traditional 'bottom up' approach. It is much easier to talk about committed resources for a small number of large units — the business sectors — than it is for a much larger number of smaller units — the profit centres — where inevitably common use of assets is much more prevalent.

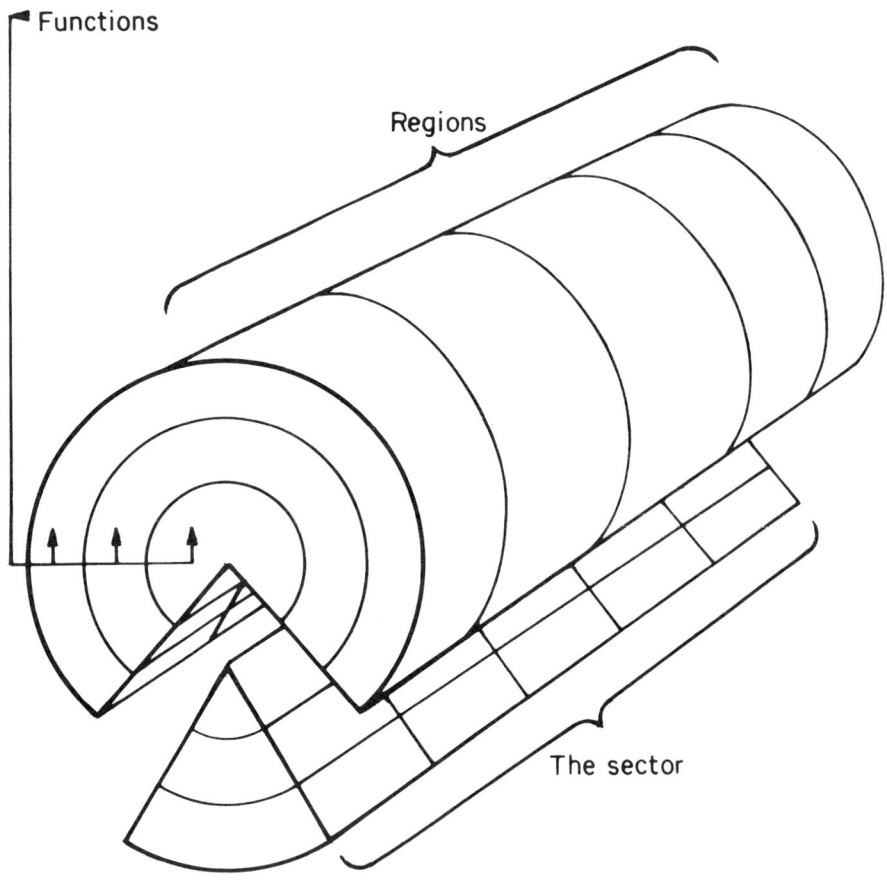

Figure 4.1 The sector cuts across both region and function

4.4 Infrastructure

Within the overall system, the treatment of infrastructure, a major element of joint cost, is particularly interesting. Here, again, the system relies on a relatively simple but managerially direct form of attribution between the sectors known as prime user costing. The main features of this are:

(1) The establishment of a prime user sector for every railway route: Inter-City takes the primacy on something over 2000 miles comprising the trunk routes from London, NE/SW and a few other lines over which Inter-City is the only passenger sector; London and SE takes the primacy on the whole of the Southern Region and Liverpool Street Division of the Eastern Region, with the exception in both cases of freight only lines, together with a relatively small number of lines on the London Midland and Western Regions; Provincial takes the primacy on all other routes used by passenger trains; Freight takes the primacy on 'freight only' lines alone.

(2) Having established primacy of use on a particular route the analysis proceeds on a 'top down' basis. Those assets avoidable to Freight and Parcels, if any, are first determined. Then, and in addition, those assets avoidable to the secondary passenger sector or sectors, if any, are isolated. Everything remaining including route structures is charged to the prime user sector.

(3) The hierarchy of hypothetical service withdrawal, having first isolated the sector in the primacy which, of course, remains till the last, is:
Freight
Parcels
Provincial
London & SE
Inter-City

This dependence on hierarchy is important because a change in the ranking would have a significant effect on the level of costs identified with each of the sectors.

The procedure is not able specifically to isolate surplus capacity but exhausts all costs of the current infrastructure over one or other of the sectors.

The issues of hierarchy and surplus capacity are still under study within British Rail. This is as it should be in what is after all the division of truly joint costs where universally right solutions do not exist.

Though the prime user convention causes some problems concerning joint costs and requires careful corporate treatment, it hands down clear management responsibilities and incentives to economy of use. No longer can infrastructure slip into being 'nobody's responsibility' in terms of bottom line impact.

4.5 The new planning system

The sector information system is but one part of the management information revolution spawned by the new management philosophy. Equally important have been the changes to the Board's corporate planning system which recognise the pre-eminent role that the sector directors must adopt in strategic planning if they are to be successful.

BR have been engaged in corporate planning since 1970 and have benefited a good deal from that process. In particular, the plans for each of the businesses, notably railways, have been at the centre of the ongoing dialogue between government and the Board on most matters of significance such as passenger grant levels, investment programmes, funding, quality of service and levels of output. However, in 1982 a major review of the planning procedures for the production of the corporate plan of the rail business (known as the Rail Plan) was undertaken largely in recognition of a need to ensure greater attention to achievement of plan forecasts and, of course, the development of sector management. The review was undertaken in conjunction with consultants Price Waterhouse Associates.

As a result of the review, it was established that six main inadequacies had existed in varying degrees in the plans produced up to 1981: (i) inadequate development of objectives and related goals; (ii) lack of attention to risk analysis and contingency planning; (iii) absence of action plans and, consequently, the commitment of regional management which, in the final analysis, comprises the only people who can actually implement large elements of the plans; (iv) inadequate plan monitoring procedures; (v) inadequate interface with annual budgets; and (vi) over-optimistic forecasting, particularly receipts growth and investment.

Additionally, and most importantly, it was urgently necessary to revise the planning procedures to recognise the primary role of the newly created sector directors. It was considered that the planning process should be one of the main means of making sector management work effectively.

With the assistance of Price Waterhouse Associates, changes to the planning systems were developed in 1982. They were partly introduced in the production of the 1982 Rail Plan and completely introduced in 1983 in the production of the 1983 Rail Plan which covered the base year 1983 and contained forecasts for the years 1984 to 1988. The revised process involves BR headquarters sector and functional directors, and regional general managers and their functional managers to the full and is summarised in Figure 4.2.

It can be seen that the revised corporate planning process is preceded by 'strategy studies'. The studies are essentially long-term (10 to 25 years) and are intended to examine the main strategic options and arrive at the key decisions on the general strategic direction of each business or sector before the rail or subsidiary business plans are prepared. Becuase of the complexity of such studies, no more than two or three are ever running at the same time, with each taking between six months and a year to complete.

Sector directors are in the lead in conducting studies confined to their own sectors. All of the studies require coordinated physical and financial evaluation and, in some cases, use of sophisticated simulation or regression models.

Returning to the elements of the revised corporate planning process, and concentrating on the procedures for the production of the five-year rail plan, it is best to describe the arrangements by reference to its three main stages of production:

4.5—1 Preparatory stage

This involves the preparation of five-year strategy papers by each of the sector directors which record:

(1) The 'bottom-line' objectives set by government or the board in respect of each sector's share of the Passenger Service Obligation (PSO) grant and related quality of service objectives. The PSO grant carrics, basically, thc combincd nct loss sustaincd by the Passenger Sectors.
(2) The strategic direction to be followed based largely on the longer-term strategic studies last produced;
(3) The investment intentions, identifying all major projects;
(4) The predicted financial results in constant prices (plus/minus any real price changes) incorporating a comprehensive functional input for working expenses identifying such items as major cost reduction initiatives, with supporting physical facts. The functional input is provided by the functional directors.
(5) Performance aims covering key non-financial outcomes and financial/non-financial performance derivatives compatible with the financial and physical facts forecasts.

These are discussed and formally approved/amended by a board committee — the strategy committee, who have earlier approved key 'plan assumptions' relating to macroeconomic indices, real staff cost and fuel price changes and extremely large events such as those relating

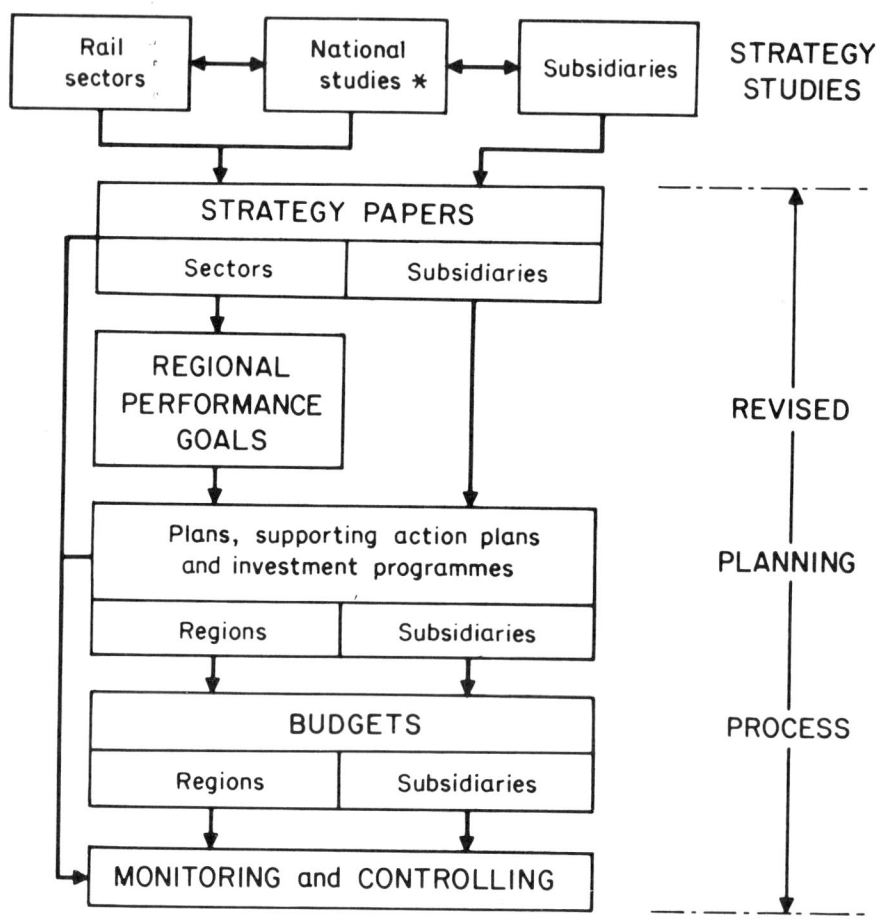

* e.g. main line electrification and Channel Tunnel

Note: All rail forecasts, action plans and monitoring statements are analysed by sector, function and region

Figure 4.2 Corporate planning

to main line electrification and Channel tunnel.

The next step is to analyse these forecasts to region (by sector within function) translating them into Regional Performance Goals. These RPGs and the detailed contingent decisions and calculations on which they are based are then negotiated as being broadly achievable with the five regional general managers at a 'Railway Planning Conference' attended by the sector directors, functional directors and regional general managers. Any significant variations would be reported back to the strategy committee for reconsideration of the decisions they had taken earlier. In respect of the 1983 Rail Plan, the Railway Planning Conference discussions resulted in an improvement in the strategy paper forecasts.

4.5—2 Detailed planning stage

This is essentially a bottom-up process whereby the forecasts are eventually measured against the criterion of the 'top-down' regional performance goals. The regions are required to produce, functionally, five-year forecasts, based on the guidance they have received, and to analyse the year-on-year changes to sector. The forecasts for the first three years are produced by first producing detailed action plans for each cause of change indicating, apart from the essential physical and financial data, the manager responsible for its achievement and the dates by which key events will occur.

These will be summarised from 1984 by an integrated computer system with terminals in each region but, in 1983, were dealt with by a temporary headquarters based computer system. The forecasts for the remaining two years are estimated by the regions on global action plan forms which do not require any of the detail needed in respect of the first three years.

4.5—3 Final stage

This involves six steps:

(1) Critical appraisal of regional forecasts by the sector and functional directors and the Financial Planning Department by reference, mainly, to the comparison with the regional performance goals;

(2) Discussion of the forecasts at a Railway Planning Conference in the light of these appraisals;

(3) Production, at headquarters level, of a risk analysis and related contingency plans. This involves the sector and functional directors in assessing not only the key upside and downside risks but the probability distributions relating to receipts by sector and working expenses by function. The risk profiles are aggregated using a

'Monte-Carlo' simulation model and an estimate made of the 'post contingency plans' outcome at selected risk levels.

(4) Re-cycling of action plans and summary forecasts as required;
(5) Consideration of the Rail Plan, in draft, at the Strategy Committee prior to consolidation with the plans of the subsidiary businesses into the Corporate Plan;
(6) Approval of the Rail/Corporate Plan by the Board.

Progress in respect of each of these three stages is reported to the Board at appropriate intervals to obtain their approval and advice. Additionally, Department of Transport officials are kept informed and the views expressed are discussed at Strategy Committee.

One of the significant benefits of these arrangements is that there is an almost automatic interface with the annual budget for the first forecast year of the plan in that the budget will also be produced 'bottom-up' by the same people. Indeed, the criterion for reviewing regional budgets and the overall sector/functional summaries is now the detailed compatibility with the first forecast year of the Rail Plan. This means that a large part of the monitoring of plan implementation is achieved through the monitoring of budget variances. However, it has been established that it is insufficient merely to monitor and control through evaluation budget variances since many of the action steps taken in year 1 do not produce financial benefits until later years. Consequently, the monitoring arrangements have been supplemented by monthly exception reporting on the individual action plans and the related investment programme. This culminates in a quarterly plan monitoring report designed to act as a trigger for implementation, where necessary, of the established contingency plans.

To conclude discussion of the revised planning process, it should be noted that, in preparing forecasts for the strategy papers and the final plans, (including a number of the action plans) considerable use is made of forecasts of national economic statistics as an important element in determining year-on-year changes. These are forecast by the Board's economist and summarised in a statement of planning assumptions produced prior to the preparation of the sector strategy papers.

The key elements considered are: (i) UK population projections by region, age and household size; (ii) UK hours of work and leisure; (iii) UK economy in terms of gross domestic product, industrial production, real personal disposable incomes and retail prices; (iv) world economy in terms of gross domestic product and consumer prices; (v) UK competitive environment in terms of car population, car ownership per person and the costs of heavy goods vehicle operation; (vi) UK energy prices for petrol, derv, gas, oil, marine and aviation fuel oil, electricity for traction, and gas and coal for industry; and (vii) UK real staff cost increases.

4.6 Performance indicators

One important common denominator in all of the planning and management information systems within BR is the identification and use of key performance indicators as an aid to management in measuring relative performance of the whole and parts of the business. Performance management through the use of performance indicators now forms an integral part of British Rail's management processes. A system based on a hierarchical structure of performance indicators — the 'analytical framework' — has been developed. The framework enables performance trends to be measured in a comprehensive and accountable manner at all organisation levels for the total railway business and its component parts. Results at one level in the structure can be disaggregated for further, more detailed examination and analysis at lower levels. The system aims to achieve better control space by placing emphasis on management by results rather than management by method.

A standard breakdown of total performance is applied throughout the analytical framework utilising six basic disaggregations: (i) total results into unit receipts, unit costs and quality of output; (ii) unit receipts into average loads and charges; (iii) unit costs by functional responsibility; (iv) unit functional costs by activity; (v) unit activity costs by cost element (staff, materials, expenses); and (vi) unit cost element costs into productivity and price.

This standard breakdown of total business performance is applicable to the business as a whole or any part of the business which might be regarded as a business unit in its own right, with both receipts and costs responsibilities, e.g. sector or sub-sector, region or sub-region. The indicators take the form of system input/output ratios utilising input and output measures specific and appropriate to the performance element and organisation level in question. Thus functional and sector indicators relate to total units of saleable output, e.g. seat or train miles whilst activity indicators relate to units of activity output (e.g. vehicles maintained, train miles crewed, etc.).

The management of performance is achieved by: (i) using relevant performance indicators to monitor past and future performance trends; (ii) comparing performance levels and trends at relevant locations or with some internal or external standard or benchmark; (iii) analysing selected variances in order to determine cause; (iv) identification of appropriate remedial action; and (v) planning, budgeting and monitoring implementation.

The relevance of any resulting managerial action depends on the quality of the information and analysis available. The information must be appropriate to the manager's needs, sensitive to the emerging variances and capable of accurately determining the cause.

The advantages of the system with the emphasis particularly on unit costs are that it enables the effects of many changes which affect any part of the business to be brought together and evaluated in a simple statistic, enables the potential for further improvement to be more easily identified and provides a consistent basis for setting future targets and subsequent monitoring of results achieved.

It is not necessary to develop initially the framework in its entirety nor to report regularly all the performance indicators. The disaggregation below sector and functional activity costs are intended primarily to assist, when required, business and line managers to manage their activities and to provide explanations for higher level performance trends to BR HQ. Also suitable input/output measures have not yet been developed for all the activities in such a large complex organisation as British Rail with its added complexities of shared resources and assets, multiplicity of asset types and wise geographical spread of activities. However, over 200 sector and functional responsibility indicators are regularly reported to BR HQ to review business and functional performance. A subset of the 200 indicators — the key 50+ indicators — are used to monitor results regularly in the budget, plan and sector evaluation processes. A further subset of about 35 performance indicators agreed between British Rail and the Department of Transport is used to report BR performance to the Department of Transport and for publication in the Board's Annual Report and accounts.

Performance indicators feature heavily in the Rail Plan and budgets in the form of secondary objectives, i.e. performance aims. The key performance indicators are used to: set performance aims based on the strategies prepared by the Sector Directors; and compare the detailed planning process results to the performance aims to ensure that targets are being met and to provide a benchmark against which to monitor future actual performance.

The indicators used measure sector receipts, functional responsibility costs and staff productivity per train mile. Quality of service for each of the business sectors is also specified in terms of punctuality and cancellation standards. The indicator values are calculated to a current year constant price level using GDP deflators and graphically presented as indices together with the historic values to give a complete trend. A detailed analysis and commentary highlighting key issues and areas of risk is prepared to accompany the statistical data for management discussion.

Part II
Costing

5 Rail cost analysis*

W. G. WATERS II

5.1 Introduction

> God Almighty did not know the cost of carrying a hundred
> pounds of freight from Boston to New York.
>> Arthur Twining Hadley, 1885

> Almost a century later, this quote can only be challenged
> in a theological context ...
>> Canadian Transport Commission, 1978

What makes railway costing such a complicated and little understood
subject? What are the purposes and methods which guide analysis of
railway costs? What are the major recent developments in rail cost
analysis? These are the guiding questions for this chapter.

5.2 The costing problem

Cost analysis for decision-making of any kind must identify and

*The author has benefited from comments and conversations with several persons expert in
various aspects of rail cost analysis. An author remains responsible for the interpretations and
views expressed, but I wish to thank without implicating: Pierre Casgrain, CN Rail; J.F. Folk,
Conrail; G.R. Green, Western Pacific (ret.); George Hariton, Canadian Transport Commission;
Kevin Horn, University of North Florida; R.W. Lake, Transport Canada and Canadian
Transport Commission; Paul Posey, Association of American Railroads; Denver Tolliver, North
Dakota State University; Walter D. Vliet, Interstate Commerce Commission; Abdul Waheed
Mian, Southern University of New Orleans; and my UBC colleagues: Garland Chow, T.D.
Heaver, Tae Hoon Oum, and Michael W. Tretheway.

measure the costs associated with doing one thing as opposed to another, i.e. the opportunity costs. The incremental costs are relevant for contemplated expansions in services supplied; for contemplated reductions in output the relevant concept is avoidable costs. Fixed costs are irrelevant. The variability of costs is the central characteristic to determine the relevance of costs for decision-making. In practice, however, especially for railways, the concept of cost-variability is ambiguous. A cost item can be variable in one sense but not in another.

The difficulty of identifying the variable costs associated with a specific movement reflects a number of characteristics of rail operations: (i) railways are multi-product enterprises; (ii) there are various indivisibilities in the production process of railways; (iii) railways employ fixed assets with differing lives, hence the variability of these cost items varies with the time horizon of the decision to be taken; and (iv) limitations exist in the accounting and management information system of railways. The implications of these characteristics are elaborated in turn. But all contribute to an unavoidable lack of precision in rail cost estimates.

5.2—1 Railways as multi-product enterprises

Railways normally supply a multiplicity of services. Various costs are incurred on behalf of the multiple outputs. It may be impossible to identify portions of total costs with a specific part of total traffic. The most vivid illustration is the joint cost of the fronthaul and backhaul. The supply of transportation involves round trips whereas the demand for transport is unidirectional. Many of the variable costs of running a train (and many other expense categories as well) are incurred jointly for the two directions. The crew incurred on the backhaul journey are not solely attributable to that portion of the round trip. The backhaul costs are inseparable from the fronthaul costs. There are other costs incurred on behalf of multiple outputs where those outputs can vary in proportions without affecting the level of costs incurred. These are common costs.

The joint and common production of rail services implies an inescapable interdependency between the costs of handling one traffic and the costs of handling others. Conceptually, it is impossible to identify the total costs of one movement separately from the costs of other traffic. Certain expense items may be uniquely attributable to specific traffic, but a major portion of total railway costs do not fall into this category. But neither are all of the latter costs totally unattributable except to all traffic taken together. There is a nested hierarchy of cost categories: certain costs are related solely to the handling and carriage of specific traffic; other costs are attributable to an aggregation of that traffic with a few others; still other costs are identifiable with still larger aggregations of traffic, for example, all traffic along a line or in a region. Some costs may be identifiable only with all traffic taken together, for example central administration. The important point is that the ability to identify specific costs with a specific movement is not a simple yes/no distinction.

In principle, the interdependence of costs for different outputs requires that optimal price-output decisions must be made simultaneously for all products. This is impossible. It is necessary for railway management (and regulators) to examine individual movements and various parts of the whole system. Therefore, estimates are made of the costs associated with specific traffic. It is impossible to calculate a true and precise measure of cost; estimates must be made of the cost of one traffic based on explicit or implicit assumptions about the volumes and patterns of movement of other traffic. The object of a costing system is to produce as reliable estimates as possible without being so complex and costly as to make the exercise not worthwhile.

5.2—2 Indivisibilities in railway operations

Railways are capital intensive, and a variety of capital inputs are employed. Typically, these various capital inputs can be expanded but only in 'lumpy' or indivisible increments. At the most basic level, the unit of supply is a rail car of certain capacity — the demand for movement is rarely forthcoming in full rail cars. The incremental adjustments in supply may exceed the additional demands for service. Similarly, once trains reach maximum size, additional capacity is gained by supplying an additional train load. A more extreme example is the need to double track as single track operations reach capacity. At some point the incremental costs of capacity expansion are substantial. The implications of this are that the costs of handling additional traffic may be very low if excess capacity is present; however, the costs may be substantial if various capital items are fully utilised at present. In other words, costs may be variable for large increments of output but not for small changes.

5.2—3 The time horizon

The short run and long run is an important conceptual distinction in economics: the planning period is either sufficient for all inputs to be varied or only some. But in practice, time is not a dichotomous concept. There are a variety of inputs employed with different lives. The need to expand these inputs to handle additional traffic depends on the time horizon of the decision and the remaining useful life of these various capital inputs. The appropriate measure of variable costs would be different for a once-only movement compared to traffic which is expected to be handled for an indefinite period. In the former case, the appropriate concept of costs is 'short run' in nature, whereas long-run costs are appropriate for the latter. However, there are numerous in-between cases; that is, traffic which is more than a single journey but is not expected to continue indefinitely. An example would be estimating the variable costs of carrying supplies for a major construction project. The implications of this discussion is that the identification of 'variable costs' differs according to the time horizon of the decision. (Generally, long-run variable cost estimates are sought.)

5.2—4 Limitations of accounting and management information systems

The detail and structure of accounts and statistics of rail operations can obscure the causality between rail services performed and the costs incurred. Cost accounts must serve different purposes, a traditional one being simply the recording and classifying of expenses for purposes of financial record keeping and management. Expenses tend to be categorised by type; for example, wages, fuel expenses, taxes. But a similar type of expense is normally associated with different services rendered. Consequently, the connection between a variety of costs and the handling of some specific traffic may be obscured. The danger is well-known and modern cost accounting seeks to prevent this from happening. But railway accounting classifications have changed little during the twentieth century. Even the recent revisions to regulated rail accounting classifications in North America (the first major revisions since early in the twentieth century) may still be deficient for some managerial purposes.

5.2—5 The ambiguity of rail cost estimates

In theory, the interdependence between costs for different traffic means that optimal prices and service decisions can only be found simultaneously for all traffic. As noted, this is a practical impossibility. It is necessary to make price and service decisions for individual commodities. To do so, the appropriate *concepts* of costs must be identified and specific procedures for *estimating* the various costs must be established. This is the purpose of a railway's costing manual. A costing order is the analogous document for a regulatory agency. Both types of document must be predicated on the goals for the organisation: management's goal would normally, in the North American context, be to maximise profits for the railway company. Economic efficiency, consistent with commercial viability of carriers, but subject to government social and political policies, are potential objectives for a regulatory agency. However, precedent and various notions of equity may also be a factor — explicitly or implicitly — in regulatory decisions.

The various purposes of rail cost analysis affect both the cost concepts and procedures for costing. Inevitably, railway costing is an arcane and contentious subject because of the unavoidable uncertainty which surrounds rail cost estimation. A costing system is a pragmatic procedure to do the practically impossible. This is not to say that one cost estimate is as good as another, only that there are unavoidable limitations in the precision which can be expected in cost estimates.

5.3 Purposes of rail cost analysis

Costing refers to the procedures for estimating the costs associated with a particular activity. The relevant concept of costs is that of opportunity costs but these have different, specific interpretations in different circumstances. The purpose or end-use of cost analysis can influence costing approaches and methods of analysis.

Several purposes of rail cost analysis can be identified, for example: (i) costing for commercial enterprises; (ii) costing for public service obligations; (iii) costing for regulatory decisions; (iv) social costs and government decision-making; and (v) cost analysis for economic research.

5.3—1 Costing for commercial rail enterprises

Here we are concerned with management decisions in a railroad pursuing profitability. This includes private rail companies as well as public enterprises which are given substantial pricing freedom and a mandate to function in a 'business-like' manner. Three categories of cost analysis can be identified.

(a) *Financial planning and budgeting.* This category refers to estimating the costs associated with budget units such as departments in a company or regional offices. These types of cost estimates can serve various managerial purposes, such as be part of an appraisal of departmental performance, or, more commonly, for projecting budget requirements of departments and operations. This type of cost analysis can be fairly simple. Straightforward projections of past expenditure levels are common. This might be supplemented by linking departmental expenditure levels to forecasts of company or regional traffic volumes and/or manpower projections.

(b) *Traffic costing.* This is the main purpose of cost analysis in most railroads. The task is to estimate the costs associated with particular traffic or types of service. This could refer to existing or prospective traffic; for short or long periods of time; and for individual movements or various aggregations of traffic. While both the concept and measurement of variable costs is ambiguous for railways rail management still needs to estimate whether the company is better off with certain traffic than without it. An estimate of variable costs, therefore, provides a floor for rate-making purposes. Normally, a rate will be somewhat above this level, but, for price-sensitive traffic, it is necessary to know the minimum rate which would be acceptable to the company. Because much traffic can pay a rate well above variable costs, precise cost estimates may not be too important. A 'quick cost formula' may be sufficient to assure that particular traffic is remunerative. For price-sensitive traffic and other special cases, more detailed cost analysis will be carried out.

Often it is desirable to cost aggregates of traffic movements, e.g. assessing the profitability of a traffic type or operations on a branch line or in a region. Such cost analysis is necessary for investment decisions on equipment or infrastructure needed to serve blocks of traffic.

For the most part, costing a collection of traffic movements is simply an aggregation and expansion of costing individual movements. But it is important to note that some costs which cannot be identified as directly variable with individual traffic may be variable for traffic taken together.

(c) Facility or project costing. Special costing studies are needed for major investment decisions. The types of decisions are several, for example: analysis of the costs of alternative types of equipment; analysis of the costs of investments to reduce delays of train operations; estimation of trade-offs between capital improvements and lower maintenance costs. These costing needs often involve new equipment, hence, historical cost experience by the company may not be appropriate. Such studies normally are carried out on an *ad hoc* or special study basis rather than follow the routine procedure used for costing traffic.

5.3–2 Costing for public service obligations

These costs are not always seen as a distinct categorisation. It is used here to refer to unremunerative services required by government mandate. Most rail passenger services in North America fit this category and it could also include provision of small shipment service and/or service to some small communities. In principle, costing for this category of services may seem little different from commercially-viable services. But special problems can grow out of the different managerial perspectives on these types of services.

The distinctive feature is the lack of commercial attractiveness. The lack of commercial pressures may reduce incentives for efficiency. Lacking profitability as a goal, management must articulate (or have articulated for them) goals, targets, criteria, etc. This is easily left vague and accountability and performance hard to assess.

Two types of cost analysis can be identified: cost accounting for auditing and general managerial control; and cost analysis to assess managerial performance. Neither are straightforward. The inevitable ambiguity in rail costs is inconsistent with auditing purposes, i.e. it is not easy to establish direct links between various costs incurred and the particular services rendered. If the mandated services are under-written by public subsidies, managers have an incentive to state costs generously, or at least ensure that no indirect costs affected by an unremunerative service be overlooked.

In contrast, regulatory or other supervisory agencies seek to minim-ise the payment of scarce public funds. There is a long history of dis-agreement in negotiating compensation for unremunerative services and trying to assess managerial performance in supplying such services poses even greater administrative difficulties. In sum, considerable time and expense may be involved in disputes over costing details for mandated unprofitable services; costs which might not arise in a purely commercial environment.

5.3—3 Cost analysis for regulatory purposes

Different regulatory concerns may require different types of cost analysis. The primary costing needs can be identified with following regulatory activities.

(a) Cost analysis for minimum and maximum rates. Maximum and minimum limits on rates are very different regulatory issues but can be addressed together. Regulations may require that rates be 'compens-atory', i.e. not permit destructive competition caused by rates below costs. Maximum rates may be restricted to some multiple of the variable cost estimate. (Just what the multiple might be is not at issue here.) In either case costing procedures must be agreed to or prescribed by the regulatory agency.

The inevitable ambiguity of rail costs provides a platform for debate among accountants, legal counsel, economists, rail operating officers, consultants, commission staff, etc. But endless debate cannot be permitted. A 'costing order' or equivalent prescribed procedures (e.g. in the USA there is the ICC's Rail Form A) must be drawn up. The analagous problem gives rise to a railway's costing manual; indeed, the regulators' and railway procedures could be identical. No single formula can, however, be ideal for the variety of circumstances which arise in different railroads and thus for regulatory purposes, accuracy and specificity for individual roads is sacrificed for administrative convenience. The dissatisfaction with Rail Form A, for instance, was widespread in the USA for years, and it is inevitable that many similar criticisms will persist with the newer Uniform Rail Costing System. Broad standardised treatment of rail costs cannot be consistent with a costing system which is highly flexible and adaptable in its application by different railroads. Railroads may increasingly rely on their own versions of accounting and information systems and costing procedures separate from that required by regulatory agencies.

(b) Costing for rail abandonments. Another long-standing source of controversy in railways and cost analysis concerns abandonment of services or branch lines. While various arguments may be in mind, the dominant reason for a proposed abandonment is lack of profitability. Where entry and exit are regulated, railroads must seek permission to abandon services. Controversy surrounds the estimation of costs to compare with revenues to establish the extent of losses incurred and opponents of the abandonment usually tend to argue that costs are overstated. The relevance of various overheads and other indirect costs are debatable, and questions associated with the inclusion of effects associated with branch operations arise. A more general controversy involves appropriate costing of assets which may have limited alternate use, as well as determining the appropriate rate of return which should be permitted on these assets.

(c) Costing for subsidy payments. This often arises out of situations where abandonment is not permitted, or it may arise out of long-standing requirements to provide specified unprofitable services in exchange for compensation. There is a need here to agree on the actual losses incurred as a basis for subsidy payment. The most controversial areas are, again, the relevance of various overheads or 'constant costs', as well as the valuation and allowed rates of return on assets associated with the service many of which may have limited alternate use.

5.3—4 Estimating social costs

Governments are expected to hold broader perspectives of costs and benefits than the strictly financial perspectives of private firms. Effects on communities, environmental impacts and other externalities may be considered by government. These are costing concerns, however, normally beyond the primary interests and responsibilities of rail management. They are not routinely monitored or costed in a firm. Different information sources are necessary and costing intangible benefits and costs to society are inevitably controversial. Yet these are valid concepts for economically-optimal decision-making in government. The social costs and benefits can be larger than the financial costs incurred by the railway. The savings in automobile pollution, congestion and necessary road investments which would otherwise be necessary to accommodate rail commuters might far outweigh the revenue shortfalls of such a service.

There have been substantial developments in both the principles and application of social benefit cost analysis or similar evaluation approaches to public projects including rail services. These involve costing procedures and controversies beyond those normally identified with rail operations and management. They are not addressed in this section.

5.3—5 Cost analysis in economic research

There is a long tradition of research on rail cost characteristics by academic economists. The focuses are on hypothesis testing and refining the methodology of cost estimation. Modern studies tend to employ sophisticated econometric methods and often methodological rigour seems more important than the specific numerical results. These studies generally limit their analysis to high-level generalisations about cost-output relationships across railroads and/or over time. Most of these cost functions are highly aggregated and contrast to the emphasis on disaggregated cost estimates used by rail management and regulators. Nonetheless, these aggregate cost functions can have practical policy relevance, e.g. verifying the presence of economies of scale in railroading lends support to a liberal merger policy.

5.4 Costing methods

Costing techniques must be used to estimate the specific relationship between outputs and costs when that relationship is not obvious from available information. There are three basic approaches to costing: accounting, engineering and statistical. These may be combined into 'hybrid' costing procedures.

5.4—1 Accounting costs

The accounting approach compiles the cost categories or accounts relevant to a particular output being supplied. The cost information is used to estimate the costs associated with a change in the level of output. This is generally the cheapest and most convenient method of costing, providing data exist. However, this approach has several potential shortcomings.

The first problem, that recorded values of assets may not be a reliable indicator of their opportunity costs, is a familiar difficulty. Opportunity costs are the relevant concept for decision-making so accounting figures may need modification to reflect actual opportunities forgone.

A second shortcoming of accounting costs arises if fixed and variable costs are not distinguished. Dividing total costs by an output measure is an overestimate of unit variable costs if some of those costs are fixed. It is necessary to estimate what portion of costs in an account actually vary with changes in output.

Another potential problem is that the accounting process could obscure the causality between particular outputs and cost categories. This is not necessarily the fault of the accounting system. If costs are incurred in common with supplying several outputs it may be impossible to identify costs with specific outputs regardless of the accounting system employed. Aggregation in the accounting system, however, can give rise to additional misleading instances of common costs. Accounting categories also tend to be determined by the nature of an expense (e.g. fuel, labour expenses, etc.) while revenues are recorded to the types of service provided. There may be little correspondence, though, between cost categories and revenue accounts.

Despite these dangers the use of accounting information generally is indispensible. Often there is no alternative and accounting information provides the basic data for statistical cost studies. The principal situation where accounting costs may not need to be used is with engineering costing.

5.4—2 Engineering costing

This approach to costing focuses on the technical relationship between inputs and outputs. Combining these technical coefficients with the cost of those inputs yields the cost function for the particular output. (If inputs are substitutable there is the additional step of seeing that inputs are combined in optimal proportions.)

There are two approaches to engineering costing. One is to derive the technical coefficients from physical laws or precise engineering relationships (e.g. DeSalvo 1969). The second is to establish empirically the technical relationship by controlled experiment. (An example of the latter would be carefully recording the speed and weight on axles passing over a section of track, and relating this to the actual rate of rail wear. This will establish wear coefficients which can then be tied to the costs of providing and maintaining the track and roadbed.) The two approaches to engineering costing can be used in conjunction with one another.

The major disadvantage of the engineering approach is that it tends to be data- and time-intensive, making it rather costly, especially if repeated studies are necessary to reduce measurement error. The results should be highly accurate, however, and it is employed in instances where the desired accuracy warrants its cost. Such costing, however, necessarily deals only with outputs and inputs which can be linked in a physical way, which implies that costs are necessarily traceable to outputs. Engineering costing will not, therefore, eliminate situations where multiple outputs exist.

5.4—3 Statistical costing

The third costing method, and one which has found extensive use in transportation, is statistical costing. Basically, it is the use of statistical techniques (usually multiple regression analysis) to infer cost-output relations from a sample of actual operating experiences. Instances of different cost-output levels (and/or different combinations of multiple outputs) are analysed statistically to identify the variability of costs with output measures. Statistical costing generally uses accounting information (with possible adjustments such as disaggregating cost categories, revaluation of assets to equal their opportunity costs, etc.). The sample of observations consists of cost-output experience relevant to the relationship being estimated. Observations tend to consist of a comparison of different branches of a firm's operations, experience over a period of time, or a cross-section of the cost-output experience of different firms. Each of these sets of observations has particular advantages depending upon the purpose of costing, but each also entails disadvantages in that it may introduce a systematic bias to the estimate of cost-output relations.

Statistical costing is not necessarily an ideal costing method. It is generally used because more direct methods are not feasible, or as a substitute for costly engineering studies. Statistical cost studies are not precise measurement devices; they only provide estimates of cost coefficients. The degree of precision depends on the sample size, the predictability of the relationship being investigated, the correct specification of the variables measured, the accuracy of measurement, and the validity of the assumptions which underlie the statistical method employed. This last influence is very important and if one or more of the underlying assumptions is not satisfied, this will undermine the accuracy of the estimated cost function. The validity of the results depend upon whether subtle, but important, underlying statistical conditions are satisfied.[1]

Statistical analysis of rail costs has been carried out for many years. In the last couple of decades, however, there has been a growing split between two types of statistical costs studies of railways. There are what might be termed 'operational cost studies' carried out by railroad and regulatory staff. These are disaggregate cost functions for various railway accounts, and are used in conjunction with other cost information to develop estimates of the costs of various specific rail services. These are the procedures embodied in regulatory costing orders or railroad costing manuals. In contrast are econometric studies of rail costs carried out by academic researchers and some public policy analysts. Typically, these are aggregate rail cost functions but are characterised by a rigorous specification of cost-output relationships and sophisticated econometric techniques are employed in their estimation. We now turn to look at recent advances in this econometric analysis.

5.5 Recent developments: econometric analysis of rail costs[2]

The modifier 'econometric' is used here to identify statistical cost studies that stress methodological rigour in the formulation and estimation of rail cost functions. Econometric studies are characterised by the precise formulation of input—output—cost relationships consistent with economic theory, and rigorous examination of underlying assumptions and data characteristics as they affect the choice of statistical techniques for estimation. These studies generally seek only high level generalisations about rail cost characteristics, e.g. confirming the presence or absence of economies of scale has been of primary interest. These studies generally employ highly aggregative data; the total annual costs of a railroad typically constitute one data point. This is in contrast to disaggregate studies of individual railway accounts which are employed by railway companies and regulatory agencies.

5.5—1 The development of econometric analysis of rail costs

It is not appropriate to survey the entire development of econometric analysis of rail costs, but a brief reference to pioneering works is in order. The statistical analysis of railway costs can be traced to Clark (1923) who, in turn, relied heavily on the earlier work by Lorenz (1916) of the US Interstate Commerce Commission. But the first studies which would be labelled econometric would be those of Klein (1953) and Borts (1952, 1954, 1960). Klein's pioneering text on *Econometrics* included estimating a rail production function with two outputs (net ton miles of freight and passenger miles) based on 1936 data. His estimates indicated the existence of economies of scale. Borts (1952) estimated rail production functions separately for linehaul and switching operations using a cross-section of US railroads for 1948. His findings were inconclusive regarding scale economies. Subsequent contributions by Borts (1954, 1960) were conceptual rather than empirical and he rigorously examined the potential pitfalls in attempting to empirically determine the presence of scale economies in railroading.

Numerous statistical cost studies for railroads appeared in the late 1950s and 1960s. They were carried out by railroads (e.g. Stenason and Bandeen 1965; Poole 1962; Association of American Railroads 1964) and government agencies (Royal Commission on Transportation 1962), as well as by academic economists (e.g. Healy 1961; Meyer *et al.* 1959). These studies focused primarily on disaggregate cost accounts and employed straightforward statistical techniques. Meyer *et al.* (1959) and others (such as Griliches 1972) included a methodological critique of ICC costing procedures. The ICC approach regressed costs per mile of track (or mile of road) as a function of gross ton miles per mile of track. Deflating the output measure by miles of track could induce spurious correlation between them. It was shown to be preferable to test for the effect on costs of output variables and miles of track separately.

The next major reformulation of rail cost estimation was by Friedlaender (1971). She estimated an aggregate long-run cost function from a cross-section, stratified by region and time period, as well as a short-run cost function estimated from quarterly data. Combinations of the cost elasticities of the two cost equations were used as evidence of excess capacity in her estimates of the social costs of inefficient regulation of the US railroad industry. A Cobb-Douglas production function of aggregate rail services was employed to estimate the impacts on rail output which would come from more efficient use of capital stock.

Keeler (1974) was critical of Friedlaender's (and Borts') cost functions and calculations of cost elasticities because of implicit contradictory assumptions. The long-run cost function is estimated on the assumption that firms are operating on their long-run cost function, whereas the short-run cost function estimated for the same companies assumes that operations are not at long-run planned output levels. If this were not so, there would be no short-run variations in costs and outputs from which to estimate a short-run function. Keeler's own approach was to postulate a Cobb-Douglas production function for passenger and freight operations and treat track as a fixed input (to be allocated between passengers and freight operations). The function was estimated on pooled cross-sectional and time-series data (1968 through 1970) for 51 US class I railways. He employed a weighted non-linear least squares regression. Given his estimate of the short-run total cost function (i.e. track fixed) he could generate the long-run cost function for various amounts of track. Then, similar to Borts and Friedlaender, he compared short-run and long-run cost elasticities and concluded that an 'enormous amount of excess track capacity' was present in US railways — a strong criticism of railroad regulation in the US. His results implied constant returns to scale although increasing returns from increased density of use. Distinguishing between economies of density or utilisation and economies of scale per se is important. Some railways get better utilisation because they are fortunate in having better traffic patterns, e.g. larger markets and better directional balance of traffic. These cost advantages should not be confused with pure economies of scale.

The idea of density as a factor explaining rail cost differences was also important in Griliches' (1972) critique of ICC costing methods. Griliches used a cross-section of US railways, averaged over the period 1957–61, with railways divided into two size classes, those above or below 500 miles of track. He found no evidence of economies of scale and, anticipating Keeler, drew attention to the importance of distinguishing between economies of scale (the change in costs with equiproportionate increases in all traffic) as opposed to increasing utilisation of indivisible plant by expansions in *some* but not all traffic.

Harris (1977) took up the issue of economies of scale versus density. His results show density to be a very important factor explaining variations in unit operating costs among US railways.

5.5–2 *Flexible functional forms: the translog*

Further advances in the econometric analysis of railway costs emerged in the late 1970s. A major advance has been the formulation of more general cost functions — and the necessary econometric techniques for estimating them — capable of incorporating more of the underlying cost interrelationships among inputs and outputs for multiple product firms. Most notable is the so-called translog cost function (an abbreviated form of 'transcendental logarithmic'). Building on the work of earlier researchers (notably Shephard 1953, and Diewert 1971), the translog function was introduced by Christensen, Jorgenson and Lau in 1973 and first applied to railways in 1976 by Brown, Caves and Christensen. The properties of the function are particularly relevant to transport studies.

A cost function reflects properties of the underlying production function, e.g. economies of scale means that output expands in greater proportion that equiproportionate increases in all inputs. The cost function reflects this by total costs increasing less than proportionately with increases in output. There are many properties of production functions which economists normally expect to hold, but multiple product industries raise additional possibilities about interrelationships among multiple outputs, outputs and inputs, along with the traditional possibilities of substitution or complementarity among inputs. The traditional *ad hoc* linear or log-linear cost functions make restrictive implicit assumptions about the underlying nature of production technology.

The translog is a formulation which imposes as few restrictions as possible about the underlying production technology. First, postulate a general production function in implicit form:

$$O = F(X_i, I_j) \tag{5.1}$$

i.e. a production frontier for a number of outputs X_i employing inputs I_j. Assuming cost minimisation, there is a cost function E dual to the above production function which can be expressed in terms of outputs and input prices w_j:[3]

$$E = e(X_i, w_j) \tag{5.2}$$

An extension of this general notation is to include firm-specific technology variables which influence its production and costs relative to other firms. Examples for railways might include terrain (Huenemann 1981), demand and network conditions such as highly seasonal traffic and empty backhauls, for imposed public duties such as serving low density routes (Spady 1977; Friedlaender and Spady 1979).

Some specific form of this general cost function must be chosen for empirical implementation. The traditional cost functions for railways are of a very simple form which must assume particular types of technological relationships among output and input variables rather than test empirically for these relationships. The translog is written in logarithmic form but includes coefficients for the effects on costs of the interaction of all variables in the cost function. Its formulation of a cost function with two outputs X_1 and X_2 and two inputs with prices w_1 and w_2 is expressed as follows:

$$
\begin{aligned}
\ln E = {} & \ln a_0 + a_1 \ln X_1 + a_2 \ln X_2 + a_3 \ln w_1 + a_4 \ln w_2 \\
& + a_5 (\ln X_1)^2 + a_6 (\ln X_2)^2 + a_7 (\ln w_1)^2 + a_8 (\ln w_2)^2 \\
& + a_9 \ln X_1 \ln X_2 + a_{10} \ln X_1 \ln w_1 + a_{11} \ln X_1 \ln w_2 \\
& + a_{12} \ln X_2 \ln w_1 + a_{13} \ln X_2 \ln w_2 + a_{14} \ln w_1 \ln w_2 + e
\end{aligned} \tag{5.3}
$$

The complexity of the translog function is readily seen. Further, adding one more output variable to the cost function with n variables already specified gives rise to n + 2 additional coefficients (6 in the above example).[4] Note that if the coefficients a_5 through a_{14} were found to be zero, the above translog formulation reduces to the familiar log-linear form.

The translog function offers the opportunity to test for subtle cost interrelatedness among variables. For example, the standard linear or log-linear functions must assume separable technologies for the multiple outputs. But this is often contrary to what we expect since there may be economies or diseconomies in the production of some of the multiple outputs. The translog form implies no such assumption but it may be tested for. These economies of common production or economies of scope (Panzar and Willig 1975) are thought to be important in explaining the existence of multi-product firms. On the other hand, some pairs of multiple products could have cost increasing effects on one another, e.g. passenger and freight operations might interfere with one another.[5]

The great number of coefficients to estimate is a disadvantage of the translog. The values of some parameters might be imposed by knowledge of the underlying production relations or otherwise constrained in the values they can take. As an example of the latter, all cost functions must be homogeneous of degree one (so doubling prices for the same inputs would yield twice the costs).

There is one additional step before the translog functions are actually estimated. The cost function can also be written

$$E = \sum_j w_j I_j \tag{5.4}$$

i.e. total costs must equal total factor payments made. For cost minimisation, the derivative of the expression for total factor payments with respect to input prices must equal the cost minimising input levels in the earlier cost function (this is Shephard's lemma, 1953) and this can be identified as the factor's share of total cost S

$$\frac{\partial \ln E}{\partial \ln w_j} = \frac{w_j I_j}{E} = S_j \tag{5.5}$$

The share equation for factor one is

$$S_1 = a_3 + a_{10} \ln X_1 + a_{12} \ln X_2 + a_{14} \ln w_2 + e_1$$

The translog cost function is estimated jointly with the factor share equations.

116

Returning to the review of the literature, the first use of the translog for railways was Brown, Caves and Christensen (1976, 1979). They applied this functional form to Klein's (1953) 1936 data on US railways. Their study followed one by Hasenkamp (1976). Hasenkamp used more general functional forms than Klein's Cobb-Douglas form but not as general as the translog. Both Hasenkamp and Brown et al. verified Klein's finding of economies of scale but also concluded that Klein's formulation was restrictive. Hasenkamp had assumed a restricted (homothetic) functional form but Brown et al. found that Hasenkamp's formulation was too restrictive as well.

Applications of the translog to more recent data soon followed. Friedlaender and Spady estimated translog cost functions for American railways and trucking in their study of intermodal competition. Spady (1977) and Friedlaender and Spady (1979, 1980) made several innovations in their estimates of cost functions. They employed the translog form including firm-specific technological variables — specifically, low density route miles and freight tons per train — as reflecting exogenous characteristics of a railway's route structure, demand patterns, and imposed public obligations. They also disaggregated the freight traffic into four categories: agricultural, coal, manufactures and other bulk. They further addressed the heterogeneity of freight traffic by introducing (hedonic) quality adjustments for average length of haul and average load. Spady (1977) estimated the functions for a sample of railroads carrying both passengers and freight for the period 1968–72. These studies found some diseconomies of scale in terms of freight ton miles, but economies of route density, train and load consolidation.

In their final report, Friedlaender and Spady (1980) reduced their rail sample to 20 US railroads and 57 observations for the period 1968–70. They extended the hedonic adjustment to passenger travel, i.e. passenger miles adjusted for passenger density and average travel length. The empirical results were similar to those of Spady (1977) with some evidence of diseconomies with respect to freight ton miles but economies of route density. These results were used in conjunction with estimates of US trucking costs and estimates of the demand for truck and rail travel to examine the implications for economic efficiency and reallocations of traffic among the modes following regulatory reform.

One reason for the limited sample size of Freidlaender and Spady (1979) was that freight-only railroads could not be included with those carrying both freight and passengers because the translog function could not handle data with zero values for output. Caves, Christensen and Trethaway (1978, 1980) overcame this by formulating a generalised translog function. It is the same as previous translog formulations except that the logarithm of output variables was replaced by the more general Box-Cox expression which has a linear and log-linear form as a special case. Their sample was a 1963 cross-section of 41 US railroads carrying passengers and freight, plus 15 freight-only roads. Output variables were freight revenue ton miles and passenger revenue miles with three inputs: capital, fuel and labour. Combining passenger and freight with freight-only railways resulted in a cost elasticity less than unity (i.e. evidence of economies of scale).

The next extension of the model was a generalised translog function to estimate rail productivity over time. Caves, Christensen and Swanson (1979, 1980) estimated total factor productivity for a sample of US railroads from 1951 to 1974. The basic approach is to add a time variable to the general cost function, i.e.

$$E = E(X_i; w_j; T) \qquad (5.6)$$

where the notation is as before, x_i refers to outputs however defined, w_j are factor prices, and T is the time variable. Total differentiation of the log of the cost function with respect to time results in an expression which allocates the growth rate of cost among changes in outputs, input prices and time. Output variables were freight and passenger ton miles as well as average lengths of haul. Input indices included labour, way and structures, equipment, fuel and materials.

The result showed the sum of cost elasticities less than unity for every year indicating economies of scale in overall rail operations. Their estimates of productivity growth were noticeably less than previous empirical estimates, about one-half. Previous studies of rail productivity had used revenue shares of passenger versus freight operations as the weights to apply to the two types of output. But 'the revenue share from passenger service greatly understates its cost elasticity. Similarly the revenue share from freight service greatly overstates its cost elasticity.' (Caves, Christensen and Swanson 1980: 180). They calculate average rate of total factor productivity at 1.5 per cent per year; employing conventional input and output weights would have yielded 3.6 per cent.

Caves and Christensen (1978, 1980) extended their total factor productivity estimates to the two transcontinental Canadian railways by combining Canadian data with the cost experience estimated for US railways. The hypothesis of constant returns to scale could not be rejected. The rate of total factor productivity for the Canadian railways was on the order of 3.0 per cent annually, about twice as high as for US railways. Of interest was that the performance of the publicly owned Canadian National rivalled and even surpassed that of the privately owned CP Rail (Canadian Pacific).

Their studies of rail productivity in the two countries prompted more specific studies comparing the performance of US with Canadian railways (Caves, Christensen and Swanson 1980; and with Trethaway 1982). The Canadian railways started from lower absolute productivity levels in the 1950s and have accelerated past US railroads, including some of the most efficient US railroads. The relative performance of railways in the two countries is presented as evidence in support of deregulation. The acceleration in Canadian rail productivity has come about in the essentially unregulated Canadian environment (see also Heaver and Waters 1982).

5.5—3 *Findings and future directions*

In reviewing the advances in econometric analysis of rail costs, it may seem curious that the debate over the presence or absence of scale economies in railroads has not been resolved. But this should not be interpreted as a shortcoming of the empirical analysis. What is apparent is that scale economies, if they exist at all, are not a predominant characteristic of rail operations. But there is general agreement that the significant economies to be realised in rail operations come not from size per se but from economies of density or utilisation. It is the ability to exploit under-utilised fixed facilities or equipment which is the major source of declining average costs in railways. Also significant is the increasing ability to identify economies (or diseconomies) associated with multiple outputs. These may be more important than economies of scale in explaining rail cost characteristics. The application of these flexible form cost functions to individual rail line operations may prove more revealing in measuring economies of scale per se.

There is a need for more research in this area. As complicated as the translog formulations are, they are still confined to only a few output measures. Much greater disaggregation may be necessary to measure more accurately the diversity of output and cost characteristics in railways. The other area for research is to incorporate more of the modern advances in econometric techniques into practical railway costing. It was academic research which originated the application of statistical methods to rail cost analysis. The standard regression techniques are now in widespread use by railroads and regulatory agencies. One can expect the newer econometric techniques increasingly to penetrate practical rail cost analysis.

5.6 Recent developments: railway costing and regulatory agencies

The major regulatory needs for rail cost analysis have been outlined above. Establishing the costs of service often is a prominent component of regulatory proceedings. If rates are, for instance, deemed to be 'too high', some measures of costs generally are needed to evaluate these rates. Cost-price comparisons are relevant even where political or equity considerations dominate economic ones. The issues of regulatory overview are relevant primarily to countries with privately owned railways, namely Canada and the United States. There can be 'arm's length' regulation of government owned railways by other government agencies, but most such railways are not in this situation. The presumption is that potential conflicts between the public and private interest do not arise where the enterprise is under direct government control. (This may be an excessively charitable view, but it is not explored in this chapter.) There have been important developments in railway costing for regulatory purposes in both the United States and Canada. They are addressed in turn.

5.6—1 Regulation and rail costing developments in the United States

Although there is some state regulation of intra-state rail operations, the majority of US rail traffic is under the jurisdiction of the federal Interstate Commerce Commission. There is a long history of detailed rail regulation and controversy in the US. Recently, however, significant deregulatory moves have taken place and with them rail costing procedures are undergoing major re-examination and modification.

The late 1970s and 1980s have seen considerable re-examination and reform of regulatory costing procedures in the US. In the eyes of many this reform was long overdue. The ICC had made only minor revisions to their costing methodology since the development of Rail Form A just prior to World War II. A cross-sectional analysis was employed to estimate the per cent variable of rail costs. Application of this percentage to total rail costs in Rail Form A was used as an estimate of out of pocket or variable costs (ICC Docket 34013). Strictly speaking, Rail Form A was never an official costing procedure requiring strict adherence to its principles (further, different cost concepts and procedures were necessary for abandonment disputes). Its unofficial status for rate disputes and regulation was a source of additional uncertainty.

As costs became a more important factor in rate-making and regulation, greater emphasis on costing methodology was inevitable. The development of rail cost analysis goes hand in hand with the modernisation and increasing commercial orientation of rail management.

Various pressures lead to re-examination of ICC costing procedures. There were internal pressures in the ICC, but many criticisms came from outside. Various economists had been critical of ICC costing methodology over the years (e.g. Meyer *et al.* 1959; Friedlaender 1969,

1971; Griliches 1972). The reorganisation of the bankrupt Penn Central into the Consolidated Rail Corporation (ConRail) and the accompanying Regional Rail Revitalisation (3R) Act in 1973 was a stimulus for reform. The Federal Railroad Administration was set up to help plan for the rail industry, and a Rail Services Planning Office was formed in the ICC. Comparing revenues with costs incurred in rail services became more important than ever.

The ICC was already reviewing rail accounting procedures when the Railroad Reform and Revitalisation (4R) Act was passed in 1976. It explicitly increased ICC responsibilities for rail cost funding. The ICC and consultants issued an interim report reviewing various theories and issues in costing in 1977, and a new uniform system of accounts (USOA) was introduced. The new USOA was more detailed, e.g. expenses were now separated by car types. Greater use of statistical analysis was recommended to determine rail cost variability and various parties were involved in consultation in the review of costing methods which was subjected to comment and discussion (e.g. see Interstate Commerce Commission 1977).

The Staggers Act of 1980 explicitly increased the role of cost analysis in rate regulation. Instead of continuing to allow shippers or carriers to protest any new rate or change in rate, rate-making freedom is permitted within a zone. Rates cannot be protested as too high unless they exceed a certain percentage above variable costs; hence determination of such costs becomes more important than ever.

The Staggers Act also provided for a Railroad Accounting Principles Board to oversee development and reform of rail accounting systems. These events coincided with the ICC's development of the new Uniform Railroad Costing System (URCS).

The URCS was a combined effort of ICC staff and consultants. The URCS is in the tradition of Rail Form A, but offers greater flexibility in establishing cost relationships and in using them. There are several phases in developing URCS estimates. Phase I combines statistics on rail operations and expenses employing regression analysis to estimate cost-output relationships. Phase II develops cost coefficients in a series of work tables, to be used for costing traffic movements (Phase III). These components of URCS are illustrated in Figures 5.1 and 5.2. URCS procedures offer some flexibility in formulating the regressions in Phase I and in developing the work tables in Phase II. URCS can be employed for their own costing purposes by railroads, but it is likely that most already have or will develop even more 'situation-specific' information for their traffic costing.

The new URCS is not without its critics. First, economists can find fault with the specification and estimation of cost relationships (e.g. McBride 1982, Crew and Horn 1981). They do not meet the methodol-

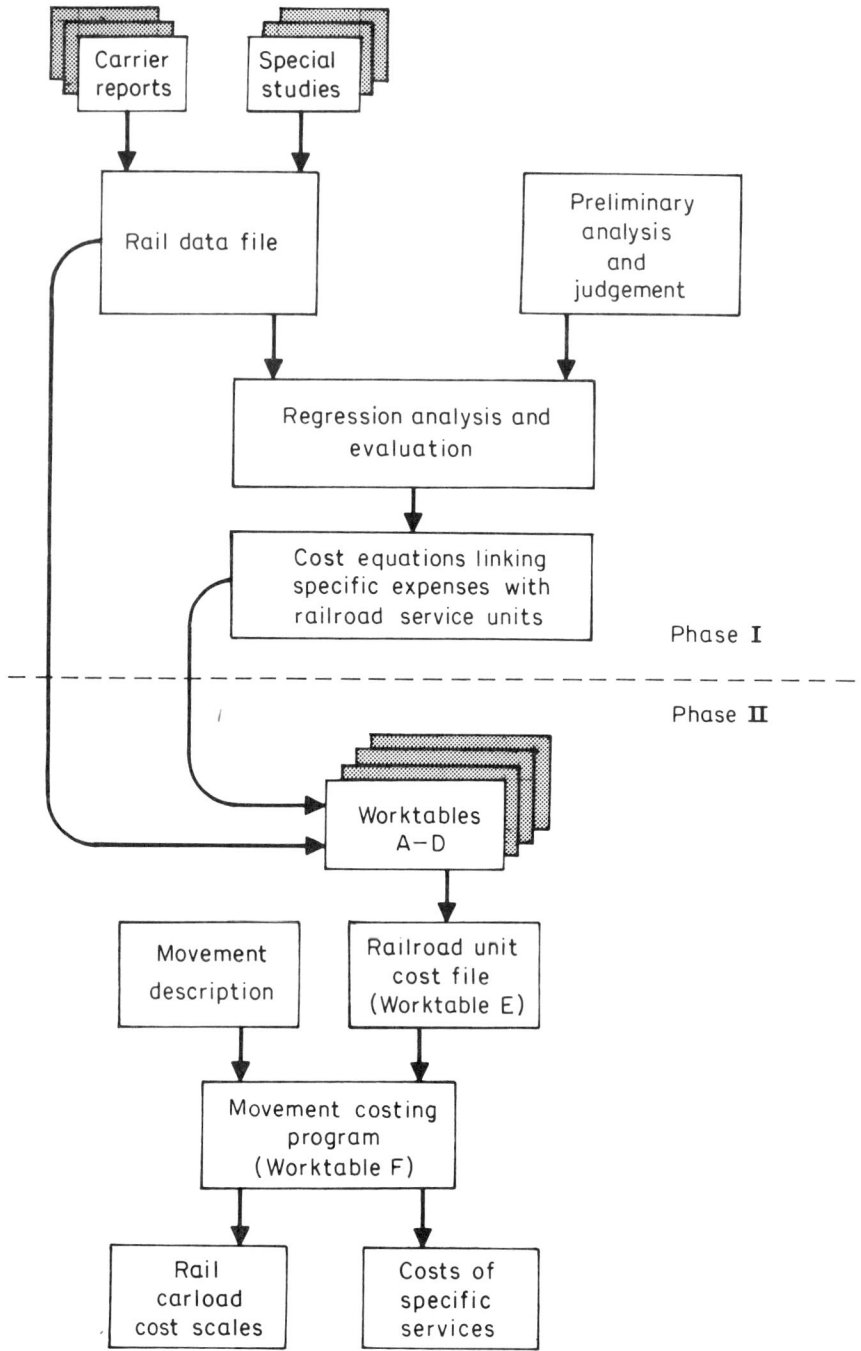

Figure 5.1 URCS overview

Source: Interstate Commerce Commission, Bureau of Accounts (undated)

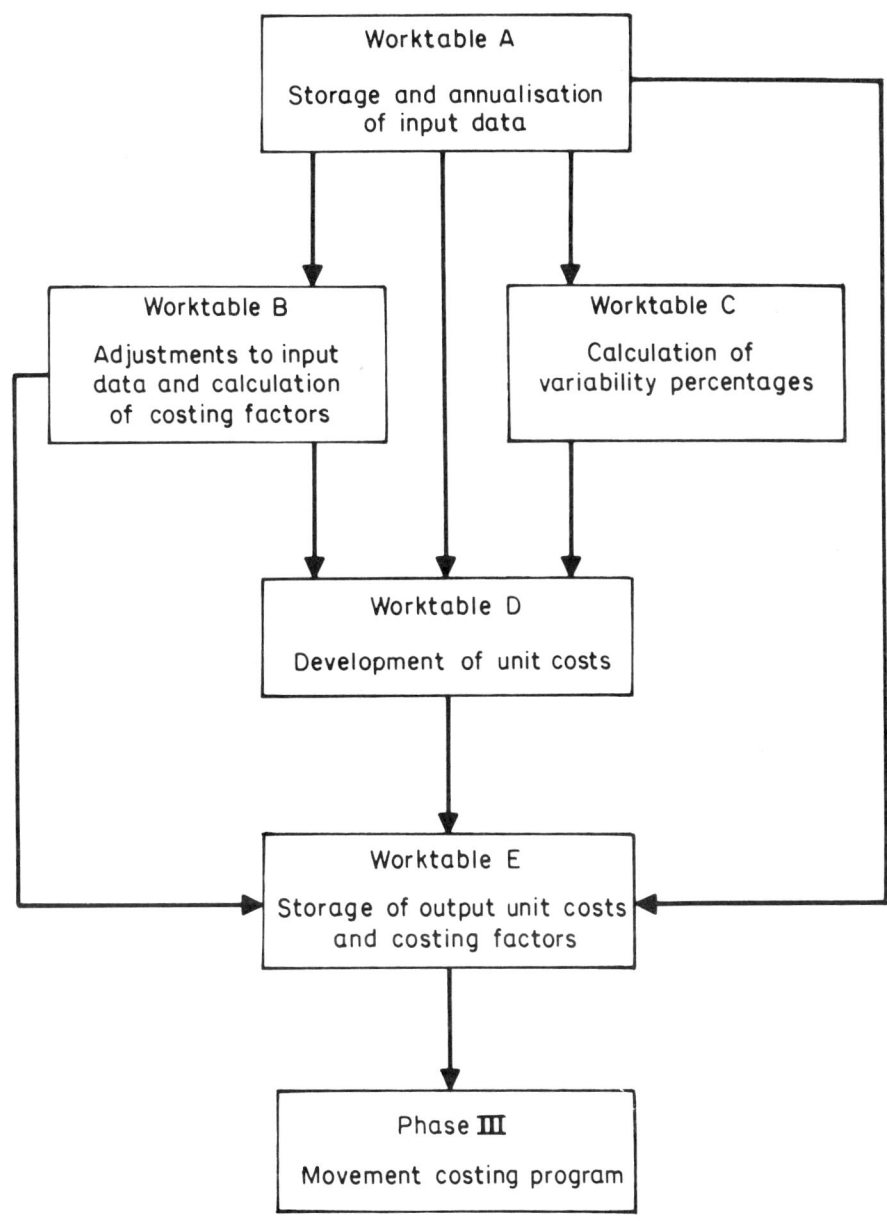

Figure 5.2   URCS worktable functions

Source: Interstate Commerce Commission, Bureau of Accounts (1982)

ogical standard of current econometric research on rail costs. A second group of criticisms arises from practitioners accustomed to working with former ICC regulatory procedures (e.g. see statements on behalf of the Western Coal Traffic League and the National Industrial Traffic League in ICC Bureau of Accounts 1977). These groups tend to focus on particular features adverse to their interest. In particular, objections were raised against including an allowance for income taxes and normal returns for capital employed in rail services. They contend that this is a pricing rather than costing matter. Normal returns, however, are a recognised opportunity cost in economics, although one might question how accurately variable capital costs will be identified in specific situations. If sunk or otherwise unassignable capital costs are included, then the validity of such cost estimates are in doubt.

As with most other contentious issues in rail costing, there probably is some validity to all parties' positions. URCS is a definite advance over the old procedures. It is also not surprising if a regulatory costing system does not incorporate the latest methodological advances, nor resolve long standing disagreements in rail cost analysis. The need for widely applicable costing procedures to facilitate regulatory analysis is inconsistent with a highly flexible costing system capable of reflecting situation-specific influences on costs.

URCS is designed to be employed in several ways. The first official use of URCS will be for joint rate surcharges. URCS will also be used for routine assessments of rates, although additional cost evidence probably will be admitted where extensive hearings or litigation are involved. An additional use of URCS will be in determining ICC jurisdiction over rates; this is a more novel role for cost analysis. The Staggers Act allows rail pricing freedom unless the railroad is market dominant. URCS will provide the cost estimate to compare with rail rates to determine if the markup is indicative of extensive market power. The allowable markup (called 'cost recovery percentage') may vary over time. This depends on the overall revenue adequacy of the railroad. If overall traffic is not generating sufficient net revenues to cover constant costs, the ICC will tend to be more lenient in interfering with maximum rates. URCS may be used to calculate the overall cost-revenue relationship for individual railroads.

URCS may have non-regulatory uses as well (O'Connor, Robinson and Huneke 1983). Shippers may, for example, make use of URCS and related analysis to assist in rate negotiations, although cost information is not always that useful in bargaining over freight rates.

In sum, URCS is a major revision in ICC rail costing methods. Some critics would prefer a sharper break from the old Rail Form A, but the improvements are significant in any event. It is a costing system less tied to system averages, and it may lend itself to be adapted to quite specific applications by adjusting cost estimates for particular situations. An example would be the work by Tolliver (1983) adjusting ICC (Rail Form A) cost estimates to better reflect low density line cost conditions. But the major source of any further refinements in rail costing for managerial purposes is likely to come from rail companies rather than the ICC.

5.6—2 Regulation and railway costing developments in Canada

Canadian railways were prominent in the development of rail costing methods. Work was undertaken during the 1950s and extensive efforts were prompted by the MacPherson Royal Commission of 1958—60. Further work on costing methods was carried out in the next few years (Stenason and Bandeen 1965).

The National Transportation Act of 1967 effectively deregulated Canadian railways with the specific exception of export grain traffic as well as restrictions on abandoning service. The primary regulatory matters requiring cost analysis are setting minimum and maximum rate restrictions, and determination of compensation for providing unprofitable services. Minimum rates must be compensatory (i.e. cover variable costs) and maximum rate limits can be imposed at 250 per cent of variable costs. Payment of subsidies for unremunerative services was to be based on actual losses by the railways. However, the Act did not provide for explicit subsidies for losses on export grain; those costs were borne internally by the railways until the recent Western Grain Transportation Act, 1983.

General regulatory costing principles are outlined in the Canadian Transport Commission's (CTC) *Reasons for Order R-6313*, issued in 1969. Specific railway costing procedures (manuals) must be approved by the CTC.

The primary regulatory use of costing has been to determine subsidy payments; minimum and maximum rate cases are virtually non-existent. The railways are permitted to agree on prices, and they are multi-modal companies themselves; hence there is little prospect of predatory pricing either among railways or against other modes. The costing procedure for maximum rates employs a relatively small carload size (30,000 lbs) but because much traffic moves in larger loads per car, the procedure results in high estimates of costs and therefore afford little protection for shippers.

The costing procedures have been used regularly to determine subsidy payments for passenger and branch line services which railways sought to abandon but were ordered to continue by the CTC. Rail passenger operations, like those in the US, are now handled by a separate corporate entity which contracts to the railways for use of rail tracks and facilities.

During the 1970s, pressures for a review of costing methods arose. The railways internal costing and information system began to depart from the regulatory approved procedures; in particular, the railways tended to use replacement costs for internal purposes rather than the historical costs required for regulatory purposes. Major changes began in the late 1970s. A new uniform classification of accounts was developed under the jurisdiction of the Rail Transport Committee of the CTC. In addition, a major review of rail costing methodology was undertaken by the Research Branch of the CTC. A Phase I review (1978) examined costing principles and methods relevant to rail costing. Phase II (1979) investigated various cost categories and components and made recommendations for changes. Some proposed changes met with mutual acceptance by the railways and are under implementation, e.g. estimation of road and track maintenance costs. Other topics have proved more controversial, notably the costs of capital and hearings are still underway on this issue.[6]

Further analysis and revision of costing procedures are likely in the near future. The Western Grain Transportation Act provides for explicit subsidies to the railways for losses associated with export grain. Monitoring the costs of the vast network collecting and transporting grain likely will entail greater specificity of costing than other recent regulatory costing requirements. The rising expenditures on unremunerative passenger services may also prompt closer examination of the costs associated with such services.

5.6–3 Regulation and publicly-owned railways

The regulatory issues discussed apply to North America. The issues have some relevance to other countries, but there are some important differences. Other countries generally have publicly-owned railways, and most are not subject to regulatory overview by separate government agencies. In effect, any regulatory function is presumed to be internalised in railway administration and/or left to Cabinet review. This is quite different from the open forums and legislated appeal processes characteristics of North American (primarily US) rail regulation. The implication is that the equivalent of regulatory costing issues for publicly-owned railroads are less visible.

A second important characteristic of most non-North-American railroads is that most have major passenger operations. Some costing problems are less acute for passenger services. Passengers move themselves to, from and between trains, hence railways avoid most of the handling and interchange costs associated with freight operations. Rail passenger services are almost invariably unprofitable; hence there is not the close analysis of incremental costs and revenues necessary for commercial rail companies. Rail passenger services are judged on social benefits and costs, not financial returns. Passenger cost analyses tend to be aggregated for service types, regions or branches in connection with abandonment or investment decisions. This is in contrast to the need to cost a myriad of individual freight services. (For example, British Rail identifies about 700 profit or cost centres, about half of which are various passenger services.[7] This is fewer than the number costed in large North American roads.)

In sum, the costing issues that have arisen in North America are of some relevance to publicly-owned railroads in other countries, particularly in assessing commercial viability of various freight services. The evaluation of passenger operations is not, however, a simple profit and loss analysis. Particular types of cost analysis are necessary. There are also special problems associated with cost analysis of unprofitable services in connection with evaluating the social merit of the services. Social benefit cost analysis or related public evaluation frameworks are the appropriate frameworks for this purpose, as they are for passenger operations. This type of analysis is different from the emphasis on commercial freight services which characterise North American rail cost analysis.

5.7 Recent developments: cost analysis and railway management

Cost analysis of various types and extents have been employed by rail management for years.[8] Rather than describe specific approaches by specific firms, this final section speculates on a few current and prospective developments in cost analysis for rail management.

There is growing interest in rail cost analysis, and this is likely to increase. This is partly the inevitable result of experience with the use of statistical as well as accounting methods in developing cost estimates. Recent years have also seen increased effort devoted to cost analysis of mutual interest to railroads sponsored by the Association of American Railroads (AAR), the Cost Analysis Organisation of North American railroads (a branch of the AAR), and studies sponsored by the US Federal Railroad Administration. There are now additional developments which will make cost analysis even more important in rail management.

One traditional obstacle to advances in cost analysis for managerial purposes has been the close identification of cost analysis with regulatory issues. That is, there has been a tendency for railway management to regard cost analysis of traffic movements as a necessary exercise in regulatory disputes, but not an integral part of rail management.

Debates on costing methods have too often centred on what would be accepted by regulatory agencies, and/or whether a particular costing approach would produce larger cost estimates. Thus, the concern has been how a costing exercise would facilitate regulatory procedures and their outcome, not with the inherent accuracy of the cost estimates. Reducing regulatory restrictions on rail management can be expected to lead to a more enlightened attitude toward cost analysis.

Deregulation of railways has two profound effects on rail management style. First and foremost is freedom to market rail services without protracted legal controversy and delay. Railway management becomes free to pursue business, identify customer needs, tailor services to that need, and negotiate a price without extensive regulatory interference or equity concerns. This may be termed 'selective service design and pricing' (Heaver and Waters 1982). Growing out of this marketing freedom is a second (but more speculative) outcome, namely increased emphasis on detailed cost analysis. As competition increases and as customers are pursued who may not be able to pay high freight charges, there will be an increasing need for accurate cost estimates for specific services. Obtaining an extra dollar from a customer has the same effect on profits as cutting costs by a dollar. As railways adjust to their increased pricing freedom, it is not surprising if marketing efforts receive the first attention. But one can expect a renewed interest in cost analysis to be the next stage.

It should be noted that the growth of interest in cost analysis by rail management will not be confined to the rail mode. It is equally important to have reliable estimates of the costs of competitive modes of transport to assist in devising competitive pricing and marketing strategies. Organisations such as the Association of American Railroads have sponsored cost studies of truck and barge operations for several years. Many railroads now have cost models of competitive modes as part of the responsibilities of their cost analysis departments.

Another force which may contribute to increased cost analysis of various types is the continuing proliferation of inexpensive yet powerful computers. Most cost analysis requires access to centralised data bases in a company, so there will be a continuing need for certain centralised information. But the spread of microcomputers and their user-friendly software enables research and analysis to be conducted in a highly decentralised manner. Maintenance records for a region or a shop, for example, can be analysed for trends or correlations; complex cost calculations can be routinely redone to test the sensitivity of cost estimates to changes in operating procedures or input prices.

The general trend toward increased specificity in cost analysis has been mentioned. Most obvious is the necessity of costing unit train operations differently than for other rail operations. This can be extended to costing different train services, e.g. express versus way freights. It is increasingly possible to develop some regional and yard-specific cost information. The trend will certainly continue. The only uncertainty is how quickly. This will depend on the market environment and managerial attitudes in the next several years.

Some specific cost categories have been of particular interest to rail management. There has been considerable research and revision in costing methods for maintenance of way and track. These costs are increasingly estimated using engineering formulae which relates track wear directly to the amount of use, taking into account track weight, the amount of rail traffic, etc. The impact of axle-loads or weight on rail is increasingly thought to be significant. This topic has been the subject of task force studies organised through the Association of American Railroads (e.g. Green 1981).

Fuel costs are coming under increasing attention from North American Railroads. They have long used formula from engineering data or simulation models to predict fuel consumption with loads, grades, curves, etc. The rising fuel costs in recent years has prompted interest in ways to reduce fuel consumption. Better train control, better scheduling and control of train speeds (to minimise acceleration, deceleration and stops) could save railroads millions of dollars per year.

A topic of periodic debate regarding costing for rail management is where this activity best fits into corporate organisation charts. Costing is a staff function but one which often overlaps established line functions. A variety of departmental organisation structures exist. Cost analysis may be included under an accounting department. Certainly access to accounting records and knowledge of account classifications are essential in developing cost estimates, but the importance of non-accounting approaches to cost analysis can conflict with traditional accounting concerns (e.g. statistical cost estimates are not auditable).

Alternatively, cost analysis can be a part of a department responsible for management information systems. Certainly the design, compilation and use of information are critical to reliable cost analysis. On the other hand, cost analysis often needs quite close liaison with end-users of cost analysis, e.g. marketing departments. Cost analysis departments can be housed in marketing departments, the rationale being that cost estimates are important in determining profitability and designing marketing strategies. There is a potential conflict of interest in that cost analysis is often a balancing force to ensure that sales-maximising objectives of marketing departments do not lead to soliciting unprofitable traffic. Some think that costing departments should be separate from marketing departments in order to ensure that cost estimates are not compromised to suit sales objectives (e.g. Waters and Green 1977).

Cost analysis is housed in the finance department of some railways.

In other railroads, cost analysis may be a separate department reporting directly to a senior executive of the company. A similar arrangement is to combine cost analysis with a research department. The latter arrangement has the advantage of facilitating coordination of cost analysis with ongoing research to increase understanding of cost causality with rail operations. This type of organisation also facilitates regular reassignment of people to different projects which is necessary for special costing studies. The disadvantage of a separate cost analysis department is the difficulty of maintaining credibility and influence relative to other departments. The corporate environment of railroads tends to have quite sizeable departmental organisations.

It is difficult to discern trends in organisational structure of such a specialised function. But the likely outcome is increased use of separate cost analysis and research departments, primarily because of the importance of ongoing investigation and research into cost-related matters for railroads; that is, the research function may be as important as the routine costing assignments during the next several years.

Notes

1   The conceptual validity of the ordinary least squares regression model requires a number of assumptions about the interrelationships among variables (e.g. explanatory variables must be independent of one another) and the behaviour of stochastic components which inevitably appear in our non-deterministic world (e.g. errors or disturbances to the hypothesised relationships must be randomly distributed with a mean value of zero and a constant variance). For specific reference to rail cost analysis see Canadian Transport Commission, 1978.

2   This section draws from a more complete review of econometric analysis and railway costing in Waters and Woodland (1984). Keeler (1983) also reviews econometric applications to rail cost analysis.

3   As Keeler (1974) has pointed out, the assumption of cost minimisation in railroading is difficult to accept given the common restrictions on the ability of railways to abandon unprofitable traffic and various 'feather-bedding' practices of labour unions. However, if such constraints persist unchanged over time (or across firms) they are constant, exogenous influences on the firm as though they were part of the technological conditions of production. Railway management may be free to cost-minimise in other dimensions. Hence the underlying assumptions of efficient operation may be legitimate providing the cost function is recognised to

reflect imposed institutional restrictions on production relations.

4   Adding another input variable also increases the number of coefficients by n + 2 but it also adds one more factor share equation (discussed below). The factor share equations constrain the values that coefficients can take hence the impact on degrees of freedom of adding input price variables is not as severe as it first appears. (However, there is also the matter of one more factor share equation to be estimated.)

5   The multi-product Cobb-Douglas cost function implicitly allows for interaction among costs and multiple outputs but they are constrained to be positive, i.e. economies of scope are inconsistent with the Cobb-Douglas formulation (Hasenkamp 1976; Huenemann 1981).

6   For an informative review of rail costing procedures and their application in Canada see Hariton 1984.

7   The British Rail Costing procedures are outlined in British Rail 1978 (it should be noted that their costing procedures were under review during 1983).

8   A widely cited reference to cost analysis for rail management is Poole 1962. A relatively early example of extensive statistical analysis of costs by railways can be seen in Stenason and Bandeen 1965. For one outline of the types of cost analysis and their use in modern rail management see Folk 1982.

References

Association of American Railroads, Bureau of Railway Economics (1964), *A Guide to Railroad Cost Analysis* (AAR, Washington, DC).

Borts, G.H. (1952), 'Production relations in the railway industry', *Econometrica*, January, pp.71–9.

Borts, G.H. (1954), 'Increasing returns in the railway industry', *Econometrica*, pp.316–33.

Borts, G.H. (1960), 'The estimation of rail cost functions', *Econometrica*, pp.108–31.

British Rail (1978), *Measuring Cost and Profitability in British Rail* (British Rail Board, London).

Brown, R.S., Caves, D.W. and Christensen, L.R. (1976), *Estimating Marginal Cost for Multiproduct Regulated Firms*, SSRI Workshop Paper 7609 (Social Systems Research Institute, University of Wisconsin-Madison).

Brown, R.S., Caves, D.W. and Christensen, L.R. (1979), 'Modelling the structure of cost and production for multiproduct firms', *Southern Economic Journal*, July, pp.256–73.

Canadian Transport Commission (1978), *Railway Costing Study*, Report on Phase I (CTC, Ottawa).

Canadian Transport Commission (1979), *Railway Costing Study*, Report on Phase II, 5 Volumes (CTC, Ottawa).

Canadian Transport Commission, Railway Transport Committee (1969), *Reasons for Order No. R-6313, Concerning Costs Regulations* (Queen's Printer for Canada, Ottawa).

Caves, D.W. and Christensen, L.R. (1978), *Productivity in Canadian Railroads, 1956–1975*, Discussion Paper No. 7825 (Social Systems Research Institute, University of Wisconsin-Madison).

Caves, D.W. and Christensen, L.R. (1980), 'The relative efficiency of public and private firms in a competitive environment: the case of Canadian railroads', *Journal of Political Economy*, LXXXVIII, pp.958–76.

Caves, D.W., Christensen, L.R. and Swanson, J.A. (1979), *Productivity in U.S. Railroads, 1951–1974*, Discussion Paper #7909 (Social Systems Research Institute, University of Wisconsin-Madison).

Caves, D.W., Christensen, L.R. and Swanson, J.A. (1980), 'Productivity in U.S. railroads, 1951–1974', *Bell Journal of Economics*, Vol.11, pp.166–81.

Caves, D.W., Christensen, L.R. and Swanson, J.A. (1981a), 'The High Cost of Regulating U.S. Railroads', *Regulation*, January/February, pp.41–6.

Caves, D.W., Christensen, L.R. and Swanson, J.A. (1981b), 'Economic performance in regulated and unregulated environments: a comparison of U.S. and Canadian railroads', *Quarterly Journal of Economics*, November, pp.559–81.

Caves, D.W., Christensen, L.R. and Swanson, J.A. (1981c), 'Productivity growth scale economies and capacity utilization in U.S. railroads, 1955–74', *American Economic Review*, December, pp.994–1002.

Caves, D.W., Christensen, L.R., Swanson, J.A. and Tretheway, M.W. (1982), 'Economic performance of U.S. and Canadian railroads: the significance of ownership and the regulatory environment', in W.T. Stanbury and F. Thompson (eds.), *Managing Public Enterprises* (Praeger, New York).

Caves, D.W., Christensen, L.R. and Tretheway, M.W. (1978), *Flexible Cost Functions for Multiproduct Firms*, Discussion Paper No. 7818 (Social Systems Research Institute, University of Wisconsin-Madison).

Caves, D.W., Christensen, L.R. and Tretheway, M.W. (1980), 'Flexible cost functions for multiproduct firms', *Review of Economics and Statistics*, Vol.62, pp.477–81.

Charney, A.H., Sidhu, N.D. and Due, J.F. (1977), 'Short run cost functions for class II railroads', *Logistics and Transportation Review*,

Vol.13, No. 4, pp.345–59.

Christenson, L., Jorgenson, D. and Lau, L.J. (1973), 'Transcendental logarithmic production functions', *Review of Economics and Statistics*, pp.28–45.

Clark, J.M. (1923), *Studies in the Economics of Overhead Costs* (University of Chicago Press, Chicago).

Crew, J.G. and Horn, K.H. (1981), 'The impact of rail rates or costs upon waterway project planning: an uncertain future', *Transportation Research Forum*, pp.432–40.

DeSalvo, J.S. (1969), 'A process function for rail linehaul operations', *Journal of Transport Economics and Policy*, January, pp.3–27.

Diewert, W.E. (1971), 'An application of the Shephard duality theorem: a generalized Leontief production function', *Journal of Political Economy*, 79, pp.481–507.

Folk, J.F. (1982), 'Cost systems at Conrail', *Transportation Research Forum*, pp.369–74.

Friedlaender, A.F. (1969), *The Dilemma of Freight Transport Regulation* (Brookings, Washington, DC).

Friedlaender, A.F. (1971), 'The social costs of regulating the railroads', *American Economic Review*, May, pp.226–34.

Friedlaender, A.F. and Spady, R.H. (1979), *Equity, Efficiency and Resource Allocation in the Rail and Regulated Trucking Industries*, Report No. 79–4 (MIT Centre for Transportation Studies, Cambridge, Mass.).

Friedlaender, A.F. and Spady, R.H. (1980), *Freight Transport Regulation: Equity, Efficiency, and Competition in the Rail and Trucking Industries* (MIT Press, Cambridge, Mass.).

Green, G.R. (1981), 'Heavy cars — the real costs', *Modern Railroads and Rail Transit*, September, pp.54–6.

Griliches, Z. (1972), 'Cost allocation in railroad regulation', *Bell Journal of Economics and Management Science*, Spring, pp.26–41.

Hariton, G. (1984), *Railway Costing: A Review* (Research Branch, Canadian Transport Commission).

Harmatuck, D.J. (1979), 'A policy sensitive railway cost function', *Logistics and Transportation Review*, Vol.5, No. 2, pp.277–315.

Harris, R.G. (1977), 'Economics of traffic density in the rail freight industry', *Bell Journal of Economics*, pp.556–64.

Hasenkamp, G. (1976), 'A study of multiple-output production functions: Klein's railroad study revisited', *Journal of Econometrics*, pp.253–62.

Healy, T. (1961), *The Effects of Scale in the Railroad Industry* (Committee on Transportation, Yale University).

Heaver, T.D. and Waters, W.G. II (1982), 'Public enterprise under competition: a comment on Canadian railways', in W.T. Stanbury and F. Thompson (eds.), *Managing Public Enterprises* (Praeger, New York), pp.152–60.

Huenemann, R. (1981), 'The Dragon and the Iron Horse: The Economics of Railroads in China, 1876–1937', Ph.D. Dissertation, (Harvard University).

Interstate Commerce Commission, Bureau of Accounts (undated), *An Introduction to the Uniform Rail Costing System: Its Development, Functions and Regulatory Role* (Washington, DC).

Interstate Commerce Commission, Bureau of Accounts (1977), 'Improved regulatory costing methodology for railroads', notes from September 15–16, 1977 meeting.

Interstate Commerce Commission, Bureau of Accounts (1981), *Uniform Rail Costing System: Preliminary 1979 Rail Cost Study* (Washington, DC).

Interstate Commerce Commission, Bureau of Accounts (1982), *Uniform Railroad Costing System: 1980 Railroad Cost Study* (Washington, DC).

Interstate Commerce Commission, Bureau of Accounts (1983), *Uniform Railroad Costing System: Phase III — Movement Costing Program User's Manual* (Washington, DC).

Johnson, M.A. and Yevich, S.C. (1982), 'An overview of the ICC's uniform rail costing system', *Transportation Research Forum*.

Keeler, T.E. (1974), 'Railroad Costs, Returns to Scale, and Excess Capacity', *Review of Economics and Statistics*, pp.201–8.

Keeler, T.E. (1983), *Railroads, Freight and Public Policy* (Brookings Institute, Washington, DC).

Klein, L.R. (1953), *A Text Book of Econometrics* (Row, Peterson & Co., Evanston, Illinois).

Lorenz, M.O. (1916), 'Cost and value of service in railroad rate-marking', *Quarterly Journal of Economics*, XXX, pp.205–32.

McBride, M.E. (1982), 'Economic costs, railway costs and the uniform rail costing system', *Transportation Research Forum*.

Meyer, J.R. *et al.* (1959), *The Economics of Competition in the Transportation Industries* (Harvard University Press, Cambridge, Mass.).

O'Connor, T., Robinson, J.M. and Huneke, W.F. (1983), 'The uniform rail cost system: implications for transportation management', *Transportation Research Forum*, pp.368–75.

Panzar, J.C. and Willig, R.D. (1975), *Economies of Scale and Economies of Scope in Multi-output Production*, Discussion Paper No. 33 (Bell Laboratories).

Poole, E.C. (1962), *Costs — A Tool for Railroad Management* (Simmons-Boardman, New York).

Report of the Royal Commission on Transportation (MacPherson

Commission) (1962), Vol.III (Ottawa).

Shephard, R.W. (1953), *Cost and Production Functions* (Princeton University Press, Princeton, New Jersey).

Stenason, J. and Bandeen, R.A. (1965), 'Transportation costs and their implications: an empirical study of railway costs in Canada', in *Transportation Economics* (National Bureau of Economic Research, Washington, DC).

Spady, R.H. (1977), 'An hedonic translog cost function for U.S. railroads, 1968–72' mimeo (MIT Centre for Transportation Studies).

Tolliver, D.D. (1983), 'Economies of density in railroad cost-finding: applications to rail form A', *Transportation Research Forum.*

Waters, W.G. II and Green, G.R. (1977), *An Examination of the Costing Procedures Used by the British Columbia Railway* (Centre for Transportation Studies, University of British Columbia).

Waters, W.G. II and Woodland, A.D. (1984), *Econometric Analysis and Railway Costing* (Centre for Transportation Studies, University of British Columbia, and North Oxford Academic Press, UK).

6 The consistent treatment of rail and road freight costs in Australia

K. W. OGDEN

6.1 Introduction

Australian railways, like those in many other countries, more or less paid their way on operating costs until the early 1970s. Since then, however, railway deficits have soared, and now exceed $AUS1 billion annually.

This situation has caused governments[1] to review their policies towards rail, and to examine critically the role of each mode of transport. While there are variations in detail, a common theme which is emerging is that *freight* services on all modes should 'pay their way'. This has been most explicitly articulated in the policy statement of the Victorian Labour government, elected in April 1982, which states, *inter alia*, that

> freight transport should not be subsidized by the
> taxpayer in general, nor should it subsidize other areas

> the State Transport Authority[2] will be acquired to phase
> out freight subsidies as soon as possible ... but there are
> to be no subsidies for road freight

This section examines the question of subsidies, and in particular the cost elements (for both road and rail) which may be labelled as a subsidy. It does not address the policy initiatives which might be necessary to eliminate such subsidies, nor the consequences of eliminating them (e.g. in terms of market share, employment levels, rail network, etc.). The context is Australian, but the conclusions and applications should be applicable to any transport system where rail and road are in competition and where there is a desire to eliminate freight subsidies for both modes.

6.2 Cost recovery

The policy objective that there should be no subsidy for freight services may be labelled as a 'cost recovery' objective. This is not the same as a policy for the optimum allocation of resources within the freight sector. The latter requires that:

long-run marginal costs, including costs external to the operator, are fully covered, and
each competing mode has the same price to marginal social cost ratio (McCloskey 1982).

It is well understood that an economic efficiency objective requires that prices be set equal to (long-run) marginal costs. This causes few difficulties in so-called increasing cost industries (where average costs are less than marginal costs) since competition will usually drive prices down to marginal cost. However with decreasing cost industries (i.e. marginal costs less than average costs), marginal cost pricing will mean that they will operate at a financial deficit.

Rail is generally regarded as a decreasing cost industry, as is the road system (as distinct from the road freight industry). Thus in both cases, financial deficits may be expected to result from the strict application of marginal cost pricing.

In these circumstances, economic theory would suggest that the deficit be made good from taxes. However, as Taplin (1982) has noted 'in our actual world, government usually takes the view that all or most of the tax to make good the deficit of a particular public enterprise should be collected from its users ... the usual policy is that each public enterprise should pay its own way, which means making up the deficit from additions to fare and freight rates'.

The point here, in the context of this section, is that the cost recovery objective is not identical to an economic efficiency objective, and thus pricing and other considerations need to be seen in the light of this more arbitrary cost recovery objective.

6.3 Resource costs

The resource costs associated with freight services may be divided into three categories, as follows (Hicks 1977).

Transport operation costs, which are the day-to-day costs of operating the freight system, as charged to the account of the railway, or as incurred by a private road operator (including profit).

Community costs, which the community incurs only because of the existence of freight services. For rail, it includes freight revenue supplements, capital grants, tax exemptions, and the opportunity costs of assets employed but not otherwise accounted for (e.g. railway land). For road, the main community costs are due to the provision of roads, and relevant policing, enforcement and regulatory costs — to the extent (if any) that these are not covered by what may be regarded as charges on the industry.

External costs, which are costs, usually non-monetary and often non-quantifiable, imposed upon third parties as a result of freight operations. They include noise, air pollution, traffic congestion, and accident costs to the extent that they are not covered by insurance premiums and direct payouts.

The following sections address these cost elements for both rail and road.

6.4 Transport operation costs

6.4—1 Rail operation costs

Rail operation costs are the costs of operating the freight component of the system, as charged to the railway's accounts. They thus include all relevant freight working expenses, and other expenses such as interest on borrowings etc. As discussed below, while there are some methodological problems involved in enumerating these costs (e.g. accounting for costs which are joint between passengers and freight), these are capable of resolution, and the railway freight operation costs can be established.

To the extent that freight revenues fail to cover rail's transport operation costs, a 'subsidy' is involved in the form of a revenue supplement (see section 6.5—1.1).

Railway operations are complex, with few instances of a one-to-one correspondence between *inputs* (e.g. capital, labour, fuel, track or vehicle maintenance) and *output* (e.g. a particular freight or passenger service, over a particular line). The prevalence of these joint and common costs means that the determination of cost recovery for particular 'outputs' is not an easy task. Moreover, the task is further complicated by the fact that railway accounts are typically concerned with 'inputs' rather than 'outputs'. The relevant costing concepts and their use are outlined as follows.

(1) *Avoidable costs*   These costs are uniquely associated with a particular output. If that output were not produced, the costs would not be incurred. It is generally recognised that the avoidable costing approach is the appropriate one to use in obtaining levels of cost recovery for particular 'outputs' (e.g. Transmark 1981; ARRDO 1981). That is, unless the cost of providing a particular 'output' is *at least* covered by the resulting revenue received, the railway is better off not carrying the traffic. Avoidable costs may thus also be considered as a floor to prices, since to charge less than the avoidable cost is to carry at a loss. There is scope for argument about when to use short-run or long-run avoidable costs,[3] but the avoidable cost principle is well established.

(2) *Common costs*   These are shared costs which occur when two or more outputs are produced in controllable proportions. (For example, if 50 per cent of the gross tonne-km of traffic on a line is a particular commodity, it is reasonable to allocate 50 per cent of the fuel used on that line to that commodity.) Because these costs are allocatable, they can be included in the avoidable costs for the relevant output.

(3) *Joint costs*   These, too, are costs which are shared between two or more outputs, but differ from (2) in that they do not vary with the quantity or proportions of the relevant outputs. (For example, the costs of signal maintenance along a line section do not vary if the proportions of traffic in different commodity groups vary.) Hence, joint costs are not avoidable between outputs.

The extent to which costs are joint across outputs depends upon the level of disaggregation; the more disaggregated, the higher the proportion of costs which are joint. (For example, if a line section carries only, say, wheat and barley, there will be joint costs if these two commodities are regarded as separate outputs. However, if the output is considered to be 'grain', there will be no joint line section costs, all costs being allocated to grain.)

While avoidable costs may provide a price floor, obviously all outputs cannot be priced at such a level if the railway *as a whole* is to fully recover its costs; all or some outputs must make a contribution towards joint costs, and the sum of such contributions must cover the sum of joint costs.

(4) *Fully distributed costs*   These are the costs attributed to various outputs, with the joint costs being allocated across output in an arbitrary fashion. (By definition, any allocation of joint costs, e.g. on a gross tonne-km basis, is arbitrary.) This is the usual basis of railways public accounts, but such costs are of little relevance to policy.

In the context of this section, costing of rail freight activities is of importance because if revenues for a particular traffic do not cover the relevant costs, a 'subsidy' for that traffic may be said to result. This aspect is pursued in section 6.5—1.

6.4—2 *Road operation costs*

Little needs to be said here about road operation costs. Since the road freight industry is in the private sector in Australia, as in most other western countries, it can be confidently stated that revenues earned by a trucking firm must cover operation costs, taking one year with the next. If they did not, the firm would go out of business. (In fact, many trucking firms in Australia are doing just that at this time. The high rate of bankruptcy in the industry is a current concern, but discussion of the reasons for and ramifications of that situation are beyond the scope of this section.)

The relevant operation costs faced by a road freight operator include

- depreciation
- insurance
- interest and finance
- registration and government charges
- maintenance
- tyres
- fuel and oil
- returns on capital
- wages and administration

The most significant of these are fuel, wages and depreciation (McDonell, 1st Report, 1980). A reasonable profit margin should also be considered as a valid part of road freight operation costs.

6.5 Community costs

As noted in section 6.3, community costs are those costs which the community incurs only because of the existence of freight services.

6.5—1 Rail community costs

Community costs for rail freight are of three types:

- revenue supplement;
- capital grants;
- tax relief.

6.5—1.1 Revenue supplement

To the extent that revenues from freight operations do not cover the (avoidable) costs of freight operations, an unambiguous public subsidy, or community cost, is involved. In addition, in the Australian context, it is reasonable to consider that some of the joint passenger-freight costs should be allocated to freight; in fact, ARRDO (1981) implicitly allocates all joint costs to freight.

As an example, Table 6.1 shows the financial results for the Victorian Railways for 1981/82. These results are based upon fully distributed costs (which involve an arbitrary distribution of joint costs) allocated across six business segments. It can be seen that on this basis, the total revenue supplement to freight was $Aus 93.4 million, including $Aus 84.4 million for Victorian freight and $Aus 9.0 million for interstate freight. Victoria's population in 1981 was 3.95 million.

Table 6.1 VicRail financial performance, 1981/82

Business category	Receipts (Aus$m)	Expenditure (Aus$m)	Government contribution (Aus$m) (%)	
Metropolitan services — passenger and parcels	74.2	148.8	74.6	50
Inter City — passenger and parcels	25.2	63.7	38.5	60
Inter Urban — passenger and parcels	5.5	15.8	10.3	65
Intersystem — passenger and parcels	15.3	29.2	13.9	48
Victorian freight	110.4	194.8	84.4	43
Intersystem freight	33.5	42.5	9.0	21
Total	264.1	494.8	230.7	47

Source: VicRail, *Annual Report, 1981—1982*

Two questions arise when rail freight revenues do not cover rail freight costs. Firstly, which traffics are incurring the deficit (and therefore, in the context of this study, may be competing 'unfairly' since they are subsidised), and secondly, if governments set a cost-recovery objective for rail freight, how can railways price their activities to achieve this objective?

To take the first question, it is fair to say that Australian railways understand their costs much better now than they did only a few years ago. However, the prevalence of joint costs, and the fact that railways operate in a commercial environment and therefore do not wish to publicise their costs, mean that the results of much of this costing analysis are not in the public domain. However, such information as is available indicates that many Australian rail traffics are net revenue earners, and that the freight deficit is incurred by a relatively few traffics (ARRDO 1981). For example, a recent study in the State of New South Wales (McDonell, 1st Report, 1980) found that the group of traffics which comprised LCL, general merchandise, specialised and 'smalls' accounted for

- 11 per cent of the freight tonnes;
- 22 per cent of the freight tonne/km;
- 26 per cent of the freight revenue;
- half of the freight costs;
- all of the freight deficit.

Detailed consideration of the second question (pricing for cost-recovery) is beyond the scope of this section. However, the principles may be stated quite succinctly (Taplin 1982; Rees 1976). Firstly, revenues should always cover marginal costs.[4] If they do not, charges should be raised at least to this level, and if the traffic cannot bear even these charges, the operation should be closed. Secondly, if government policy dictates that prices should exceed marginal costs (which will be necessary to achieve a 'cost-recovery' objective — see section 6.2), then prices should be set according to what the traffic will bear.

The implication of these observations is that there is scope in Australian railways to abandon certain 'loss-making' traffics with significant effects upon the rail deficit. As Taplin (1981) has noted, much of the deficit arises because railways 'are required by government to do a lot of things a commercially oriented enterprise would not do — most of them silly, pointless and conferring little benefit to anyone'. Both economic theory and financial imperatives lead to the conclusion that these loss-making activities should be abandoned to road. Perhaps, fortuitously, these same pressures lead to the conclusion that there are other traffics presently dominated by road which should be transferred to rail (see section 6.5—2).

6.5–1.2 Capital
Sources of capital for railway investment are of three types:

- *Loan funds*   Some capital expenditure is provided from borrowings. Interest and redemption on these funds are usually included in railway accounts.
- *Leverage leasing*   A recent innovation, leasing has the effect on railway accounts of charging 'capital' to 'working expenses', and thus such charges are reflected in railway accounts.
- *Grants for government*   From a railway accounting viewpoint, these are regarded as a 'free gift'.

While there are some technical issues in the allocation of depreciation etc. (see for example, Transmark 1981), essentially the first two of these are accommodated within the railways' accounts, and thus in its transport operation costs, as discussed in section 6.4.

The third item — capital grants — constitutes a community cost, in the sense that there is an element of public expenditure which is additional to that included in the revenue supplement. As an example, of Victorian Railways' total capital investment of $Aus 109 million in 1980/81, $Aus 9.3 million was spent on freight services, and a further $Aus 23.6 million on infrastructure, much of which would be relevant to freight (VicRail 1982).

In addition, it could also be argued that to be truly comparable with road transport, returns on investment in rail freight facilities should not only be sufficient to cover interest and redemption, but show a net return as well. Private section expectations would be that invested funds would show a return, while in Victoria the government requires its energy utilities to show a net return on invested capital.

6.5–1.3 Tax relief
The third category of community cost lies in the revenue forgone by the public exchequer by virtue of the tax relief which the railway may enjoy but which its chief competitor (road) does not.

It is not possible to generalise about this, since the extent to which it may occur will vary from place to place. In Victoria, however, the railway is exempt from two significant taxes: sales tax on the purchase of goods, and state diesel taxes (although the latter may properly be regarded as a charge on road vehicles for the provision of roads — see section 6.5–2.3 — and rail's exemption is thus appropriate).

6.5–2 Road freight

6.5–2.1 Introduction
At the outset, it must be said that it is very difficult to estimate the

costs associated with trucking, and in particular, with the costs which trucks impose on the road system. Taplin (1981) has drawn attention to these difficulties, noting that:

> The road services are used in a way which, though not unique, differs greatly from what is normally regarded as the provision of service. The railway, or even the telephone system, takes what is consigned on it and carries it to its destination. An electricity authority provides a flow of electrical energy which is consumed. A road does none of these things, but merely provides a way by which the user can provide his own service, the carriage of people or goods. From the point of view of the road authority, all that is used up is wear and tear to the road.

By comparison, railway costs are straightforward; Taplin commented that 'the failure of railways to correctly identify costs, in some cases, has arisen more from inadequate methods than from any inherent inaccessibility of information'.

On the other side of the ledger, revenues are no less ambiguous, or difficult to assign.[5] In particular, the question arises as to which taxes on the road freight industry may be considered as a charge for the provision and use of road space, and which are general revenue taxes; this is clearly of significance to cost recovery questions.

The review of costs, revenues, taxes and subsidies presented in this section is thus not definitive. However, an attempt has been made to identify the main cost categories, since these carry with them the potential for subsidy if revenues do not cover costs. Revenues are also examined, discussing (as noted above) the arguments concerning their being considered as charges or otherwise. A discussion on resultant subsidy follows.

6.5—2.2 Road freight — community costs
In principle, it is undeniable that the presence in the road system of heavy vehicles imposes costs on the system which would not occur if those heavy vehicles were not present. These costs included design and construction elements (wider lanes, flatter grades, stronger bridges, deeper pavements, etc.), maintenance elements (pavement maintenance, shoulder maintenance, etc.) and reconstruction elements (accelerated pavement deterioration).

To go beyond the principle however, and to try and enumerate some of these cost elements, poses major conceptual, scientific and economic questions. These questions have been the subject of study in many places: for example McDonell (1980), Taplin (1981) and SWATS (1978) in Australia; Ministry of Transport (1968) and Armitage (1980) in UK; Haritos (1973) in Canada; and the Department of Transportation (1982) in the USA. The answers to the questions are neither straightforward nor agreed upon, with the result that there is no unique, unambiguous and agreed answer to the question: 'what proportion of road track costs should be attributed to trucks?'.

The problem has been well summarised by Lawlor (1982) who stated that:

> different classes of vehicles each impose their own demands on road provision and those demands have different cost consequences. Since the demands are met jointly rather than separately, in the context of road construction and maintenance, the separate costs of each demand — and hence of each user class — cannot be determined on any technical engineering basis.

More specifically, some of the major problems are:

- separable costs that may be attributed to trucks are different for each cost category (e.g. vertical alignment, horizontal alignment, pavement strength, etc.);
- for those that are vehicle-size related (e.g. pavement strength), the relationship is a continuous one in the sense that there is not a discrete distinction between 'heavy' and 'light' vehicles (this usually means that several classes of vehicle, arbitrarily defined, must be considered);
- not all heavy vehicles are freight vehicles (consider passenger coaches, service vehicles, etc.);
- it would be very difficult to relate vehicle classes with commodities or traffics.

Nevertheless, by using an arbitrary allocation of vehicle classes, it is possible to allocate avoidable (or separable) costs amongst those classes according to valid technical criteria. The main avoidable cost item is the pavement cost. It is reasonable to say that virtually all pavement deterioration of roads can be attributed to heavy vehicles. These pavement costs represent perhaps 10 per cent of total road system costs. Other avoidable costs attributable to heavy vehicles (e.g. bridges, enforcement, etc.) represent approximately a further 10 per cent of road system costs (see section 6.5−2.4).

The joint costs (i.e. those costs which would not be avoided if the specific vehicle classes were removed from the road system) cannot be so treated. Allocation of those costs is, by definition, arbitrary, though often some quasi-scientific basis is used. For example, the following bases have been used to allocate joint costs. (The percentages refer to the approximate allocation to heavy vehicles which would result from the use of each criterion):

- fleet size (10 per cent)
- vehicle-km of travel (15 per cent)
- vehicle-km, weighted by the number of 'passenger car units' per vehicle (e.g. one truck might equal three or four cars) (20 per cent)
- gross tonne-km of travel (25 per cent)
- a 'benefits' basis (50 per cent)
- a 'capacity to pay' basis (80 per cent)

Which of these is correct? There can be no unique answer to that. However, as will be seen below, perhaps 70—75 per cent of total road system costs are 'joint' between heavy and light vehicles, so the decision as to which of the above values to use is of critical importance.

Finally it is pertinent to note that the amounts allocated for expenditure on roads is as much a political as a technical decision. That is, although trucks may 'cause' road damage, that damage does not directly 'cause' roads expenditure, since such expenditure is what politicians decide it will be. While much effort over recent years, in Australia and elsewhere, has been devoted to technical studies on the level of road funding, it nevertheless remains that any allocation of road costs to heavy vehicles is an exercise in allocating an arbitrary amount.

6.5—2.3 *Road freight — public revenue*

Various taxes and charges are associated with road use, including those levied on trucks and the road transport industry. In Australia, as in most countries, they are of four main types, as follows, and are levied by both State and Commonwealth governments.

(1) *Taxes on the industry* (corporate tax, payroll tax, stamp duty on non-vehicle transactions, and driver licence fees)   It is generally agreed that these should not be counted as a contribution of the industry towards road infrastructure. These are general revenue taxes, not peculiarly levied on the road freight sector, and as such should probably be regarded as revenue sources rather than as road charges; even the road transport industry appears to accept this view (McDonell 1980, 2nd Report; Blakiston 1977).

(2) *Taxes on vehicle ownership* (sales taxes, custom duties and tariffs, stamp duty on new and used vehicle purchases, etc.)   There is no consensus in Australia as to whether these taxes should be counted as part of the charge on the industry when assessing cost recovery. On the one hand, some argue that they are general revenue taxes of the sort that are levied against most industries, and are not therefore to be used to offset against road infrastructure costs. On the other hand, others (and in particular the

road freight industry) argue that in considering the question 'does the industry pay its way?', it is unreasonable and illogical arbitrarily to refuse to allow some of the taxes which the industry does in fact pay, since these enter the industry cost structure and effect its competitive position. The pros and cons of this argument are reviewed in McDonell (1980, 2nd Report).

(3) *Motor vehicle registration charges*   There is a general consensus that these charges are a charge on the industry which may be regarded as part of its contribution towards the provision of infrastructure.

(4) *Fuel excise, state fuel franchise fee, tolls*   Like the previous category, there is general consensus that these charges should be considered as a charge against road provision and use. (However, there is a further element of this category which is contentious in Australia. This is the Oil Import Parity Pricing Levy. This is a levy imposed by the Commonwealth Government on 'old' (pre 1976) crude oil production in Australia to bring its price to refiners to a level commensurate with world crude oil prices. The extent to which portion of this is a charge on the road freight industry is contentious. Most economists would argue that the levy is merely a device to reflect the resource cost of the crude oil; if it were not used domestically it would be traded internationally at its ruling market prices and thus domestic users should also pay this price. On the other hand, the industry argues that it is a real cost to be faced and constitutes a substantial tax payment.)

Table 6.2 shows, by way of example, the available information in respect of road payments by Victorian motorists, and by Victorian truck owners. By way of illustration it is pertinent to note that the 'average' Victorian large articulated vehicle, exceeding 11t tare mass (which according to the *1979 Survey of Motor Vehicle Usage* travelled 91,300 km/year at a fuel consumption of 55.6litres/100km; ABS 1981) paid some $9600 in fuel taxes and about $1300 in registration fees in 1981/82.

6.5–2.4 Road – community cost recovery
In section 6.5–1, the question of the community costs of the rail freight system was addressed, and the conditions which would need to be satisfied in order to comply with a 'no subsidy' policy were outlined. This section has a similar aim in respect of the road freight sector, but since, as noted in section 6.5–2.1, the identification of neither the costs nor revenues (taxes) on the road freight industry in Australia are straightforward, it is not possible to be as precise here.

Table 6.2 Taxes and charges on the road freight industry, Victoria, 1981/82

Source	All vehicles (Aus$m)	Trucks (Aus$m)	Jurisdiction
Taxes on ownership			
Sales tax new vehicles and parts	754	?	Commonwealth
Customs duties Tariffs (vehicles)	?	?	Commonwealth
Vehicle registration	152.0	30.6	State
3rd party insurance surcharge	5.2	0.2	State
Stamp duty, vehicle purchase	74.5	15.0	State
Taxes on use			
Fuel excise	224.5	37.7	Commonwealth
Oil parity pricing	426.7	88.3	Commonwealth
Fuel franchise fee	87.4	13.8	State
Bridge tolls	6.8	1.1	State

Source: Ogden 1983

Several studies have been conducted in Australia in recent years in an attempt to shed light on this question. Perhaps the most definitive was the aforementioned Enquiry into the New South Wales Road Freight Industry (McDonell 1980).

Table 6.3 shows McDonell's estimates of the cost recovery position of three classes of truck (light rigid, heavy rigid, and articulated) in New South Wales using 1977/78 data. Pavement costs were allocated using a fourth-power relationship, and other joint costs were allocated across vehicle classes on a passenger-car-unit basis. Revenues were divided into fixed (e.g. registration) and variable (e.g. fuel excise) components.

It can be seen that this estimate would indicate that trucks as a whole do not 'pay their way', with the heaviest trucks being most heavily subsidised, and the lightest trucks (along with private cars)

149

Table 6.3 Comparison of truck costs and revenues, New South Wales, 1977/78

Costs	Rigid trucks			Articulated trucks	Total trucks
	less than 4.1t	greater than 4.1t	Sub total		
Total (Aus$)					
Costs: Separable:					
pavement	1.9	18.5	20.4	36.8	57.2
other	13.6	32.4	46.0	15.2	61.2
Truck share of joint costs	29.2	26.9	56.1	31.5	87.6
Total	44.7	77.8	122.5	83.5	206.0
Revenues:					
Variable	15.1	25.3	40.4	34.2	74.6
Fixed	38.8	36.1	74.9	21.3	96.2
Total	53.9	61.4	115.3	55.5	170.8
Per truck (Aus$)					
Costs: Separable:					
pavement	30	363	179	2809	449
other	215	637	403	1160	481
Truck share of joint costs	461	528	491	2405	688
Total	706	1528	1073	6374	1618
Revenues:					
Variable	239	479	345	2611	586
Fixed	613	709	656	1626	756
Total	852	1188	1001	4237	1342

Source: McDonell 1980, 2nd Report, p.3/46

making a positive contribution. This general result has been indicated in a number of other recent Australian studies, e.g. SWATS 1978; Taplin 1981; Both 1980; ARRDO 1981. A somewhat similar conclusion, using a different method, has also been recently reached in the United States (US Department of Transportation 1982).

In summary, McDonell concluded that, of total road expenditure in New South Wales in 1977/78 of Aus\$116 million:

- 7–12 per cent was pavement separable costs of trucks (over 4.1t capacity);
- 8 per cent was other separable costs of trucks;
- 11 per cent was separable costs of other vehicles;
- 70–74 per cent was joint between vehicle classes, allocated as follows:
     10–15 per cent to rigid trucks
     5–7 per cent to articulated trucks
     80–85 per cent to other vehicles.

The implication of these results in the context of cost recovery and road-rail competition is that road vehicles should be paying much more for long-distance inter-regional and interstate movements.[6] It is precisely these movements which, along with bulk freight (grain, minerals), are suited to rail. The potential for a significant rationalisation of freight activities in Australia thus exists, with rail abandoning much LCL and short distance general freight to road (see section 6.5–1.1), and road taxes being increased for the large vehicles typically engaged in longer-distance hauls with the potential for significant shifts of traffic from road to rail (Young *et al.* 1983).

6.6 External costs

As noted in section 6.3, external costs are costs, often of a non-quantifiable or non-financial nature, imposed upon third parties as a result of freight operations. They are of four main types:

- accident costs;
- air pollution;
- noise;
- traffic congestion.

6.6–1 Accident costs

Most of the costs associated with accidents, for both road and rail modes, will be covered by insurance or by direct payments. To this extent, they are covered in the transport operating cost component discussed in section 6.4. (McDonell 1980, 1st Report, suggests that insurance represents about 5—6 per cent of operation costs in the road freight industry.)

To these costs should be added additional factors not covered, such as a proportion of hospital and ambulance costs, that portion of accident costs not covered by insurance but 'written-off', and an allowance for pain and suffering.

However, with the possible exception of pain and suffering, these accident costs are probably small, for both modes, in relation to other community costs.

6.6—2 Air pollution

Air pollution has an adverse effect upon human health. The emissions from diesel engines are a relatively small contributor to overall vehicular air pollution (Armitage 1980). Both road vehicles and railway locomotives use diesel fuel, although the former are more significant contributors. Andrews and Lacey (1980) estimated that pollution from non-urban truck travel in Victoria costs around 0.06 cents per tonne-km. Rail air pollution is probably negligible.

6.6—3 Noise

Noise, like air pollution, is an external cost which is difficult to measure and attribute. Andrews and Lacey (1980), using methods based upon those developed in the UK by Llewelyn-Davies et al. (1973) suggest that truck noise might be perhaps three times the cost of air pollution. While this estimate is of doubtful validity, it perhaps provides an order of magnitude estimate. Again, the overall cost of rail noise is probably negligible.

6.6—4 Traffic congestion

In Australian conditions, traffic congestion is rarely a problem outside the major centres, i.e. in situations where road and rail are in competition. Long-distance trucks probably make a negligible contribution to urban traffic congestion, and thus any congestion costs associated with such trucks are probably very small.

6.6—5 Implications for cost recovery

Externalities of the sort mentioned above probably have very little effect upon cost-recovery. In effect, the cost of most of the externalities are internalised through such measures as compulsory third party insurance, emission standards, vehicle design rules, noise level standards, and (to an extent) regulations on driver licensing and permitted hours.

6.7 Conclusions

Analysis of road and rail freight from the viewpoint of examining consistent cost-recovery objectives is difficult, for three reasons:

(1) For rail, the nature of railway accounts, and the fact that much cost and revenue information is properly of commercial confidence, mean that it is difficult to allocate costs to traffics and/or market segments. Moreover, becuase of the jointedness between business segments of many railway costs, an overall freight cost recovery position may be difficult to achieve; pricing principles dictate that a traffic should be carried if it meets its avoidable costs, but the railway has to ensure that it has sufficient 'premium' traffics to generate a margin over their avoidable costs such that the joint costs are covered.

(2) For road, there are considerable conceptual, scientific and economic difficulties with cost recovery analyses — on both the cost and also (in Australia and other countries which do not hypothecate road user taxes to roads expenditure) on the revenue side of the ledger. On the cost side, determination of infrastructure and maintenance costs, and their allocation to vehicle classes, is a complex and ultimately an arbitrary undertaking. On the revenue side, there is difficulty in designating which of the taxes that the industry pays are 'charges' for the provision and use of road space, and which are general revenue 'taxes' levied on the industry and analogous to revenue taxes on any other industry.

(3) Even if these issues could be resolved, there is the further difficulty that what results is a cost recovery allocation based upon *vehicle classes* for the road side, and upon particular *traffics* or commodities on the rail side. In this circumstance, it is difficult to ensure equitable treatment across the modes. The best that can probably be achieved is to aim for full social cost recovery across all vehicle classes and traffics for both modes.

However, within these boundaries, this paper has discussed the questions of cost allocation and recovery as between road and rail freight using Australian experience as an example. It has suggested, in quantifiable terms where possible, what cost and revenue sources should be included if a stated policy of full cost recovery for both freight modes is to be achieved. The main conclusion is that neither road nor rail achieve full cost recovery overall. Rail's shortfall appears to be principally in LCL and intrastate general freight (although the treatment of rail capital complicates the issue). The road freight industry does not appear to 'pay its way', particularly for the larger vehicles typically used in long-distance interregional and interstate hauls.

The result is that the community, and both modes, would be better off through a rationalisation of traffics, with much intrastate and LCL traffic being abandoned by rail to road, and road user charges on the larger vehicles being increased. The cost recovery positions of both modes would improve, and traffic would likely tend to move by the mode to which it is best suited.

Notes

1   Four of the five government rail systems in Australia are owned by State governments (Victoria, New South Wales, Queensland and Western Australia). The fifth is owned by the Commonwealth, and operates in South Australia, Tasmania, Northern Territory and the Australian Capital Territory.
2   The STA has operated non-urban rail in Victoria since July 1983. Prior to that the operating authority was the Victorian Railways (VicRail), to which reference is made at various points in this section.
3   For example, withdrawal from a particular traffic in the short term may save very little — say a small fuel cost saving. However, in the long term, savings in labour, locomotive and wagon fleet requirements, track maintenance and perhaps even whole line sections may be available.
4   Marginal costs and avoidable costs are not synonymous, but they will usually be similar over the same time period.
5   This applies to countries, like Australia, which do not have roads expenditure funded from taxes which are hypothecated for road purposes. For those countries which fund road works from explicit, hypothecated taxes (e.g. most US and New Zealand road taxes), much of the agreement in this section does not apply.
6   The Australian Constitution puts some impediments in the way of governments in taxing vehicles engaged on interstate trade. Discussion of this issue is beyond the scope of this section.

References

Andrews, J. and Lacey, G. (1980), *The Total Resource Costs of Road and Rail Freight in Victoria* (Environmentalists for Full Employment, Melbourne).

Armitage Committee (1980), *Report of Enquiry into Lorries, People and the Environment* (HMSO, London).

Australian Bureau of Statistics (1981), *Survey of Motor Vehicle Usage: Commercial Vehicle Usage, 12 months ended 30 September, 1979* Cat. 9208.0 (Canberra).

Australian Railway Research and Development Organisation (ARRDO) (1981), *1981 Report on Rail* (Melbourne).

Blakiston, H.P. (1977), 'The Australian road transport operator's attitude to forms of roads funding in Australia', *Proc. International Road Federation of Australasia* (Road Conference, Melbourne).

Both, G.J. (1980), 'Road costs and tax payments attributable to trucks', in *Victorian Transport Study* (Melbourne).

Haritos, Z. (1973), *Rational Road Pricing Policies in Canada* (Canadian Transport Commission, Ottawa).

Hicks, S.K. (1977), 'Urban freight', in D.A. Hensher (ed.), *Urban Transport Economics* (Cambridge University Press, Cambridge).

Lawlor, L. (1982), *Road Pricing and Cost Recovery: A Review of Approaches to Allocating Road System Costs*, Reference Paper 38 (Bureau of Transport Economics, Canberra).

Llewelyn-Davies, Weeks, Foresher-Walker and Bor (1973), *Freight Transport and the Environment: Local Studies of Road and Rail* (UK Department of Environment, London).

McCloskey, D.N. (1982), *The Applied Theory of Price* (McMillan, New York).

McDonell, G.J. (1980), *Report of Commission of Enquiry into the NSW Road Freight Industry* (two Reports, plus Supplementary Papers) (Ministry of Transport, NSW, Sydney).

Ministry of Transport (UK) (1968), *Road Track Costs* (HMSO, London).

Ogden, K.W. (1983), *Freight Benchmark Review* (Victorian Ministry of Transport, Melbourne).

Rees, R. (1976), *Public Sector Economics* (Weidenfeld and Nicolson, London).

Southern Western Australia Transport Study (SWATS) (1980), *Final Report* (Perth).

Taplin, J.E. (1981), *Pricing Tasmania's Roads* (Transport Economics Center, University of Tasmania, Hobart).

Taplin, J.E. (1982), 'A pricing framework for cost recovery', in D.N.M. Starkie, M.R. Greening and M.M. Starrs, *Pricing and Cost Recovery in Long Distance Transport* (Martinus Nijhoff, The Hague).

TRANSMARK (1981), *Rail Cost/Pricing Options*, Report prepared for the Victorian Minister of Transport (Melbourne).

155

US Department of Transportation (1982), *Federal Highway Cost Allocation Study* (Washington).

VicRail (1982), *Annual Report*, plus *Appendices* (Melbourne).

Young, W., Richardson, A.J., Ogden, K.W. and Rattray, A.L. (1983), 'An inter-urban freight mode choice model', *Transportation Planning and Technology*, Vol.8.

Part III
Forecasting, Evaluation and Investment

7 The determinants of fixed-rail transit demand — an international cross-sectional comparison

P. GORDON AND R. WILLSON

7.1 Introduction

Though travel demand forecasting is by now one of the largest fields of applied urban research, it is still subject to sharp criticisms. Various authors have noted conceptual problems found in conventional forecasting models (McGillivray 1972); others have challenged the quality of the forecasts (Wohl 1976); Wachs (1982) has added the complaint that the context in which these models are used is open to certain ethical dilemmas. We agree with the three challenges and add that surprisingly little is known about how the demand for transit trips interacts with generalised city descriptors as well as with characteristics of the population, and transit system referents. This study looks into these interactions for the light-rail and the heavy-rail transit modes — with the goal of increasing understanding and improving travel demand forecasts.

There are two additional observations which motivate the study. The first is the paucity of knowledge about the possible international transferability of what is known about travel demand. We are able to make a contribution here by analysing an international cross-section.

The other problem area is the concentration within the travel demand literature on cross-sectional studies which rely on observations taken from *within* individual cities. This limits the understanding of the effects that general city descriptors have on travel demands. (There do exist studies of transit demand based on cross-sectional samples of urban areas, by Pushkarev and Zupan (1977; 1980); these studies are restricted to North American cities and lump the light and the heavy-rail mode together; many of the forecasts derived are similar to those derived here).

The international cross-sectional data are used here to estimate single-equation demand models. That framework suffices since there is little or no relationship between transit provision (supply) and the relevant economic variables: there is little chance of an identification problem since supply has for the most part been independent of fares and most of the other predictors. Rather, transit provision has been in response to political factors. Put another way, fixed-rail transit is now thought to be so inefficient that its continued provision can not really be rationalised by economising behaviour (Hilton 1974). We are left with a simple relationship between the various system characteristics and levels of usage.

Separate models are estimated for two fixed-rail modes: heavy-rail (subways mostly) and light-rail (streetcars and trams which run largely at-grade).

The wide-ranging international cross-section shows us some remarkably stable relationships; in light of the great heterogeneity, this finding supports the idea of model transferability. The models developed here are also utilised to evaluate forecasts of demand for urban rail systems now being developed in North America. These forecasts (and confidence intervals) provide some perspective on the official forecasts: not only are they found to be optimistic, but many can be construed as outliers with a low probability of occurrence. Given the well-known tendency of official forecasts to overestimate demand, this finding enhances the credibility of our models.

Finally, the much suspected relationship between population density and ridership is specified — as are some other similarly useful associations.

7.2 Conventional travel demand forecasting

Conventional travel demand forecasts in the US and Western Europe often flow from UTPS (Urban Transportation Planning System) type models. The drawbacks of this package are well-known: the possible inconsistency between inputs and final outputs; the lack of linkage between land markets and 'markets' for transportation (Berechman and Gordon 1983); the problem that policy tests can best be conducted in the mode-choice module, leaving total trip volume unaffected; none of the difficulties are really met if/when a modern multinomial logit model replaces a more traditional mode-choice model.

160

These criticisms help to motivate the search for alternate forecasting techniques. The international sample may be especially useful now that more cities have reached a similar state of advanced development, allowing the testing of forecasting tools based on cross-sections of cities.

7.3 Methodology

The statistical model used was linear multiple regression; we also studied the influence statistics (Belsley, Kuh and Welsch 1980). That procedure allows a more deliberate examination of the sample, in part making up for the lack of some important explanatory variables. Our interest was in explaining demand: passengers per-kilometre-per-day. The choice of predictor variables was constrained by those reported for a large enough sample, in the *UITP Handbook of Urban Transit* (UITP 1981).

The Handbook reports data for approximately 150 transit systems world-wide. It is a consistent data source for a quite large international sample. The choice of predictor variables was, however, restricted by the nature of the Handbook; not all cities apparently supplied values for all variables, which also limited the sample size.

The variables selected for testing flowed from conventional urban theory: income per capita, per capita auto registration, average station distance, average fares, urban population densities, etc.

There are other variables which would have been useful; we were not able to find data on CBD employment, CBD floor-space, nor were there detailed descriptors of urban structure. It is well-known that the former are very hard to find in comparable form; there is no agreement on what the latter should be (corridor descriptors are not widely available nor are there accepted definitions of corridors; descriptors of the degree of policentrism remain to be agreed on).

The variables used are listed in Table 7.1. Populations for the US cities were taken from the 1980 US Census. Per capita incomes are from the *Handbook* and a 1979 United Nations source. These were national readings which we applied to the cities of the sample. For the US cities, the national per capita income figure was applied to San Francisco (the high-income US city according to the 1977 *City and County Data Book*). The other city readings were then scaled, down from San Francisco's assigned $8612, in proportion to their 1977 standing. Similar income data for the light-rail investigation were regional data for the US cities. The latter had just become available as the light-rail investigation was undertaken. The two readings are similar and perform equally in the equations.

Table 7.1   Variable definitions

PASSKM	passengers per kilometre of route per day
CPOP	city population
CDEN	gross city population density (per square kilometre)
INCOME	national income per capita
FARE	average trip fare in 1980 (US$)
PCMAREG	per capita auto registration (metropolitan area)
PCCAREG	per capita auto registration (city)
STADIS	average km distance between stations (heavy-rail)
STOPDIS	average km distance between stops (light-rail)
US	dummy variable for US observations
COMM	dummy variable for Eastern-bloc observations

Notes: Most data is from 1980 UITP Handbook, which was actually compiled in late 1978.
Other light-rail quality-of-service descriptors were collected (per cent exclusive right-of-way; total daily transport system passengers; average speed; existence of a nearby subway; maximum and minimum fares paid) these did not explain demand as well as STOPDIS.

Population data, along with area data from the *Handbook* made possible the computation of city-wide population densities. As already suggested, 'corridor' densities are preferable, yet these are not readily available. We prefer to assume that the route alignments in the sample have been advantageously placed *and* have had some time to attract complementary proximate land uses — including high density population developments. The estimated coefficients of our crude density variables must be interpreted accordingly: what is the performance of alignments 'best placed' *vis-à-vis* density in an environment with known (observed) average density?

Dependent variable readings were corroborated where possible from miscellaneous published sources as well as from personal conversations.

7.3 Estimations

Tables in this section report the estimations conducted. Throughout, the reporting convention adopted is to delete all independent variables with coefficients of less than one. Dhrymes (1980) reports that this procedure has the chance of maximising adjusted R^2 values. In addition, the risk of misspecification from deleted variables is minimised.

7.3—1 Heavy-rail sample

Table 7.2 displays the estimated equations for the heavy-rail sample; this is for cities in Western Europe, Japan, and North America. The first equation (untransformed variables) is dominated by CDEN and PCMAREG. They all have signs to be expected from available urban theory. The second model (double-log) adds the effect of average station distance. The dummy variable for US observations is not quite significant. The semi-log model (2c) includes all four independent variables significant at the 95 per cent level; auto registration per capita is the most influential; adjusted R^2 is highest. The mean value of the dependent variable for the 23 systems of this sample is 11,585 (riders per kilometre of route per day). Dividing the estimated coefficients (of 2c) by this number gives the following elasticity estimates: -0.485 (station distance), -0.416 (income), 0.263 (city population density), -0.418 (auto registration per capita). The negative effect of income represents the opportunity cost of using the more time-intensive transit alternative.

The following table (7.3) reports results for an expanded sample; the Eastern-bloc observations are added. This expansion of the sample is paid for by losing three variables not reported for those countries; income, population density, auto registration data were not available. As such, variables highly collinear with these now enter the equations — under the Dhrymes conditions, again. In these estimations, all signs are, again, as expected. The second (double-log) model (3b) is the best fitting and shows a fare elasticity of -0.204, very close to magnitudes reported in the literature on transit fare elasticities (Black 1980).

Both dummy variables in model 3b are significant at the 95 per cent confidence level. We follow Halvorson and Palmquist (1980), who have pointed out that an adjustment factor must be used to multiply the coefficients. We found that a US observation accounts for an (average) downward shift between 35 and 55 per cent — the average value of the dependent variables in this sample was 13,689. In contrast, an Eastern-bloc observation accounts for an average upward shift of transit demand of 70—80 per cent. The latter effect is probably due to the

163

Table 7.2 Heavy-rail regression results for cities in North America, Western Europe, and Japan

(t-values in parentheses)
predictor variables:

model	dependent variable	STADIS	INCOME	CDEN	PCMAREG	LSTADIS	LINCOME	LCDEN	LPMAREG	US	$\bar{R}^2$	N
2a	PASSKM	−0.894 (−1.50)		0.532 (2.26)	−24364 (−2.93)						0.52	23
2b	LPASSKM					−0.907 (−2.60)		0.285 (1.41)	−0.337 (−1.95)	−0.442 (−1.35)	0.62	23
2c	PASSKM					−5620 (−2.30)	−4824 (−2.09)	3044 (1.89)	−4847 (−3.93)		0.69	23
2d	LPASSKM	−0.709 (−3.27)		0.000044 (1.81)	−2.76 (−2.55)						0.59	23

Note: Prefix L denotes natural logarithm.

Table 7.3 Heavy-rail regression results for cities in
North America, Western Europe, Eastern Europe, and Japan

(t-values in parentheses)
predictor variables:

model	dependent variable	CPOP	STADIS	FARE	LCPOP	LSTADIS	LFARE	COMM	US	$\bar{R}^2$	N
3a	PASSKM	0.00136 (2.10)	−4421 (−1.61)	−13060 (−1.86)				11059 (2.94)	−5674 (−1.59)	0.50	41
3b	LPASSKM				0.399 (3.36)	−0.568 (−2.17)	−0.204 (−1.60)	0.579 (1.98)	−0.756 (−3.03)	0.61	41
3c	PASSKM				3901 (2.80)	−5662 (−1.58)	−3242 (−1.86)	10003 (2.41)	−4729 (−1.38)	0.53	41
3d	LPASSKM	1.24 E−7 (2.62)	−0.530 (−2.66)	−1.042 (−2.03)				0.626 (2.30)	−0.775 (−2.99)	0.58	41

Note: Prefix L denotes natural logarithm.

absence of an auto registration variable in this set of observations.

7.3—2 Light-rail sample

Similar estimations for light-rail demand were performed. The results appear in Table 7.4. The linear model is dominated by city population density, positively related to ridership, as expected. The per capita income variable is again negatively related to demand. Average station distance, a proxy for quality of service, is negatively related — as expected. The US dummy variable again has a negative effect.

The log-linear model offers higher levels of significance. Possible reasons for this result are suggested in the discussion of regression diagnostics, below.

Per capita auto registration was substituted for per capita income in model 4c; they are collinear, accounting for similar effects with the latter available for a larger number of cities. Again, all coefficients are significant with the expected signs.

Adding data on maximum and minimum fares yielded a coefficient with the expected sign but with a t-value less than 1.00. When average speed was substituted for average distance between stops, it did not improve the statistical fit. Proportion-of-line with exclusive right-of-way, yet another measure of service provided by tramways was also a less effective service predictor of demand.

7.3—3 Comparisons

Abiding by the Dhrymes conditions meant that the identical models were not specified for the two modes. Yet, comparisons are possible if it is assumed that the separate specifications are each valid. The result is that the same variables effectively predict demand for both modes; coefficients or elasticities for the heavy-rail mode's predictors were all larger. This makes perfect sense since heavy-rail demand is generally a higher order of magnitude. This result helps to corroborate the validity of the models.

7.4 Influence statistics

As already mentioned, we were able to use a large number of regression diagnostics in an attempt to learn more from the sample. The simplest of these is the studentised residual, formed by re-estimating the model with a dummy variable for each observation, there being as many re-estimations as there are observations. This procedure identifies outliers. Usually, an outlier is an observation which can be shown to be an exception to the linear specification. Deletion of any such cases

Table 7.4   Light-rail regression results – international sample

(t-values in parentheses)
predictor variables:

model	dependent variable	CDEN	INCOME	PCCAREG	STOPDIS	US	COMM	$\bar{R}^2$	N
4a	PASSKM	0.311 (7.26)	−0.255 (−1.97)		−974.531 (−1.58)	−1348.137 (−1.82)		0.69	52
4b	LPASSKM	4.46 E−5 (3.34)	−9.78 E−5 (2.21)		−0.466 (−2.21)	−0.859 (−3.30)		0.54	52
4c	PASSKM	0.355 (6.90)		−7155.437 (−2.67)	−1260.264 (−1.63)			0.74	37
4d	LPASSKM	4.27 E−5 (2.94)	−8.99 E−5 (−2.15)			−0.740 (−2.88)	0.440 (2.51)	0.43	91

Note: Prefix L denotes natural logarithm.

could be justified if there is some understanding of why one sample member ought to belong to another (non-linear) model. There are other influence statistics which can help to answer the latter question. Various 'DF-betas' measure the effect that an observation has on a coefficient estimate; 'cutoff values' of $2/n-2$ (n being sample size) signal which observations have this effect. The method of using these statistics is exemplified in what follows.

7.4—1 Heavy-rail sample

The R-student values for model 2a included a significant value for just one city, Montreal at 2.97. We take this to reveal that Montreal's actual demand levels are significantly higher than could be explained by the model. For a sample of n=23, the cutoff value is 0.417; the computed DF-beta for REGPC is 0.742, well above the critical value. This indicates that Montreal's presence in the sample pulls the negative coefficient of PCMAREG in the positive direction. Combining the two readings, we conclude that Montreal's actual subway demand is badly explained by the model; at the same time *lower* than average auto registration in Montreal does not explain the outlier. This suggests that Montreal is likely to be part of a non-linear specification. Removing Montreal from the model raised the adjusted R^2 of 2a by fifteen points.

Osaka is the only other observation which, in this particular model, shows a significant value for the DF-beta associated with auto registration. Yet, the value is negative. Probing further, we find that Osaka's studentised residual is about half of Montreal's; its unexplained residual is about 25 per cent. Osaka's auto registration per capita, 0.013, is among the lowest in the sample. We infer a much stronger link between low auto registration and high subway use than in the rest of the sample: Osaka would also fit a non-linear model.

The only other significant DF-beta in model 2a was for income, for Lisbon. The diagnostic was negative, indicating that the negative relationship suggested by the equation understated the strength of the link for Lisbon.

We do not report the equivalent discussions for the other heavy-rail models. Instead we have a few words on behalf of this sort of empiricism. At this stage, there are not enough available observations categorised into the linear or the non-linear specification, as suggested in the previous paragraphs. If there were enough, the exercise would be especially useful if there were available *a priori* hypotheses to suggest which city forms and which populations relate *non-linearly* to subway use. Urban theory available to us is not that advanced. We expect, nevertheless, that exploratory studies of this sort can be an impetus to that sort of theory building.

7.4–2 *Light-rail sample*

Similar diagnostics were computed for the light-rail models. For model 4a four outliers were found: Hong Kong (t=3.12), Kosice (2.79), Bern (2.32), the Hague (-2.03). For the case of Hong Kong, we notice a very high DF-beta associated with city population density. That city's density, upon examination, was found to be further beyond the sample's mean than was Hong Kong's ridership. Again, a non-linear association is inferred at the extremes.

By similar investigation, we found the other three cases to be departures from the linear hypothesis. Dropping them, we re-estimated the model, with the following result:

$$PASSKM = INTCPT + 0.283 \; CDEN - 0.230 \; INCOME$$
$$(8.042) \qquad\qquad (2.230)$$
$$-936.300 \; STOPDIS - 1227.810 \; US \qquad\qquad (7.1)$$
$$(1.980) \qquad\qquad (2.170)$$

adj R-square = 0.750

Again, we are not able to assert which of the non-linear associations support any hypothesis. Nevertheless, the procedure does develop partitions to be explained by new urban theory.

7.5 Comparative forecasts

The models developed in this investigation can be tested by using them to forecast rail transit demand for the many North American cities that are now establishing subway and/or tram systems. The reason why we claim this exercise is a model test, albeit an unusual one, is that it is well known that official forecasts have an almost un-blemished record of extreme optimism. Can the newer models generate forecasts which are significantly less ambitious?

7.5–1 *Heavy-rail sample*

There are now as many as six US cities with subway plans under development or in the advanced planning stages. Values of the predict-or variables which describe these systems (such as average station distance) are available from the planning documents — other variables are available from the conventional sources mentioned above. All these are reported in Table 7.5.

Table 7.6 displays the comparative forecasts. The far left column shows the official forecasts. With the exception of the first model's

Atlanta projection, the new models significantly reduce the official projections for 23 of 24 cases. Aside from our not being sanguine about the official forecasts, we note that a growing literature questions whether conventional rail transit can perform in the modern city (Hilton 1974). If so, the performance of our models in forecasting underscores their appropriateness.

Table 7.5   Values of predictor variables for selected planned North American heavy-rail systems

City	CPOP	STADIS	INCOME ($)	CDEN	PCMAREG
Atlanta	425,022	2.13	6509	1261	0.30
Baltimore	786,775	1.42	6225	3925	0.53
Honolulu	365,114	1.22	7282	1693	0.48
Los Angeles	2,966,763	1.86	6497	2498	0.54
Miami	346,931	1.64	6636	3942	0.64
Washington	637,651	1.88	8136	4390	0.48

Note: All fares are assumed to be $1.00.

The forecasting exercise is completed with the computation of confidence intervals (Table 7.7). Both the narrow (95 per cent) intervals for the *mean* forecasts as well as the wider (95 per cent) intervals for the *particular* forecasts are shown. The first and third models generated unusually wide intervals which are not shown. That is not surprising since the forecast cities are quite distinct from the sample cities. Forecasts for the other two models reveal that, with the exception of Atlanta, the high edge of the confidence interval for the mean forecast is always *below* the official forecast. This underscores the serious contrast with the official projections! Turning to the upper edge of the *wider* bands, we see that the official forecasts for Los Angeles and Honolulu are even beyond the 95 per cent band of these projections!

7.5—2 Light-rail sample

Table 7.8 summarises values of the predictor variables for the planned light-rail systems. The resulting comparative forecasts are shown in

Table 7.6 Comparisons of heavy-rail patronage projections
(passengers per day per km)

proposed system	official forecast	model 3a	model 3b	model 3c	model 3d
Atlanta (85.3 km)	3810	7786	1728	445	2873
Baltimore (12.8 km)	6484	3857	2851	3643	3240
Honolulu (13.4 km)	15,598	2941	2662	1663	3774
Los Angeles (29.8 km)	10,067	2606	1946	440	2175
Miami (32.8 km)	6159	814	2349	1617	2183
Washington (161.3 km)	5425	3609	2358	1589	2660

Notes: Official projections for the Los Angeles project are being
revised upwards.
The Washington figures are for the full to-be-completed
project.

Table 7.7 Ninety-five per cent confidence intervals
heavy-rail system forecasts
(for mean predictions and individual predictions)

proposed system	edge	model 2b forecast		model 2c forecast	
		mean	individual	mean	individual
Atlanta	low	1120	520	2065	660
	high	2665	5743	4000	9596
Baltimore	low	2216	904	2473	988
	high	3668	8995	4245	10626
Honolulu	low	1875	823	2966	1154
	high	3779	8611	4797	12326
Los Angeles	low	1434	609	1613	657
	high	2641	6220	2932	7202
Miami	low	1795	742	1540	650
	high	3074	7441	3095	7328
Washington, DC	low	1783	743	2035	809
	high	3118	7484	3477	8774

Table 7.9, again providing scaled down forecasts. Calgary's tram system is already operating and provides an additional check on the models developed there. Models 4b and 4d provide excellent projections, matching actual demand levels being experienced there. At the same time, Calgary's official forecast is about twice what has actually been achieved.

Confidence intervals were again computed (see Table 7.10). These are shown for models 4b and 4d, the two models with the most plausible forecasts. The interval calculations reveal that here too the official projections of ridership are often beyond the upper edge of our models' outputs. The same conclusions as for the heavy-rail forecasts apply — and are corroborated.

Table 7.8   Values of predictor variables for selected
North American light-rail systems

City	CDEN	INCOME	PCCAREG	STOPDIS
Calgary	1247	6930	0.42	0.81
Detroit	3616	7648	n.a.	1.41
Los Angeles	2498	6497	0.59	1.16
Portland	1506	7505	n.a.	0.96
Seattle	2287	7714	n.a.	0.65
Vancouver	3627	6930	0.46	1.81

7.6 Conclusions

Cross-sectional studies in the urban transportation field are especially timely because there are now a large number of cities at similar levels of development and in similar stages of the urban life cycle (Vining 1982). These studies are also of interest because of the demonstrated need for new forecasting tools, for a better understanding of how city descriptors interact with rail transit demand, and to what extent these

Table 7.9 Comparison of light-rail patronage projections
(passengers per day per km)

proposed system	official forecast	model 4a	model 4b	model 4c	model 4d
Calgary (12.9 km)	3100	1482	1610	242	1772
Detroit (23.9 km)	6485	103	531	—	871
Los Angeles (36.2 km)	1464	−65	563	−1052	828
Portland (24 km)	1628	−78	607	—	812
Seattle (2.1 km)	n.a.	413	712	—	820
Vancouver (21.7 km)	4608	1247	1123	−561	1958

Table 7.10 Ninety-five per cent confidence intervals
for light-rail forecasts
(for mean and individual forecasts)

proposed system	edge	model 4b forecast		model 4d forecast	
		mean	individual	mean	individual
Calgary	low	1436	836	1436	768
	high	1791	3098	2145	4085
Detroit	low	400	231	602	316
	high	704	1218	1260	2400
Los Angeles	low	437	252	602	316
	high	724	1253	1137	2166
Portland	low	479	277	615	323
	high	770	1331	1071	2040
Seattle	low	567	328	640	341
	high	894	1546	1034	1969
Vancouver	low	964	558	1275	670
	high	1612	2788	3004	5722

results are transferable.

We have found that some of the simple relationships between city, population, rail system descriptors and transit demand are remarkably strong and stable over a diverse international cross-section. Much work certainly remains to be done with refined hypotheses, larger samples, and more poignant variables. Nevertheless, we are surprised by the power of the simple hypotheses tested here.

In addition, we have tried to make the point that these identified relationships can serve as a fairly reliable, and simple, forecasting tool. The forecasting evidence, especially that from Calgary, provides support for that conclusion.

Aside from the shortcomings already mentioned, it appears that a more comprehensive system of relationships should be tested. Part of the problem facing urban analysts in that task is the long-term nature of any feedback between transit system performance and the elements of urban structure. Nevertheless, we hope that our exploratory results will generate interest in more elaborate data bases and analyses.

References

Belsley, D.A. *et al.* (1980), *Regression Diagnostics: Influential Data and Sources of Collinearity* (John Wiley & Sons, Inc., New York).

Berechman, J. and Gordon, P. (1983), 'Linked models of land use-transportation interactions: a review', presented at the International Symposium on New Directions in Urban Modelling: University of Waterloo, July 1983.

Black, J. (1980), *Urban Transport Planning* (The Johns Hopkins University Press, Baltimore).

Cahners Publishing Co. (1982), *Modern Railroads Rail Transit: 1982 City-by-City Transit Digest*.

Dhrymes, P.J. (1970), 'On the game of maximizing adjusted R-squared', *Australian Economic Papers*, Vol.9.

Gordon, P. (1982), 'The determinants of rail transit demand — an international cross-sectional comparison', University of Southern California: School of Urban and Regional Planning.

Gordon, P. and Willson, R. (1983), 'The determinants of light-rail transit demand — an international cross-sectional comparison' (School of Urban and Regional Planning, University of Southern California).

Halvorson, R. and Palmquist, R. (1980), 'The interpretation of dummy variables in semilogarithmic equations', *American Economic Review*, Vol.70, pp.474–5.

Hilton, G.W. (1974), *Federal Transit Subsidies: The Urban Mass*

Transportation Assistance Program (American Enterprise Institute for Public Policy Research, Washington, DC).

McGillivray, R. (1972), 'Some problems in urban transportation models', *Traffic Quarterly*, pp.547–58.

Pushkarev, B. and Zupan, J. (1980), *Urban Rail in America: an Exploration of Criteria for Fixed-Guideway Transit* (US Department of Transportation, Washington, DC).

Pushkarev, B. and Zupan, J. (1977), *Public Transportation and Land Use Policy* (Indiana University Press, Bloomington).

Statistics Canada (1977), *Census of Canada* (Ottawa).

Transportation Research Board (1978), *Light-Rail Transit: Planning and Technology*, Special Report 182 (Washington, DC).

Union Internationale des Transportes (1981), *Modern Light-Rail* (Brussels: 44th International Congress).

Union Internationale des Transportes (1981), *UITP Handbook of Urban Transport* (Brussels).

United States Department of Commerce, Bureau of the Census (1981), *City and County Factbook* (Washington, DC).

United States Department of Commerce, Bureau of the Census (1981), *1980 Census of Population* (Washington, DC).

Vining, D. (1982), 'Migration between the core and the periphery', *Scientific American*, Vol.247, pp.44–53.

Wachs, M. (1982), 'Ethical dilemmas in forecasting for public policy', *Public Management Forum*, pp.562–7.

Webster, F. and Bly, P. (eds.) (1980), *The Demand for Public Transport: Report of the International Collaborative Study* (Transportation and Road Research Laboratory, Crowthorne).

Wohl, M. (1976), 'The case for rapid transit — before and after the fact', in P. Gordon and R. Eckert (eds.), *Transportation Alternatives for Southern California* (Center for Public Affairs, University of Southern California).

8 An evaluation of the Tyneside Metro

B. FULLERTON AND S. OPENSHAW

8.1 Introduction

This chapter considers the development and economics of a light-rail rapid transit system which forms the core of an integrated public transport service in the Tyneside conurbation of North East England (see Figure 8.1). The Metro was constructed between 1974 and 1984 and remains the largest single investment in British urban transport during the twentieth century. The building of the Metro during a period of national economic recession in a peripheral region whose basic economy was in rapid decline provides an interesting study of the interplay between local and national planning and politics.

Section 8.2 provides a short background description of the Tyneside Metro, its geographical and historical setting, and the planning process which brought it into being. Section 8.3 reviews the original economic evaluations that were used to justify the development of the Metro. Some of the major planning assumptions and forecasts are monitored in Section 8.4. Section 8.5 examines the current use of social cost benefit analysis to determine fare and service levels on the Metro and the final section offers some broader conclusions about the performance of the Metro.

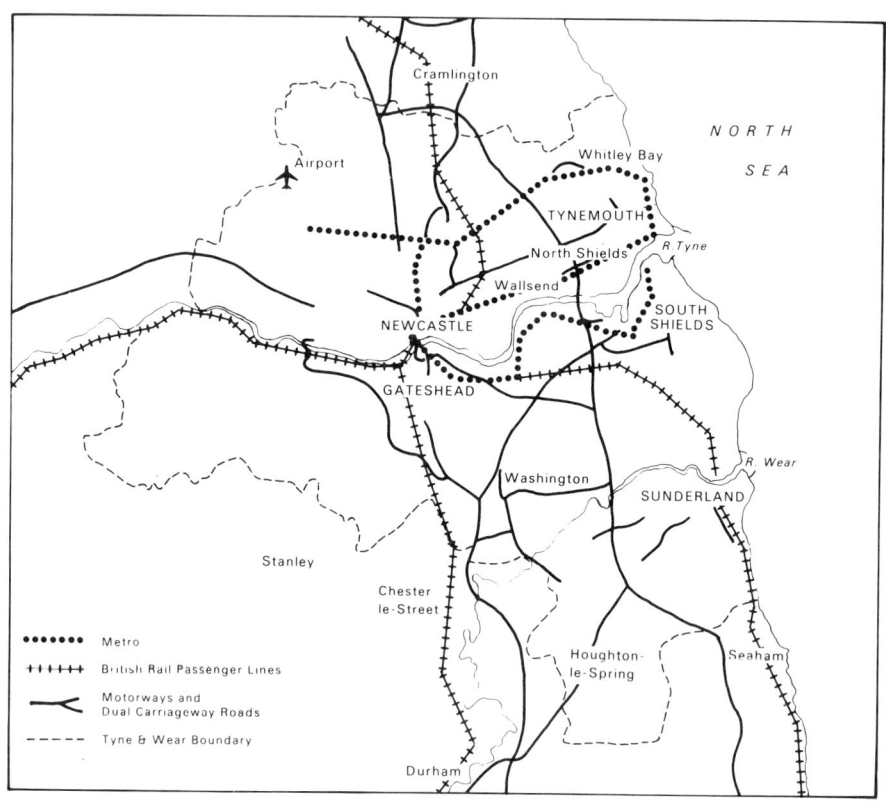

Figure 8.1   Tyne & Wear transport

8.2 Background

8.2—1 The Metro system

The Tyneside Metro is a light rapid transit system of 35 miles (56 km) of track (see Figure 8.2). Construction began in 1974, the first section came into operation in 1979 and the final 8 miles (13 km) in 1984. The central part of the system consists of a cross comprising 3.7 miles (6 km) of tunnel under Newcastle city centre; the rest comprises 25 miles (41 km) of conventional suburban railway routes and the links between them and the underground lines. The 41 stations have platforms to serve four-car metro trains and there are interchange facilities with connecting buses and car parking at eight stations. Each Metro car has a total capacity of 200 passengers and they are normally operated in two car units. They are one man operated with a maximum speed of 50 mph (80 kmp.h.). The stations are unmanned except in the central parts with automatic ticket machines and TV surveillance. The system provides for high train frequencies with 18 trains per hour each way on the central section between South Gosforth and Heworth, 12 trains per hour between St James and North Shields, and 6 trains per hour on the remainder of the system (in March 1983).

8.2—2 Geographical and historical context

Tyne and Wear County had a population in 1982 of 1.138 million. It is 267 miles (430 km) north of London and includes a number of formerly separate towns that had developed along the estuaries of the Tyne and Wear rivers. Living standards in the County are below the EEC average and unemployment averaged 17 per cent in 1982. This relatively poor performance is partly a consequence of the region's economic history and its past dependence on coal mining and heavy engineering industries.

In the nineteenth century the industrial development of Tyneside and Wearside produced a settlement pattern consisting of a number of separate colliery, shipyard, factory, and coastal towns with Newcastle and Sunderland as the major service centres. The development of transport services reflected the growth of the towns. The first suburban railways had been built in 1839 (linking Newcastle and North Shields, Gateshead and South Shields, and later Newcastle and Gateshead; a loop was also built north of the Tyne). The lines were electrified and now form the basis of the Metro system. In the 1950s the area was also served by six separate municipal and private bus companies (see Figure 8.3). Since then patronage on both systems has fallen dramatically as car ownership levels have increased, e.g. bus patronage fell by 60 per

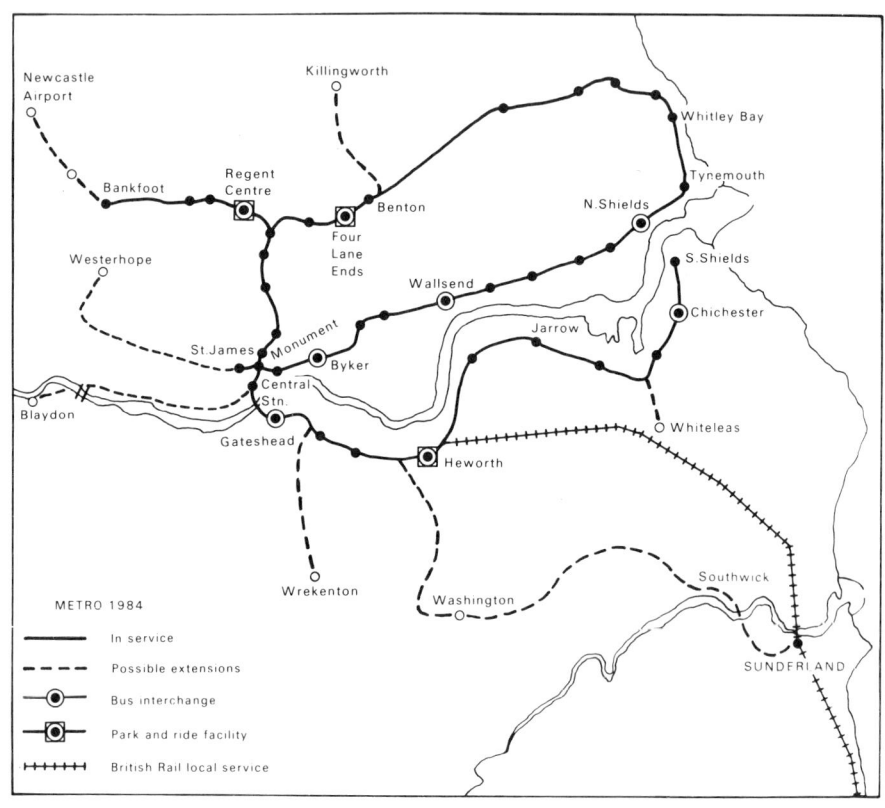

Newcastle Airport

Killingworth

Whitley Bay

Bankfoot

Regent Centre

Tynemouth

Benton

N.Shields

Four Lane Ends

S.Shields

Westerhope

Wallsend

Chichester

St.James

Monument

Jarrow

Byker

Central Stn.

Blaydon

Whiteleas

Gateshead

Heworth

Southwick

Wrekenton

Washington

SUNDERLAND

METRO 1984

——————— In service

- - - - - - Possible extensions

Bus interchange

Park and ride facility

+++++++ British Rail local service

Figure 8.2 Tyneside Metro

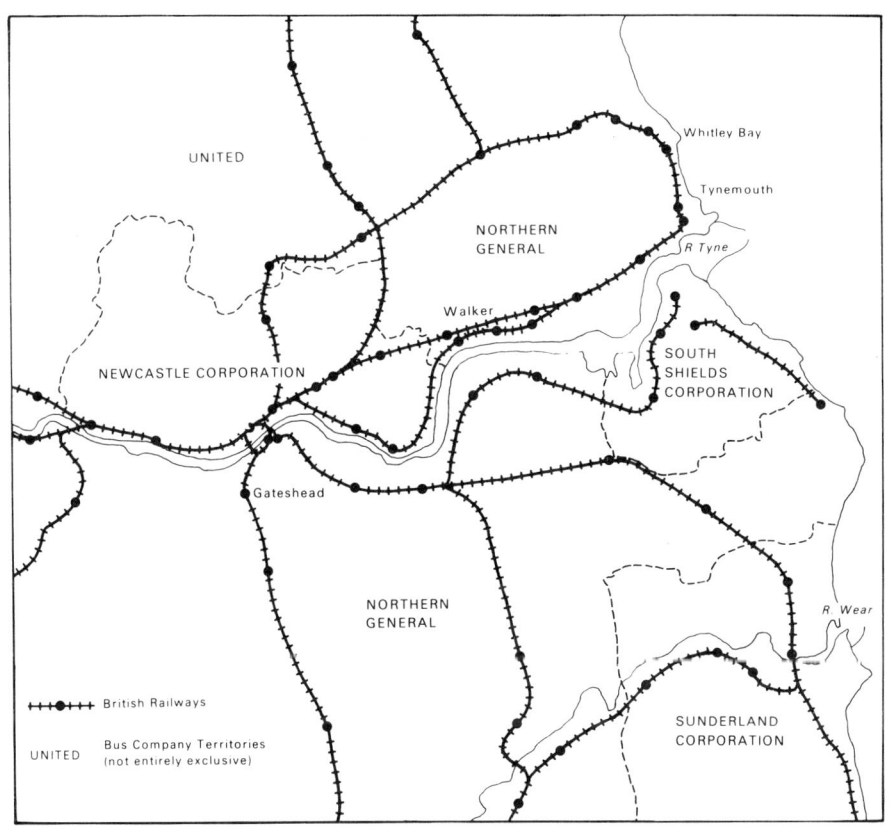

Figure 8.3   Public transport, 1950

cent in the period 1955–76. The period 1955–70 was also character-ised by a steady disinvestment in public transport on Tyneside. Eight local railway lines were abandoned and 13 stations closed while the electrified lines were replaced by diesel operation in 1967.

8.2–3 The planning and construction of the Metro

The emergence of the Tyneside Metro can be understood as the result of a number of favourable circumstances which, in combination, were unique to Tyneside. One was the willingness of British governments in the 1960s to spend money on transport infrastructure as a form of regional aid. Other contributing factors were local.

National government was becoming increasingly concerned at the rapidity of the switch to road transport. The Environment and Home Office sub-committee of the Expenditure Committee of the House of Commons suggested that '... national policy should be directed towards promoting public transport and discouraging the use of cars for the journey to work in city areas and that investigation of Rapit Transit Systems should be encouraged'. At the same time the Ministry of Transport was encouraging local government and transport interests to undertake American-style comprehensive land-use transport plans (Starkie 1976). On Tyneside a Voorhees and Buchanan consortium was appointed as principal consultants for such a plan in 1967. The 1968 Transport Act tried to foster public transport by offering 75 per cent infrastructure grants for interchange facilities, bus lanes, rapid transit and fixed track systems. It also allowed local authorities to subsidise bus fares and enabled the establishment of Passenger Trans-port Authorities in the six largest conurbations.

An argument in favour of a Metro was that the Government wanted a test site to develop a rapid transit system which could be exported. Indeed the jobs created in the West Midlands by the develop-ment of the Metro seem to have been an important political factor in gaining government support and retaining that support in the difficult period of the mid 1970s.

The 1968 Act applied to all British conurbations and the first rapid transit studies were carried out in Greater Manchester. Tyneside, the smallest of the Passenger Transport Authorities (Sunderland was not yet included, see Figure 8.4), however, had the advantage of an already existing local rail network from which a rapid transit system could be developed. At the same time the consultants' Design Report forecast that the conurbation would not be able to cope with un-restrained growth in car usage merely by building more roads if the existing urban development pattern was to be retained. The Report recommended additional investment in public transport as a solution

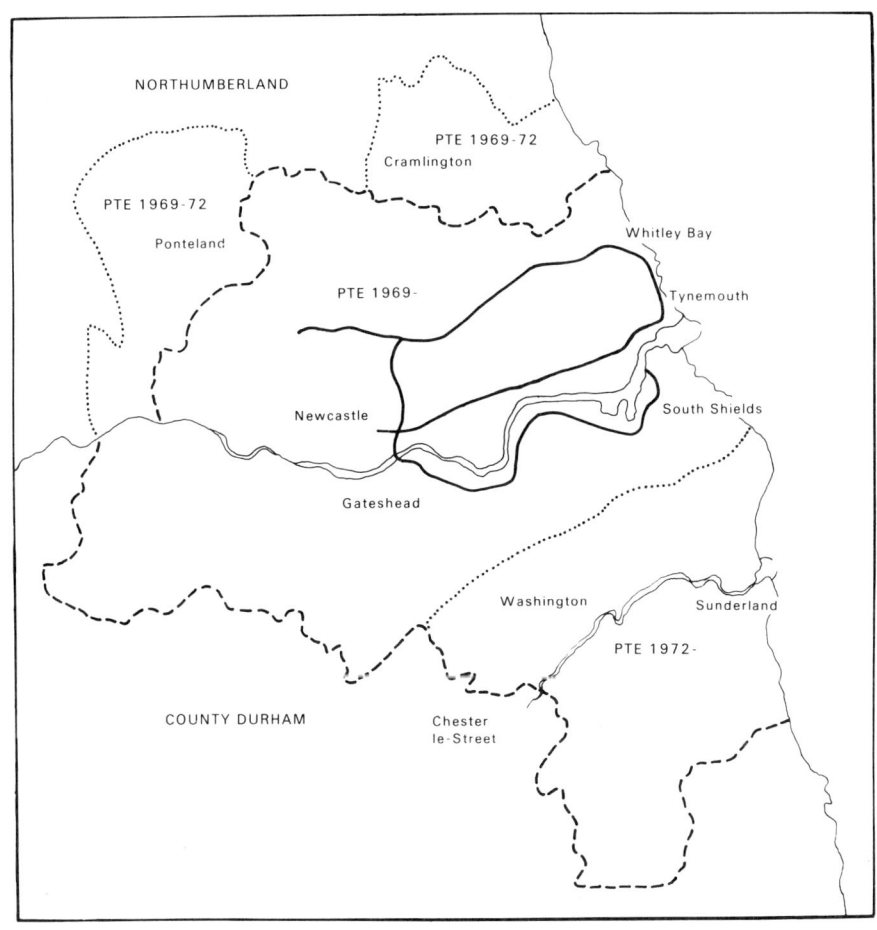

Figure 8.4   Area responsibilities of the Tyneside/Tyne & Wear P.T.E.

183

to the problem. The result was the commissioning of a major transport-ation and land use study known as the Tyne Wear Plan (Voorhees 1972c) to provide a transport plan for the mid 1980s and recommend-ations for land use up to 2000 AD.

The Tyne Wear Plan (TWP) tested a number of alternative transport strategies and advocated major expenditure on both roads and public transport. Although the latter initiative was local, national government was prepared to meet 75 per cent of the costs. In addition to £109 million already committed to road schemes, an additional £88 million was planned with £48 million devoted to a rapid transit system. Thus the capital expenditure on public transport was planned to rise from virtually nothing in 1966–71 to 38 per cent of the transport capital budget in 1971–84. The plan was approved in principle although most of the road programme was later cancelled as a result of a national economic crisis and local environmental opposition.

The public transport proposals eventually resulted in the current Metro system. The object was to provide a transport system for house-holds without cars and to provide an alternative mode of travel for those with cars. The TWP evaluated four options: an all-bus system on existing roads with the existing railways, the conversion of the local railways to express bus operation on reserved track, a bus system integrated with an upgraded railway service, and a rapid transit system based on existing railway track supplemented by interconnecting tunnels and bridges through central Newcastle and Gateshead. The rapid transit system was considered to have many economic and trans-port advantages over the other schemes although its costs were higher. It was considered to be more reliable than the alternatives, it avoided the need to revise drastically the city centre plan for Newcastle, and it was thought to be a better alternative than a bus-based system. It was doubtful whether an all bus system could achieve sufficiently attractive levels of service to compete with cars and serious practical difficulties were forecast in achieving a fast service to town centres.

A series of more detailed feasibility (Voorhees, 1972a) and costing studies (A.M. Voorhees and Associates, 1972b) were commissioned prior to a grant application (Tyneside Passenger Transport Executive, 1972). The application was successful and the Tyneside Metropolitan Railway Act was passed in 1973. Construction began in 1974. Local government reorganisation in 1974 improved the financial prospects for the Metro by increasing the size of the Passenger Transport Execut-ive to include Sunderland (see Figure 8.4) and by creating Tyne and Wear County. The new county council was able to give operating sub-sidies to public transport services as well as offer concessionary fares. It also became possible to integrate fares and control the contribution of fare revenue to all sectors of public transport (although since 1982

184

these powers have been greatly reduced).

8.3 Economic evaluation

8.3—1 Basic methodology

The justification for the Metro was twofold: it made sense from a transport engineering point of view and it could be justified by economic evaluation procedures. The latter was particularly important in order to justify the scheme to central government. The method used was a modified consumer surplus evaluation of the changes in the public transport system. Benefits come from travel time savings and greater reliability for public transport users, reduced traffic congestion and higher average speeds for car users and commercial vehicle operators, and increased revenue with decreased costs for the public transport operators. The total system benefit can then be compared with the marginal costs of implementing and operating the proposed changes so that an estimate may be made of the rate of return on the capital expenditure that would be achieved in the first year of operation. This first year rate of return could then be compared with a standard rate chosen by the national government. The technique was based on concepts developed by the then Ministry of Transport so its technical acceptability, when applied to the Metro, could be taken for granted.

This form of economic evaluation depends on the comparison of two alternative courses of action. For the Metro, there were two basic questions to be answered. The first was whether any additional investment in public transport facilities beyond that already committed was 'worthwhile', and the second was in what way should any available further investment funds be used, particularly with regard to the share allocated to public transport. At various stages in the development of the Metro, the economic evaluation process was repeated and it is interesting to examine in some detail the various evaluation exercises.

8.3—2 The Tyne Wear Plan (TWP) evaluations (circa 1969)

The Tyne Wear Plan considered two alternative transport plans for 1981 (Voorhees 1970; 1972d). Table 8.1 provides details of the basic calculations. There was some confusion over whether 1981 or 1984 was the forecast year. A relevant quote from TWP should clear up the confusion '... it was agreed that the rigidity of a particular year, namely 1981, could usefully be avoided and that the final plan should be one considered applicable to the early nineteen-eighties' without any changes in assumptions. That is, the years 1981 and 1984 can be used interchangeably because the data and the planning assumptions were the same for both years! The alternative public transport plans for 1984 were costed at similar amounts (£208 and £209.9 million) but Plan 1 incorporated a Metro system while Plan 2 involved a higher cost road plan and a lower cost public transport plan with an extended rail system but no Metro (Voorhees, 1971d). The plans were evaluated against a 'do nothing' situation in which only the current 1971 developments were included. It is interesting that in both cases the investment commitment existing in 1971 equalled the cost of the new proposals. Plan 1 was costed as involving £48.5 million of new public transport facilities and £51.4 million of new road developments while Plan 2 involved £24.1 million of new public transport facilities and £76.8 million of new road proposals; in both cases the existing road commitments amounted to £109 million.

Table 8.1   Tyne Wear Plan economic evaluation
(£ m, 1969 prices)

| | alternative plans | | |
	1	2	recommended
Base highway system	109	109	109
Base public transport system	7.4	7.4	8.5
Additional highway costs	51.4	76.8	88.0
Additional public transport costs	41.1	16.7	39.5
Total evaluated capital costs	92.5	93.5	127.5
Total user benefit	9.11	10.02	5.29
System operating benefit	0.9	0.44	0.14
Net benefits	10.01	10.46	5.43
First year rate of return (%)	10.9	11.2	11.3

Source: Voorhees (1972d)

A first year rate of return cost benefit analysis was used to compare each of the alternative plans with the no change base situation. The rate of return was calculated as

$$R = (\sum_i Bu_i + \sum_i Bo_i)/\sum_i C_i \tag{8.1}$$

where:

R is the first year rate of return;

Bu_i is the forecast net user benefit for user i in 1984;

Bo_i is the net benefit for the i_{th} operator; and

C_i is the capital cost for element i.

In order to minimise the effects of estimation errors all the quantities needed for equation (8.1) were calculated as the difference between the alternative being evaluated and the base situation, that is as marginal change. The capital cost elements take into account the estimated costs of new roads and railways, annual operating costs which were forecast for 1984, revenue forecasts from predicted 1984 fare levels, forecasts of road maintenance costs, and even the forecast costs of traffic accidents. It is worth emphasising that the cost estimates made in 1969 relate to a forecast 1981 or 1984 situation and the presence of errors in these predictions could seriously bias the economic evaluation (see section 8.4).

The net benefits to transport users were assessed based on an 'equity' value of time. Thus the user benefit for public transport trips was defined as:

$$\sum_i \sum_j \left\{0.5 \; (Tb_{ij} + Ta_{ij}) \; 0.955 \; (tb_{ij} - ta_{ij}) - (\Delta u_{ij} - \Delta r_{ij})\right\} \qquad (8.2)$$

where:

Tb_{ij} is the number of base plan public transport passengers travelling from zone i to zone j during the AM peak hour forecast for 1984;

Ta_{ij} is the forecast change in the number of passengers for the alternative plan being evaluated;

tb_{ij} and ta_{ij} are the two sets of forecast 1984 travel times in minutes;

the constant 0.955 is the 1969 Ministry of Transport equity value of time in pence (pre metric) per person per minute and incorporates an adjustment for 1984 income levels;

$-(\Delta u_{ij} - \Delta r_{ij})$ is a correction for changes in non-resource costs for the trips between i and j;

Δu_{ij} is the 1984 forecast change in behavioural costs compared with the standard equity value of time; and

Δr_{ij} is the 1984 forecast change in resource costs (i.e. cost of trip).

Equivalent methods were used to estimate user benefits for private vehicle users and commercial vehicle users. A summary of the results

187

is given in Table 8.1.

It is interesting that Plan 2 (the small public transport investment option) actually gives a better rate of return although the difference is small. Considerable significance was attached to the discovery that the public transport investments offered far higher rates of return than road investment; in Plan 1 the first year rate of return was 20 per cent compared with 3 per cent, in Plan 2 it was even higher at 45 per cent compared with 4 per cent. It would appear then that the TWP had made a good case for Plan 2, the non Metro plan. It is slightly surprising, therefore, to discover that 'The purpose of the evaluation of Alternatives 1 and 2 was not to choose one of them as the better and therefore the recommended plan. Rather it was to evaluate alternative investment policies' (Voorhees 1972d: p.198). Thus it seems that all the analysis demonstrated was that some investment in public transport is better than none at all. It may also be that economic evaluation was only one of the factors governing the decision as to what to do. It may also be that non-quantified social advantages may have led to a preference for Plan 1 despite its lower rates of return. It is impossible now to discover precisely how the preferred or recommended plan emerged; however, it was a modified version of Plan 1.

The economic evaluation of the recommended plan showed that public transport offered at least three times the rate of return of the highway system (22.6 per cent compared with 6.1 per cent), although it must be emphasised that the evaluation relates to an integrated transport system with a combination of highway improvements, public transport improvements, and restraint policies in central areas. It was almost as if Voorhees were having difficulties in preferring public transpsort *vis-à-vis* road investments. A critical caveat is the statement that 'it must be implemented as an integrated system or the overall benefit forecast will not be achieved' (Voorhees 1972d: p.128). Integration influences the economic evaluation mainly through the effects of road congestion on interzonal movement forecasts and on the associated network costs, even though it does not appear explicitly in the economic evaluation. Indeed it may be reasonable to inquire whether the available transportation models were able to cope with an integrated system.

8.3—3 *The Tyneside Rapid Transit Analysis (TRTA) Report*

A more detailed economic assessment of the Tyne Wear Plan's light rapid transit system (Metro) is provided in a 1972 report (A.M. Voorhees and Associates, 1972c) and this formed the basis for the subsequent application to the Department of Environment for a 75 per cent infrastructure grant towards the construction of the Metro

(Tyneside Passenger Transport Executive 1972). The purpose was to provide a more detailed examination of the economics of the proposed Metro system both to convince the Department of Environment and to justify changes in cost estimates since the TWP assessments of 1969/70. The revised cost of £65.5 million (January 1972 prices) can be compared with an equivalent TWP estimate of £39.5 million. The revision included an east-west tunnel under the central area of Newcastle and various other major infrastructure investments on the Metro up to 1979 when the full system was intended to be complete. The revised system was seen as offering a higher level of service than the TWP original.

On this occasion the cost benefit analysis compares the proposed Metro system, combined with a high level of bus-rail integration, with an all-bus system which was considered to be the best alternative to Metro. The all-bus alternative was regarded as providing a far better test than the 'do nothing' base plan used in the TWP because it involved major changes in bus networks in an attempt to meet the anticipated level of demand. The computer models were improved and the data were more refined than those used in the TWP. In addition, a larger number of zones were used (330 compared with 257 previously) while the capital costs and operating cost estimates were more conservative than previously (A.M. Voorhees and Associates, 1972c). Other improvements were also included.

The economic analysis was based on the recommended Ministry of Transport procedure, although the method was very similar to that used in the TWP. The planning forecasts were also based on the TWP although the forecast year was now 1979, giving an equivalence for forecasting purposes between 1979, 1981, and 1984! The user benefits for public transport trips were defined as

$$\sum_i \sum_j \left\{ 0.5\ (PTb_{ij} + PTa_{ij})\ (EQb_{ij} - EQa_{ij})\ (Vc)\ (K) \right\} \qquad (8.3)$$

where:

PTb_{ij} is the base system morning peak hour passenger work trips forecast for 1979;

PTa_{ij} is the Metro trips as forecast for 1979;

EQb_{ij} is the weighted door-to-door time in equivalent minutes forecast for flows between zones i and j for 1979;

EQa_{ij} is the same forecast for Metro;

Vc is the value of time for commuting trips; and

K is a conversion factor (5.65) to convert from peak hour to all trips.

The results of the economic assessment aggregated across all trip purposes are given in Table 8.2.

**Table 8.2   Economic evaluation of the
Tyneside Rapid Transit System (£ m, 1972 prices)**

	TRTA	PTE$_1$	PTE$_2$
Total evaluated cost	55.0	58.7	65.5
Total benefit	6.03	6.26	6.26
First year rate of return (%)	11	12.2	10.8
Discounted rate of return at 10 per cent (%)	8	9.4	8.0

Notes: PTE$_1$ excludes specific design, supervision, and conting-
                ency costs of £6.8 million
                PTE$_2$ includes these costs

Sources: TRTA from A.M. Voorhees and Associates (1972c)
                PTE from Tyneside Passenger Transport Executive
                (1972)

It is interesting that there are small differences between the Tyneside Passenger Transport Executive (1972) application and the values reported in A.M. Voorhees and Associates (1972c) from which the analysis was obtained — see Table 8.2. Of the forecast £6.03 m total user benefit in the TRTA report, it is noted that £0.8 million was attributed to a service reliability differential and £3.7 million for travel time benefits and that only £0.27 million accrued to private and commercial vehicle operators (because of reduced road congestion effects). It was emphasised in the TRTA report that the assumptions were very conservative and that the benefits were likely to remain constant until 1984; thereafter they would slowly increase. The report concluded that 'These investigations permit a confident statement that construction could be commenced in 1974 and the system could be in operation in 1979 at a capital cost very near to that assumed in this study.' (A.M. Voorhees and Associates 1972c: p.16).

8.3—4 The 1976 review

By 1975—6, the costs of construction had risen so much and the prospect of fundamental inter-union disputes loomed so large that it was feared that government would cancel their open-ended commitment to pay 70 per cent of the costs. A new study was commissioned to update the previous economic evaluations, particularly the estimates of user benefits to November 1975 prices. No attempt, however, was made to review or change any of the basic input variables (namely population, employment, car ownership forecasts), although it was acknowledged that some changes had occurred. It was assumed, for the purposes of analysis, that the system would be opened in stages between 1978 and 1981 but for comparability with the original study all the system was regarded as being operational in mid 1979 (Martin and Voorhees Associates 1976).

The 1976 review largely vindicated the TRTA study. It was found that, in general, the evaluated capital cost had increased by a factor of 2.39 and the benefits by a factor of 2.14 over a three-year period. The conclusion was 'Bearing in mind the very significant movements in costs since the original evaluation was completed the revised rate of return of 9.7 per cent shows that the project is robust' (Martin and Voorhees Associates 1976: 31). The results of the revised economic evaluation are shown in Table 8.3.

Table 8.3 Revised economic evaluation of the
Tyneside Rapid Transit System (£ m, 1975 prices)

Total evaluated capital cost	160.884
Total benefit	13.396
First year rate of return (%)	9.7
Discounted rate of return at 10 per cent (%)	7.9

Source: Martin and Voorhees Associates (1976)

The reason for the large increase in cost from £65.5 million (1972 prices) to £160.884 million (1975 prices) was attributed to inflation (£74.8 million), additional design work and consultancy fees excluded from the TPTE's grant application (£6.76 million), and a number of small increases and unexpected costs (£4.27 million). The difference of £9.554 million was attributed to a real price increase of 6.3 per cent; a cost over-run of this magnitude was considered to be reasonable for a complex project.

The analysis in Table 8.3 shows that, compared with the all-bus alternative, the Metro system still seems to be worthwhile. The alternative decision of cancellation was also considered. The unavoidable costs of cancellation amounted to £104.27 million, although at the time only £28.05 million had actually been spent. However, it was concluded that the rate of return on the avoidable expenditure (£113.360 million) was 11.8 per cent which was above the 10 per cent level then used to judge public investment decisions. Although the rate of return on the Metro investment was now below the norm of 10 per cent, it made more sense to continue because of the higher rate of return on the remaining avoidable expenditure.

8.3—5 A discussion of the possible effects of uncertainties in the economic analyses

The economic evaluation exercises used forecasts of interzonal and intrazonal flows for 1979, 1981, 1984 for either 257 or 330 zones. They each assume a fixed set of planning inputs about population, employment, and network costs. Quite simply, if these trip forecasts were much in error, then the entire basis for the economic evaluations would be suspect. It is worth reflecting on the problems and difficulties of the transportation modelling process. The models were calibrated on the 10 per cent 1966 Census journey to work data, a data set which is far from ideal for transportation modelling (e.g. it is a biased sample and provides information only about work trips). Based on this data, the models were required to make forecasts for several very different transportation plans for a period 15 years ahead. Such a task is virtually impossible if the results are meant to be accurate. At the very least the major structural changes that were being evaluated would render the models being calibrated on a very different 1966 situation worthless. It is likely that the interzonal assignments upon which the economic assessments were based are completely wrong. The use of marginal change forecasts does nothing to reduce the consequences of forecast error; indeed, it is likely that the actual changes are smaller in magnitude than the variability due to forecast errors. In theory these errors could be empirically estimated for the Metro, although whether those who have the data and the original forecasts would want to perform a detailed evaluation is doubtful.

It is now known that transport models are often incapable of providing a good representation of even the calibration year situation and are largely incapable of providing accurate forecasts of future travel patterns (Openshaw 1979a; Openshaw and Ramsey 1980). The only practical solution to this problem is to pretend that it does not exist. It is not surprising, therefore, to find no assessment of the performance of the transportation models that were used in the Metro studies. The only vague indication that problems existed was the occasional reference to inconsistencies being removed by 'revised distribution, modal split, and assignments' (A.M. Voorhees and Associates 1972c: 5). There was also the reference to 'F-factors'; for example, 'calibrated socioeconomic adjustment factors were used to reflect the local trip distribution patterns where these differ from area wide patterns' (A.M. Voorhees and Associates 1972c: 43). It seems that automatic calibration routines were not available in the transportation packages that were used. Problems also arose with: modal choice, the inclusion of congestion effects, the calculation of generalised costs, network representation especially for public transport, the estimation of door-to-door travel costs, and assignment.

To be fair to those involved, the best available models were used but they were applied in a simplistic manner. The effects of forecast errors on the robustness of the economic evaluations should, however, have been considered. The only justification for their omission is, and was, that there was no requirement for such basic and fundamentally useful information to be provided. This is not to say that the decision to build the Metro was wrong, only that the economic benefits forecast for it were suspect.

8.4 Monitoring some of the assumptions and forecasts

It is surprising that so few attempts have been made to identify the levels of forecast error that exist in the inputs to the economic assessment of transport investments. The reasons are probably that those who possess the necessary data lack the necessary will to investigate what could turn out to be their own off beam forecasts, while those with the necessary will lack the data that are needed. It is certainly true that there has been no monitoring or review of the Metro forecasts even though the results might offer useful insights for the future evaluation of large-scale projects. One problem is that, despite the very detailed studies of the Metro, there are very few published forecasts that can be checked against observed data. There is also the problem of knowing what effect forecast errors might have on the investment decision without access to the historic models and computer programs that were used; and, of course, only in very exceptional circumstances would vintage 1969—72 models still be preserved in working order. Nevertheless, an indication of some of the problems can be obtained by a limited evaluation of a selection of Metro forecasts used in the economic assessments.

8.4—1 Fare levels

An important element in the economic evaluation of the Metro is fare levels. Fares are important in modal split and thus in the forecasting of network flows. It is possible that the current zonal fare structures with through ticketing procedures were not foreseen in the early 1970s when the cost benefit analyses were performed. The fare models that were used assume a conventional relationship between travel distance and fare.

The TWP model involves

$$\text{fare (1969 prices)} = 1.5\text{p} + 0.83\text{ppermile} \tag{8.4}$$

This was based on 1966 fare levels and assumed no increase in real terms until 1984 on the premise that increases in operating costs would be offset by increased productivity. However, in the TRTA report it was reported that fares in 1972 had already exceeded the TWP forecasts for 1984. The 1972 'present day' formula was:

$$\text{fare (1972 prices)} = 2.0\text{p} + 1.1\text{ppermile} \tag{8.5}$$

An alternative, up to 50 per cent higher than the TWP fare model, was considered most applicable for a 1979 forecast:

$$\text{fare (1972 prices)} = 3.0\text{p} + 1.5\text{ppermile} \tag{8.6}$$

These three fare models were reviewed in 1976 and changed to November 1975 prices to become

$$\text{TWP fare} = 2.6\text{p} + 1.45\text{ppermile} \tag{8.7}$$
$$\text{1972 fare} = 3.49\text{p} + 1.9\text{ppermile} \tag{8.8}$$
$$\text{1979 fare} = 5.2\text{p} + 2.6\text{ppermile} \tag{8.9}$$

while the actual 1975 fare structure was described as

$$\text{1975 fare} = 4\text{p} + 4.0\text{ppermile for trips less than 3 miles} \tag{8.10}$$
$$\text{1975 fare} = 13\text{p} + 1.2\text{ppermile for trips greater than 3 miles} \tag{8.11}$$

A final alternative was the 1975 model increased by 20 per cent.

The question remains as to how well any of these historic fare models represent the 1983 fare structures on the assumption that the 1983 fares are representative of those likely to be used on the completed Metro. The various models in equations (8.7) to (8.11) can be updated to November 1982 prices and compared with actual fares (see Table 8.4). The comparison is in terms of a distance approximation to the current fares and for a selection of journeys.

It is apparent that beyond about 5 km the fares model used in the economic evaluations overpredicts the actual fares especially the long distance trips. At present, however, mean Metro trip lengths are about 4.8 km and at this distance the fares model is relatively accurate, although it does depend on the trips used in the comparison since interchanges and fare zones can distort the simple distance costs. It is unlikely that the errors noted in Table 8.4 had much effect on the

Metro evaluations although fare levels are used in the modal choice and assignment models. The principal effect may have been to inflate the expected revenues.

Table 8.4 Comparison of fare model forecasts
with November 1982 fares

distance km	current fares	fare models: TWP	1972	1979	1975a	1975b
zonal distances						
1	14	8	10	15	14	17
2	14	10	13	18	20	23
3	20	12	15	22	25	30
4	26	14	18	25	30	37
5	32	16	21	29	36	43
10	37	25	33	47	45	54
15	45	35	46	64	53	63
20	58	45	59	82	61	73
25	70	55	72	99	69	83
sample of fare						
4.0	14	14	18	26	31	37
4.7	37	14	19	27	32	38
6.1	37	18	23	33	38	46
7.7	45	21	27	39	41	49
10.8	45	27	35	49	46	55
12.2	58	30	39	54	48	58
14.6	58	34	45	63	52	62

8.4—2 Forecasts of revenues and operating costs

Another important element in the economic evaluations are the forecasts of revenue and operating costs. Various forecasts were made and these are shown against current and predicted values in Table 8.5. It is apparent that the cost estimates are relatively accurate given that at present the full costs of the Metro system are not being experienced. The 1972 cost forecast updated to 1982 prices is £79.5 million and the 1976 forecast is £99 million and these are quite close to 1980—1 observed value of £74.9 million and the 1981—2 value of £83 million given that not all the Metro is operational. The Passenger Transport's

Executive cost forecast for the completed system are: £102.9 million (1984—5), £108.3 million (1985—6), and £115.1 million (1986—7) (see Passenger Transport Executive 1983).

Table 8.5   Forecasts of operating costs and revenues

	TWP a	b	c	TRTA	MVA	actual values 1980—1	1981—2
Operating costs							
bus	50.5	13.6	12.7	61.2	84.6	64.6	70.9
rail	14.8	11.7	4.8	3.8	1.7	3.6	2.2
Metro	34.6	—	3.6	14.4	12.6	5.8	9.5
Total costs	100.0	98.5	80.7	79.5	99.0	74.9	83.0
Revenue	86.7	83.3	82.2	92.8	109.4	39.0*	41.6*
						50.2**	55.1**

Notes: Tyne Wear Plan alternative 1 (a), alternative 2 (b), preferred plan (c) TRTA based on A.M. Voorhees and Associates (1972c). MVA based on Martin and Voorhees Associates (1976)

* 1980—1, 1981—2 prices all other costs and revenues are November 1982 prices

** includes concessionary fares and education fares

The revenue forecasts have proved to be very optimistic. The Martin and Voorhees Associates (1976) forecast of £99 million can be compared with 1981—2 observed income of £39 million or £50.2 million if concessionary fares and educational grants (not envisaged when the Metro was being planned) are included. The forecasts for the completed system are also very different from the 1976 figure; £50.3 million or £71.0 million (1984—5), £53.7 million or £76.2 million (1985—6), and £53.7 million or £77.9 million (1986—7). It is perhaps no exaggeration to say that if the expected revenues had been 25 or 50 per cent smaller then the Metro would never have received government approval.

8.4—3 Forecasts of Metro usage

The Passenger Transport Executive currently attribute a lower than expected Metro ridership to high levels of unemployment, population decline, and the effects of the recession (Passenger Transport Executive

1983), none of which could have been forecast in the early 1970s. However, it seems that the TWP forecasts for population and employment are quite good. The forecast total population for the Inner Study Area for 1981 was 1,468,000 compared with our 1981 Census-based estimate of 1,351,000; an employment forecast of 612,525 (later revised to 612,349) can be compared with a 1981 estimate of 632,000. It is not possible to check the zonal disaggregated forecasts. What is interesting is that the aggregate Metro forecasts for total employment are lower than the current recession hit levels; this may be due to chance since no unemployment was forecast in the TWP. It is also interesting that the car ownership forecasts for 1981 of 429,590 cars or 0.65 cars per worker are nearly twice the estimated 1981 values of 282,000 or 0.45 cars per worker.

The most plausible explanation of the revenue forecast errors is that the transportation models predicted far more trips on the Metro and by bus than have actually materialised. Some indication of these errors is given in Table 8.6 which compares forecast and actual morning peak flows for part of the Metro network. It is emphasised that the observed figures are for a Metro system which is not yet complete but it can be argued that the substitute metro buses will have loaded onto the network most of the trips that are likely to occur. It is apparent that the forecasts are a factor of between 2 and 4 too large.

A further clue is given in a summary of the public transport assignments in A.M. Voorhees and Associates (1972c). Forecasts are given of morning peak hour boardings and passenger miles. It is possible to convert these figures into estimates of the equivalent annual figures for comparison with the Passenger Transport Executive's returns for public transport usage. The results depend on the conversion factors used and we were unable to discover the values used in the Metro studies. Accordingly, a peak hour to daily factor of 10 is used to scale up the peak hour assignments with an annualisation factor of 310. The PTE report that in 1982 the total number of boardings were 361.6 million (with a forecast of 366.2 for 1984). The TWP predicted 972 million and the TRTA forecast was 747 million. The PTE's return of total passenger miles in 1982 was 1087.9 million (with a forecast of 1110 for 1984). The TWP forecast implied about 2591 million and the TRTA about 2264 million. These values are comparable with the results in Table 8.6 and also with the very high bus frequencies that were forecast in the Tyne Wear Plan.

It seems then the level of public transport demand was seriously overestimated. It is not known how good or bad are the road traffic forecasts. It may be that 15-year forecast errors of between 200 and 300 per cent are relatively good for transportation models! Clearly some means need to be developed to aid the use of models possessed with this degree of uncertainty. The basic techniques for doing this exist (see Openshaw 1979b; Openshaw and Ramsey 1980) but are currently not used.

Table 8.6   Comparison of forecast and actual morning peak flows on Metro in March 1982

| network link | forecast | | observed | | ratio of total forecast to observe |
	a	b	a	b	
Heworth-Felling	6337	2335	2286	387	3.2
Felling-Stadium	6896	2235	2455	462	4.1
Stadium-Gateshead	6570	3251	2501	587	4.1
Gateshead-Central Station	9471	4463	4130	1020	2.7
Central Station-Monument	9037	5659	3742	1732	2.6
Monument-Haymarket	8365	3436	2337	2500	2.4
Haymarket-Jesmond	3012	9062	1443	3490	2.4
Jesmond-West Jesmond	2413	8655	1021	3598	2.3
West Jesmond-Ilford Road	2294	8164	1097	3680	2.1
Ilford Road-South Gosforth	2136	7884	1041	3626	2.1
Bank Foot-Fawdon	997	470	307	23	4.4
Fawdon-Wansbeck Road	2430	583	630	73	4.2
Wansbeck Road-Regents Centre	2952	628	818	82	3.9
Regents Centre-South Gosforth	3899	1176	1080	525	3.1
South Gosforth-Longbenton	2042	5154	839	2512	2.1
Longbenton-Four Lane Ends	1283	4992	468	2476	2.1
Four Lane Ends-Benton	1242	2536	241	1852	1.8
Benton-Shiremoor	520	2257	325	1539	1.4
Shiremoor-West Monkseaton	588	1860	374	1387	1.3
West Monkseaton-Monkseaton	1027	1234	378	1141	1.4
Monkseaton-Whitley Bay	1310	910	377	817	1.8
Whitley Bay-Cullercoats	1470	787	485	325	3.7

Notes: a is travel in one direction, b is travel in another

Source: forecasts A.M. Voorhees and Associates (1972c), observed based on Passenger Transport Executive report (unpublished)

8.5 Economic evaluation of future public transport expenditure

8.5—1 The 1983 Transport Act

Now the Metro exists, its continued use and level of use depend on, among other things, another form of economic appraisal concerned with the amount of money used to subsidise private and public transport operations. It is no longer sufficient for a local authority simply to declare that 'public transport investment is good' as is contained in the Structure Plan Annual Report (Tyne and Wear County Council 1982: 5) which states that 'the maintenance of a high level of public transport services in the county needs to continue to be given priority'. Certainly for a long time public transport expenditure levels were evaluated on an *ad hoc* basis without either any clear framework or any economic assessment techniques to aid decision-makers. The situation has changed because government is now keen to control public expenditure on transport. Previously a certain amount of control had been exercised through central government grants, but the metropolitan counties were able to supplement this finance by funds obtained from local rates. The 1983 Transport Act attempts to change this by establishing three-year public transport plans with cost-benefit analysis to assess the effectiveness of different policy options. It aims to provide a more stable basis for public transport planning and subsidies and introduces, for the Metropolitan counties, a new protection from legal challenge for levels of subsidy that do not exceed the annual amount indicated by the Secretary of State for Transport. This critical quantity is known as the protected expenditure limit (PEL) and is the amount of money that could be spent, were it available, without any legal challenge from a ratepayer.

The government's policy is to control expenditure on public transport by what it calls 'a phased return to balanced policies for public transport with levels of support rigorously justified and applied in a manner best suited to the steady adjustment of services in line with requirements' (advice by the Secretary of State quoted in Passenger Transport Executive 1983). The critical words are 'rigorously justified'; by this the Department of Transport has in mind a social cost-benefit approach as a means of evaluating the benefits of implementing those policy options needed to satisfy the theoretical limits on expenditure (PELs) set by the Minister. A statement sets out the policy: 'Ministers have made it clear during the passage of the Act through Parliament that they intend to make use of techniques of cost-benefit analysis, developed by the Department in collaboration with qualified advisers, as part of the process of assessing the proposals for levels of revenue support put forward' (Department of Transport

1982). It was not intended, however, that the results would be used in isolation but that they would be one of the factors to be taken into account. Nevertheless, the intention of the Secretary of State was that the proposals in the public transport plans had to be justified. It is probably difficult for outsiders to imagine the panic which this must have caused the Authorities and Executives responsible for public transport.

8.5—2 *The Department of Transport's economic evaluation model applied to the Metro*

It is the Department's intention that their model should be used to answer two questions. First, for a given level of subsidy, how can fare and service levels be adjusted to give the greatest benefits? This involves a question of balance which is defined as the need to adjust fare and service levels so that the effect of moving subsidy from fares to service levels, or *vice versa*, cannot bring any greater benefit from the same overall level of subsidy. The second question is to compare the 'value for money' or marginal rates of return for subsidy levels in different conurbations with a view to determining the best allocation of central government funds.

The basic technique is very simple. In the context of a fixed protected expenditure limit the effect of a change in subsidy is to force either changes in fare levels or changes in service levels in order to balance revenue and operating costs. The Department of Transport model provides a means of investigating the effects of different transport programmes based on different fare and service assumptions. The model predicts the average effect of a change in fare levels and service frequencies by estimating the change in the generalised cost to the public transport user (this is a function of changes of fares and wait times), the congestion effects on other road users (a function of changes in wait times, operating costs, and traffic speeds), and the changes in operating costs of public transport (a function of changes in service levels and congestion). The results of the evaluation are expressed in terms of the marginal net social benefit per pound of subsidy. The policy variables can also be adjusted to identify that combination of fare and service levels needed to balance the marginal rates of return and thus effectively maximise net social benefits. The argument would be that an imbalance in the marginal rates of return would indicate that different policies for bus, rail, and road should be used to move funds away from those options with low shadow prices in favour of those with a high shadow price so as to achieve a gain in benefit whilst keeping the overall subsidy level constant. In practice this may mean raising fares and reducing services on the buses and reducing fares and increasing services on rail or Metro. It is easy to appreciate the high degree of political sensitivity involved in these evaluations.

In contrast to the methods of economic evaluation used to justify the Metro decision this model operates at an aggregate level. The input variables provide an aggregate description of the entire system (e.g. average fares per mile). Many of the relationships involved in the model are dynamic with, for example, road speeds depending on bus usage while bus usage is influenced by fare elasticities, wait times, and load factors. Thus the effects of a 10 per cent reduction in bus fares would be calculated as a benefit to existing users resulting from the fare reduction plus benefits to new users who are attracted to the buses, less the loss of revenue to the operator because of reduced fares, less the cost of increased average waiting times because of higher bus load factors, less a small increase in operator costs due to the reduction in bus running speeds, and plus some time savings for car users due to less road congestion. Various empirically derived equations are used to link the various components together.

There are a number of operational problems with the model version which was available to us. First, there are a number of programming errors. Second, the empirical equations need to be calibrated for a particular area. Third, it is difficult to use it to evaluate Metro fare policies because there is no provision for either an integrated transport system or a Metro and bus system. The expedient adopted here is to assume that the Metro is a railway. A final problem concerned the data inputs needed for the model. These were obtained from the 1984–7 public transport plan (Passenger Transport Executive 1983).

The model's most relevant application is for determining optimal fare and service levels for various amounts of expenditure so as to maximise social benefits. The Department of Transport report describes a semi-graphical approach to approximately optimising these policy variables but in the version of the programme available to us this option did not work due to inherent programming errors. In fact it is slightly worrying that the recommended model is neither complete nor fully operational nor error free. The best alternative was to embed the complete model in a non-linear mathematical programming framework. The objective function is to maximise the value of social benefits subject to an expenditure constraint. The latter is most easily handled as a penalty function so that a combined function can be optimised using an unconstrained non-linear optimisation procedure with numerical calculation of derivatives. The optimisation model can be written as

$$\text{minimise } -SB + 100(R - TEP)^2 \tag{8.12}$$

where:

SB is the social benefit for a given combination of fare and service levels;

R is the difference between costs and revenues; and

TEP is the total expenditure allowed including non-revenue grants.

It should be noted that there are four parameters for which optimal values are required (percentage change in bus fares, Metro fares, bus service frequencies, and Metro frequencies). When an optimal solution is found, then the fare and service levels will be in balance. The results are shown in Table 8.7 for a range of expenditure constraints, based around the probable limit which assumes a PEL of £17.5 million, £7 million from reserves, and £22.5 million concessionary fare support. The changes in fare and service levels are forecast for 1984–5 from a 1983–4 base situation.

Table 8.7   Optimal fare and service levels

Total expenditure (£ m)	Value of benefit (£ m)	for buses (%)	Change in fares for Metro (%)	for buses (%)	Change in service for Metro (%)
44	6.9	59.5	−52.3	6.3	70.6
45	8.7	32.2	49.1	−8.8	54.1
46	7.7	58.4	−50.0	14.2	69.1
47	7.7	53.0	−50.2	13.5	69.4
48	7.8	51.3	−50.8	15.4	69.6
49	7.9	48.8	−52.3	16.2	70.6
50	8.1	53.6	−59.5	19.2	77.3
51	8.2	52.1	−60.2	21.2	77.6
52	8.2	50.7	−59.3	23.5	78.4

It appears that the more money that is spent on subsidising public transport the greater the monetary value of the benefits, but after a certain point rates of return diminish. For example, total expenditure of £47 million results in a social benefit of £7.7 million, whereas £50 million produces only £8.1 million. The value of £8.7 million for expenditure of £45 million seems to be anomalous. It seems that the model is possessed of some spectacular dynamic behaviour properties, including some kind of catastrophic behaviour and bifurcation (see

Wilson 1981). Whether this is intentional (which it should be because smooth changes would not be expected as the policy variables change by large amounts) or a result of non-convexities, rounding errors, or programming errors, is uncertain. Apart from the £44 million run, consistent trends in the policy variables emerge although the predicted changes needed to obtain the optimal levels of benefit are very large. Additionally, there is no way of knowing whether the resulting system would be stable and robust when faced with minor changes, or indeed, whether the forecasts of revenue and benefit would actually be achieved.

One problem is whether the macro model properly represents individual behaviour, especially as the policy variables are seeking to change behaviour patterns with respect to the use of public transport. It may also not adequately handle congestion effects on roads, nor does it handle public-private transport mode switching. Until this latter problem can be resolved it will not provide a good basis for simulating the effects of policy changes. It is also very doubtful whether the revenue forecasts will be sufficiently accurate to allow the model to be useful.

8.5—3 The Passenger Transport Executive's economic evaluation

A similar but much simpler form of economic evaluation is described by the Passenger Transport Executive (1983) to justify its public transport plan. It claims that the standard model cannot be used for Tyne and Wear because of the presence of the Metro and an integrated fare and transport system. As an alternative the PTE provides a direct assessment of costs and benefits in aggregate terms. The evaluation is performed against a hypothetical 1984—5 base situation in which the expected protected expenditure limit is met in order to justify the extent to which higher levels of revenue support can be justified, which is not really what the Minister had in mind. The results are summarised in Table 8.8. It is noted that the benefits forecast for 1984—5 are almost as great as those discovered by the optimisation model but in this instance very small changes are being proposed. The reasoning behind the PTE's benefit forecasts have not been published and the entire evaluation lacks a rigorous basis.

8.5—4 A discussion of some evaluation problems

There are a number of fundamental problems with the application of social cost-benefit analysis to evaluate public transport investment programmes. It is doubtful whether it is sensible to try and predict the effects of changes in fare and service levels using macro models when the results depend on changes in individual behaviour patterns. There is a need for an investigation of the possibility of using microanalytical simulation models for this purpose. Such models could probably be built using existing data sources in the metropolitan counties. Additionally, some measure of uncertainty needs to be incorporated in the results. There is a real danger that decision-makers using such models neither understand the concepts of social cost-benefit analysis nor appreciate the limitations of the results. An equilibrium is being sought between 'funny money' which is the monetary value placed on time and 'real money', for example fares, but the two are not the same. Further, the levels of uncertainty in the forecast effects of changes, marginal or otherwise, are likely to be far greater than the changes which different policies can bring about. For instance, the marginal change in costs and benefits are typically small in relation to both the total sums involved and the levels of uncertainty; for example, a 1983—4 projected cost increase of £1.6 million out of a total expenditure of £102.9 million with estimated benefits of £6.0 million. This degree of fine tuning is unrealistic, unnecessary, and impossible to achieve with current economic assessment techniques.

Table 8.8   Benefits forecast for PTE's
alternative programmes (£ m)

policy option	Value of benefits			
	1983—4	1984—5	1985—6	1986—7
Preferred	2.29	4.00	5.40	7.90
TWCC modification	3.07	6.59	9.65	13.36
Alternative 1a	2.10	−0.24	−1.47	−0.98
Alternative 2	3.07	8.98	13.72	20.22
Alternative 3	1.33	2.31	1.51	1.51

Source: Passenger Transport Executive (1983)

It is easy to demonstrate that the results of the economic evaluations are very sensitive to various critical parameters; for example cross elasticities, average fares, wait times, etc. — none of which can be accurately or reliably estimated or forecast. Further, doubts are expressed about the wisdom of using averages to represent non-normal frequency distributions. It is claimed that the Department of Transport's procedure is robust (for example, 'we are confident that the overall directions of the findings has not been distorted significantly by' (Department of Transport 1982)), but no evidence is presented to support such assertions. Indeed there are indications in Table 8.7 that the model is highly unstable. It is also easy to demonstrate that different wait times or different values of time produce major differences in the results. If the most uncertain parameters were replaced by probability distributions chosen to represent the effects of sampling, measurement, or forecast errors (see Openshaw 1979b), then the range of results can vary between one and two orders of magnitude. For example, suppose all the uncertain constants are assumed to be uniformly randomly distributed over a range of plus or minus 5 per cent of the current values, then the results have been observed to vary in a range of −18 to +20 per cent around the average. If an error of plus or minus 10 per cent is assumed, then the range is −26 to +84 per cent. Now it is possible, even likely, that many of the critical parameters possess levels of uncertainty of around 50 to 100 per cent. It is suggested, therefore, that neither the current Department of Transport model nor the equivalent PTE alternative are likely to be useful for a rigorous assessment of public transport investment programmes. A variety of more robust methods already exist and modifications based on some of these techniques should be used to incorporate risk and uncertainty effects into the economic evaluation process (Openshaw and Ramsey 1980).

8.6 Conclusions

The success of a major public transport investment may be evaluated in terms of the original objectives or judged by the extent to which it continues to render good service in changed circumstances. Tyneside was clearly a good location for a Metro experiment. The geography of the conurbation, bisected by a deep valley with infrequent crossings and with its main service centre lying west of the geographical centre, favours a public transport system based around a rapid transit core. This was appreciated when the first railways were built in the 1840s; the legacy of those decisions provides a ready-built route for the Metro of the 1970s and reduced its capital costs significantly. In the broadest terms the promise of a public transport system providing reasonable accessibility within Tyneside to those who lacked mobility by private car has been achieved. Although the Metro's contribution to the ridership of the public transport system is not as great as had been forecast, it has enabled the later development of an integrated transport system on a much more comprehensive scale than was conceived in the early 1970s.

A more detailed reworking of some of the original forecasting models shows the extent to which they depended on predictions of future travel demand. The Tyne Wear Plan (Voorhees 1972d) produced a remarkably pessimistic forecast of population and employment numbers in the early 1980s, but assumed that the 1981 population would be relatively wealthy in terms of 1970 living standards, that it would collectively own nearly twice as many cars, and would have much higher propensities to travel on public transport. The effects of the unforeseen economic recession and unemployment of the 1970s has been to depress the demand for public transport and indirectly, by drastically slowing down the growth of car ownership, to postpone the benefits of public transport as a means of reducing road congestion and as an alternative investment to building more road space.

Circumstances have changed in one other important aspect. The consensus of the late 1960s, clearly expressed in the 1968 Transport Act, was that public transport was to a considerable extent a merit good and that both the capital and running costs should be partially defrayed through national and local taxation. It was also tacitly assumed that the revenue from the taxation of a richer community would increase in real terms. In combating the recession, the national governments elected in 1979 and 1983 have sought to limit public expenditure at national and local levels and rely increasingly on national norms as a guideline for what can be spent locally. The Metro was seen as an opportunity to forestall a movement towards private transport resulting from a deterioration in public transport services, in the specific context of low car ownership on Tyneside. It can be argued that the imposition of national norms remove any flexibility of response to the differing economic and social circumstances experienced by various conurbations. Moreover, if the allowable public transport subsidies are set too low, then a downward spiral of falling ridership and declining service coupled with increasing road congestion and demands for more road investments could be precipitated. The removal of the economic context within which the Metro was designed to operate would clearly reduce its efficiency and threaten its future economic viability. This situation is not improved by the failure of available economic evaluation methods to give proper regard to the kinds of advantages offered by an integrated Metro system.

The conclusion is that the Tyneside Metro was a worthwhile investment but that its worthiness cannot be proved by the economic assessment methods that were used, or more precisely it can be, but the results are almost certainly wrong! A similar conclusion applies to the current debate about the best level of public transport subsidy. The government-preferred social cost-benefit analysis model is currently highly unsatisfactory as an evaluation tool and it is, in any case, biased against an integrated Metro bus system. Wait times on the Metro are, for example, far smaller than for buses, thus in cost-benefit analysis terms it is frequently possible to increase benefits by transferring resources from the Metro to reduce bus wait times. However, it is important to put Metro in context. It cost about £300 million over a 10-year period and that is not much by modern standards. It is true that it is a direct benefit to only a minority of public transport users with, in 1982, 77 per cent of all public transport trips exclusively by bus, 4 per cent by Metro only, and 19 per cent involving bus and Metro stages. The Metro also offers no benefits to the people of Sunderland, which is the largest of the five Districts in Tyne and Wear County, who are nevertheless subsidising Metro users from their rates. The planned demise of Tyne and Wear County as an administrative unit is a major threat to the future viability of the Metro with the prospect of a major change in financial support for it. A similar problem might also arise if public transport and road investment programmes were to compete for the same sums of money.

Despite these and other problems, the existence of Metro has had some major beneficial but perhaps non-quantifiable effects on the area. A high level of public transport usage has been retained and it offers a considerable degree of mobility within the Tyneside labour market. Both are major advantages for an area of high unemployment and low incomes. However, the full impact of the Metro has not yet been studied or identified (see for example, Transport and Road Research Laboratory 1979, Fullerton 1982) because the system is not yet fully operational. In any case it still may not be possible to identify a 'real Metro effect' because the changes involved are marginal and the area is currently in the throes of a major economic recession. Nevertheless, given the suspicion that various planning and possibly non-quantifiable social benefits do exist, then it would be sensible to give the Metro the benefit of any remaining doubts and adopt policies which would seek to make the most of what is an unique asset for Tyneside. At a capital cost of about £5 million per km the Tyneside Metro was one of the cheapest rapid transit systems in the world to build.

References

Department of Transport (1982), *Urban Public Transport Subsidies: An Economic Assessment of Value for Money* (Department of Transport Technical Report, London).
Department of Transport (1982), *Circular 1/83* (London).
Fullerton, A.J. (1982), *Shopping Travel Patterns in Tyne and Wear: A Before Metro Profile* (Crowthorne, TRRL Report 1045).

Martin and Voorhees Associates (1976), *Review of Tyneside Rapid Transit Economic Evaluation* (MVA, London).

Openshaw, S. (1979a), 'Alternative methods of estimating spatial interaction models and their performance in short term forecasting', in C.P.A. Bartels and R.H. Ketellaper (eds.), *Exploratory and Explanatory Statistical Analysis of Spatial Data* (Martinus Nijhoff, Boston).

Openshaw, S. (1979b), 'A methodology for using models for planning purposes', *Environment and Planning A*, Vol.11, pp.879–96.

Openshaw, S. and Ramsey, J.B.H. (1980), 'A method for assessing the risks in making transportation investments due to sampling and modelling errors', in *Proceedings of Transportation Planning Practice Meeting* (PTRC, London).

Passenger Transport Executive (1983), *Tyne and Wear Public Transport Plan 1984/5–1986/7* (Tyne and Wear County Council, Newcastle).

Starkie, D.N.M. (1976), *Transportation Planning Policy and Analysis* (Pergamon, Oxford).

Transport and Road Research Laboratory (1979), *Tyne and Wear Public Transport Impact Study: Study Definition Report* (TRRL SR 478, Crowthorne).

Tyne and Wear County Council (1982), *Structure Plan Annual Review* (Tyne and Wear County Council, Newcastle).

Tyneside Passenger Transport Executive (1972), *Application to the Department of the Environment for Infrastructure Grant* (Newcastle).

Voorhees, A.M. and Associates (1970), 'Method of economic evaluation', *Technical Memorandum 49* (Voorhees, London).

Voorhees, A.M. and Associates (1972a), *North Tyne Loop Study* (Voorhees, London).

Voorhees, A.M. and Associates (1972b), Evaluation of alternative strategies, *Technical Memorandum 63* (Voorhees, London).

Voorhees, A.M. and Associates (1972c), *Tyneside Rapid Transit Analysis, Technical Report* (Voorhees, London).

Voorhees, A.M. and Associates (1972d), *Tyne Wear Plan: Transport Plan for the 1980's* (Voorhees, London).

Wilson, A.G. (1981), *Catastrophe Theory and Bifurcation* (Croom Helm, London).

9 Forecasting rail freight flows in Britain

D. E. PITFIELD AND A. E. WHITEING

9.1 Introduction

Road transport dominates all other modes in the carriage of freight in Britain, and this dominance is long-standing. Table 9.1 illustrates the position since 1971 and shows that in terms of goods lifted rail only accounts for about 10 per cent of the total by comparison with road's share of 80 per cent. This pattern is echoed in terms of goods moved where the rail share by 1981 was just under 12 per cent in contrast to road's 65 per cent. Hence attempts to model freight, as a precursor of a forecasting exercise, have concentrated on road freight flows. If future flows can be determined with a reasonable degree of accuracy, then more informed decisions can be made on the allocation of invest-ment in the public sector in general and in transport infrastructure in particular.

However, rail freight is an important contributor to British Rail's revenue, comprising 49 per cent (£504 million) in 1981. Further, in the case of some commodities, rail dominates road; for example, 54 per cent of coal and coke was moved by rail in 1981 (95 million tonnes) and this amounted to 67 per cent of all freight lifted in this group in terms of tonne-kilometres. Also, it has been argued, especially in the case of trunk hauls, that the government might significantly influence future modal split in favour of rail for the sake of environ-mental issues.

It is therefore idle to expect any forecasting exercise to yield implementable policy prescriptions if such an exercise is confined to road freight and, besides, rail freight is important to British Rail. Yet recent research has suggested considerable difficulties in even adequately modelling the interzonal flows of freight in Great Britain by road. The papers by Pitfield (1978a), Gordon (1979), Pitfield (1979) and Gordon and Pitfield (1981) report the results of applying a conventional doubly-constrained gravity model to such data; provide comments on the model's efficiency and tentatively conclude that shortcomings with the data and a misspecification of the model are jointly responsible for biased results with an attendant overall poor level of goodness-of-fit. Indeed, the latest research shows that respecification of the model in multistream form (as reported in Gordon and Pitfield 1981, and Pitfield 1982) can do much to eliminate intrazonal bias and improve overall goodness-of-fit.

Table 9.1 Modal split of freight traffic
in Britain, 1971–81

| Mode | Million tonnes lifted | | | (%) | | |
	1971	1976	1981	1971	1976	1981
Road	1582	1516	1339	84.1	84.5	82.0
Rail	198	176	154	10.5	9.8	9.4
Coastal shipping	47	44	60	2.5	2.5	3.7
Inland waterway	5	5	5	0.3	0.3	0.3
Pipeline	49	53	75	2.6	2.9	4.6
Total	1881	1794	1633	100	100	100
Mode	Billion tonne-km moved			(%)		
	1971	1976	1981	1971	1976	1981
Road	85.9	95.6	97.1	64.7	67.4	64.3
Rail	21.8	20.4	17.5	16.4	14.4	11.6
Coastal shipping	21.4	20.0	27.0	16.1	14.1	17.9
Inland waterway	0.1	0.1	0.1	0.1	0.1	0.1
Pipeline	3.6	5.7	9.3	2.7	4.3	6.1
Total	132.8	141.8	151.0	100	100.3	100

Source: Department of Transport, *Transport Statistics Great Britain 1971–1981*

Yet applying conventional distribution models with power deterrence functions to rail freight flows produces far worse simulations. Improved results can be obtained by specifying a better relationship within the model between costs and distance and by also respecifying the model in multistream form. However, the resulting absolute levels of explanation still leave much to be desired. The next section of this chapter summarises this research effort before; in section 9.3 the organisation of the rail freight business in Britain is examined. It seems that for this sector of the freight market, which is characterised by sparse matrices for a few commodities, that there is no substitute for specific knowledge of the market and contractual arrangements. Consistently specified models, where only the parameter values are allowed to vary across commodities, do not provide a sufficient base to cater for the variation inherent in the data. In fact, it is arguable if any globally specified tractable model could cope with the situation.

Not only does the nature of rail freight business argue against the application of distribution models, but again in comparison with road freight, useful generation models are difficult to obtain. Benheddi (1980) explores in detail the derivation of statistically robust models for road freight by commodity, but is forced to speculate on the way in which improvements to rail freight generation models may be sought. This work is also summarised in section 9.2, for it seems that the difficulties of this modelling effort are also largely explained by the nature of the rail freight market.

Section 9.4 concludes the chapter by speculating on the role of models and forecasting techniques in guiding investment in rail infrastructure, particularly as it is commonly subject to joint-use by passenger and freight demand.

9.2 Modelling rail freight movements

9.2—1 The data

The information on interzonal freight flows used in the modelling exercises was compiled by British Rail (1975) as part of its long-term strategic planning studies. The rail freight flow data were obtained as a by-product of British Rail's accounting system and, as such, represents a 100 per cent sample. This was allocated to a commodity classification based on CSTE equivalents (Economic Commission for Europe 1965) and to a zonal system constituting mainland Great Britain taking up 134 zones based on administrative areas. Figure 9.1 illustrates these zones and their centroids. A distance matrix was derived for this same set of zones based on intercentroid road mileages, whereas intrazonal

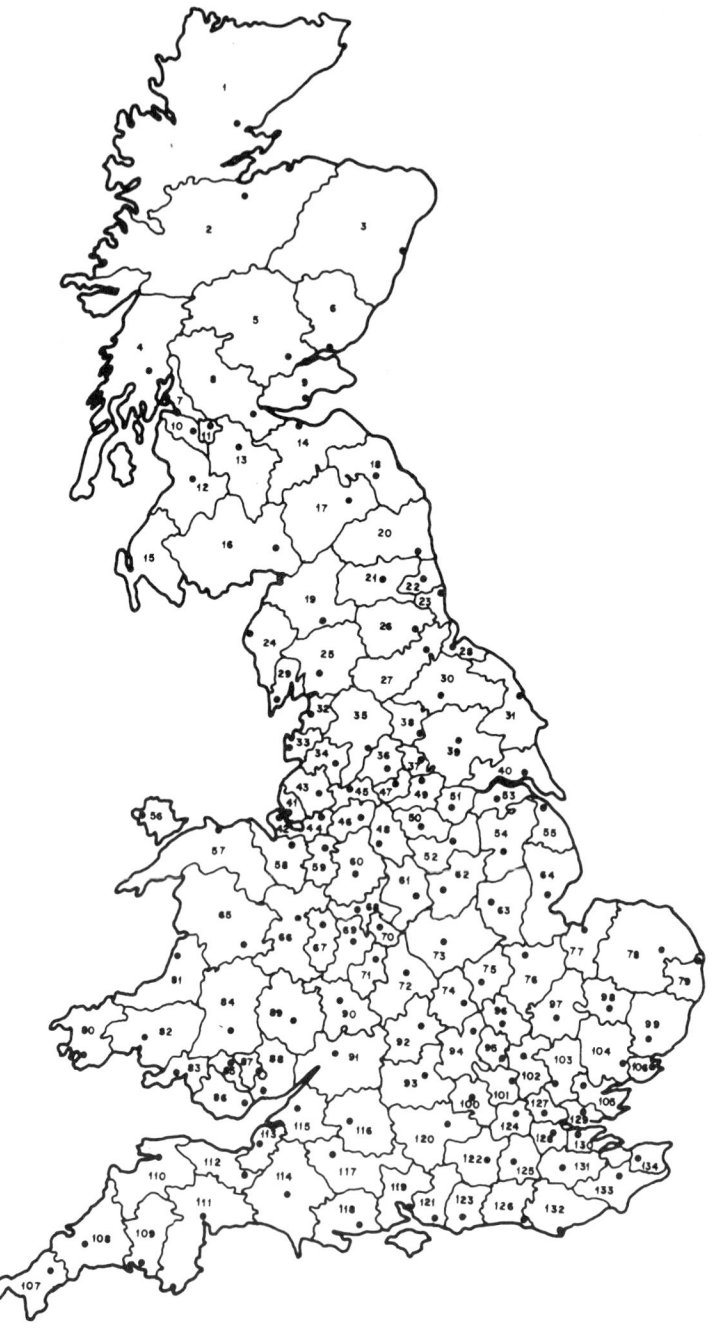

Figure 9.1   Freight traffic zones and centroids

distance was based on an analysis of total within-zone ton miles and total within-zone tonnage moved. Further information on the data can be found in Pitfield (1978b) and Pitfield (1977). It should be noted here, however, that basing distance estimates on road mileages immediately imparts a bias to any study of rail freight movements where the distance matrix is used as a data input, in particular when distribution models are estimated.

Detailed examination of rail freight flows for all 30 commodity groups is not provided in this chapter, partly because of constraints on space but mostly because the problems can be amply illustrated by the examination of a few commodity groups. In turn, it seems sensible to select these groups on the basis of some intuitively appealing criteria. In the first place, it could be argued that those commodity groups that contribute significantly to total rail flows by volume should be examined. The top nine by tonnage and their ton-mileage for 1972 are shown in Table 9.2. Table 9.2 also indicates in volume terms which groups are important in the sense that a large proportion of the total carried by road and rail modes together is carried by rail. These nine commodities account for 92.1 per cent of rail flows; that is, the other 21 commodity groups account for only 7.9 per cent of the total rail flows by volume. Further, the commodities where rail has an important market share and where ton-mileage is high are also covered by these groups. Consequently, the research reported in the following sections commenced with the objective of focusing on rail flows for these commodity classes despite the fact that a full variation in types of product is not covered, for example, manufactured products for final demand or food. Further, the spectrum of variation in value/ weight ratios is also not covered by this sub sample. Nevertheless, from the point of view of rail infrastructure investment it can be argued that it is principally important to explain (and ultimately to forecast) those flows that are important to rail and these nine commodities meet that criterion.

9.2—2 Generation models: results

The first steps in the sequential modelling framework leading to freight flow forecasts is concerned with explaining the originating (O_i) and terminating (D_i) tonnages by zone for each commodity. At the zonal level, the problem of potential explanatory variables is first encountered and in this chapter, the following variables are employed. Firstly, resident population is available, based on local authority estimates, as the zones depicted in Figure 9.1 are made up of local authority areas. Secondly, dummy variables reflecting whether the zone in question had a sea port that might influence O_i and D_i were used. Thirdly, resident population might be expected to serve the purpose of explanation less well when commodities are being studied, the demand for which is not directly a function of population. In these cases, employment in the industrial group might be expected to yield a better performance and so census data was adjusted to the appropriate areal basis with some adjustments in addition to match the SIC and MLH groups with those used in the freight data. Principal component analysis on SIC orders was also used in this context to identify employment variables that represented a significant component well so that they could be used as explanatory variables in a step-wise regression procedure (see Benheddi 1980 for further details).

Table 9.2   Aggregate indicators of the importance of
rail freight movements by commodity group

Commodity		Rail flows as a % of total rail flows	Rail flows as a % of total road and rail flows	Ton-miles	
code	Description			millions	rank
1	Coal + coke	55.9	49.7	5270.8	1
23	Fuel oil	10.4	20.4	1902.8	2
4	Ores	7.8	82.2	606.5	5
15	Earths + stones	6.3	3.6	974.2	3
2	Steel	5.5	20.0	949.1	4
7	Scrap	1.9	19.7	270.9	9
20	Cement	1.8	9.5	353.5	6
8	Waste	1.4	10.5	212.0	13
5	Lime	1.1	100.0	216.0	12

The results of these regression equations were extremely disappointing. Indeed, the results are so poor that only the best are summarised below, and these do not happen to coincide with the nine commodity groups earlier selected for special study. The median R^2 for regressions explaining rail O_i in terms of resident population is 0.007 and for D_i the equivalent figure is 0.043. This contrasts to attempts to explain road freight generation where the respective medians are 0.332 and 0.395. Table 9.3 contains the best equations.

If dummy variables are also used to reflect whether a zone contains a port the results shown in Table 9.4 are obtained. The justification for including such a variable is simply that a zone may receive more terminating tonnage or generate more originating tonnage than is

214

Table 9.3 Originating and terminating tonnage of rail freight regressed on resident population (000s)

Dependent variables Commodity code	Description	Constant b_0	Coefficient b_1	R^2	F
	O_i (000 tons)				
29	Parcels and newspapers	−6.51	0.03	0.52	141.94
30	Milk	52.18	0.64	0.37	75.98
	D_j (000 tons)				
13	Other foods	−1.36	0.02	0.42	95.17
16	Chemicals	−2.63	0.02	0.31	59.35
30	Milk	55.83	0.63	0.42	93.70

Table 9.4 Originating and terminating tonnage of rail freight regressed on resident population (000s) and a port zone dummy variable

Dependent variables Commodity code	Description	Constant b_0	Coefficients b_1	b_2	R^2	F
	O_i (000s)					
29	Parcels and newspapers	−8.08	0.03 (135.57)	4.39 (3.23)	0.53	73.78
30	Milk	49.83	0.64 (73.68)	6.56 (0.01)	0.37	37.71
	D_j (000s)					
13	Other foods	−2.52	0.01 (90.32)	3.26 (6.81)	0.45	53.08
16	Chemicals	−3.99	0.02 (55.33)	3.82 (3.35)	0.33	31.88
30	Milk	54.76	0.63 (91.02)	2.98 (0.00)	0.42	46.50

Note: F ratios in brackets

suggested by its resident population if it is heavily involved in foreign trade. Only those equations where $R^2 > 0.3$ are reported and the port zone variable is only significant at the 5 per cent level for parcels and newspapers, other foods and chemicals which seems plausible. However, in every case, the addition to R^2 seems insignificant.

Table 9.5   Originating and terminating tonnage of rail freight regressed on employment (000s)

Dependent variables		Constant	Coefficient		
Commodity code	Description	b_0	b_1	R^2	F
	O_i (000 tons)				
1	Coal + coke	16.08	2.97	0.77	461.52
18	Fertilizers	−3.55	1.01	0.56	168.00
	D_j (000 tons)				
2	Steel	33.42	0.19	0.49	92.92
13	Other foods	−0.08	0.02	0.55	167.81
16	Chemicals	−0.30	0.02	0.51	96.28

The employment explanatory variable refers to, in the case of each of the freight flow classifications:

Freight comm. code	Employment
1	MLH 101, 261
2	MLH 311, 312
13	MLH 215−217, 229, 231, 232, 239, 240
16	MLH 271−274, 277, 279
18	MLH 278

Redefining the port zone variable to indicate important ports where the ratio of imports to O_i or exports to D_j exceeds the national average when all modes are considered yields almost identical results. The only equation worth reporting is for terminating tonnage of commodity group 27, miscellaneous where R^2 on resident population alone was previously 0.27.

The equation is now:

$$D_j \text{ miscellaneous} = -1.97 + 0.02 \text{ Pop} + 12.37 \text{ Port zone} \qquad (9.1)$$
$$\qquad\qquad\qquad (37.88) \qquad (21.63)$$

$$R^2 = 0.35, F = 35.42$$

These results are generally too poor to warrant the investigation of whether the technique of ordinary least squares (OLS) regression is acceptable, for example, whether the residuals from the estimated equation are free from spatial autocorrelation or homoscedastic.

These assumptions are examined for the remaining results shown in Table 9.5. The table shows the result of regressing O_j and D_j on employment in thousands. These models have considerably improved levels of explanation but again are only worth reporting for a few commodity groups of which only two, coal and coke and steel, were earlier suggested as being flows worthy of examination from the viewpoint of rail traffic. In addition, the disturbance terms are heteroscedastic except in the case of fertilizers, although the null hypothesis of no spatial autocorrelation in the residuals is not rejected using Moran's I statistic (Cliff and Ord 1973). The results of the regressions on SIC order employment were also generally poor. The best models were derived for originating flows of coal and coke, scrap, and parcels and newspapers. These attained R^2s of 0.79, 0.56 and 0.73 respectively. The next best models were obtained for terminating tonnages of coal and coke, steel, alloys, pig iron, other foods, chemicals and fuel oil. These models yielded R^2s in the range 0.35–0.49 with, in most cases, only one significant explanatory variable.

9.2–3 *Generation models: possible improvements*

Benheddi (1980) concluded his treatment of rail freight generation by speculating on some means by which better explanations could be obtained and experimented with two of these suggestions. The first of these concerned transforming the data to reflect the fact that rail freight is concentrated on specific industries and areas so that the spatial distribution of the dependent variable is not normal but positively skewed and leptokurtic. However, logarithmic transformations of the data did not help.

The second avenue explored was to weight the employment explanatory variables on the basis that if rail was used for some proportion of industrial output being shipped from a zone, then it is logical to only use a proportion of the total employed in the relevant industrial groups by zone. Canonical correlation analysis was used to relate originating freight by commodity group against the 24 SIC orders dealing with manufacturing employment. An index was then derived from this analysis as:

$$g_i = \sum_k E_i^k / \sum_n E_i^n \qquad (9.2)$$

where the numerator represents the sum of employment over the k industries that load significantly on the canonical vector and the denominator is the sum of employment in all industries present at location i. However, using g_i as a weight to the relevant employment variable did not yield better regression results.

Overall, the 'flat' regressions (Epperson et al. 1980; Goldberger 1964) are the result of the high frequency of zero observations of O_i and D_j, for example, in some cases no more than 15 of the 134 zones have a non-zero entry. Attempts to improve the explanations by transformations, weighting or adding further explanatory variables are not likely to be successful. In these circumstances, Tobit analysis has been suggested, but to convert the data to binary form seems to represent a loss of information. A better course to explore in the future is the abandonment of models for each commodity group that are based on all the zones, in favour of the application of Q-mode factor analysis which may be used to identify significant zones and commodities. In this way, regression models may be produced for each of the significant commodities for the significant zones. However, a less mechanistic route to the same conclusion is provided by a specific knowledge of the organisation of rail freight business.

9.2–4 Distribution models: results

Distribution models of rail freight traffic are also relatively poor in comparison with road-based models and the latter are far from perfect. The transportation problem of linear programming and the doubly-constrained gravity model using a power deterrence function were used by Pitfield (1978a). The familiar transportation problem primal may be written as:

$$\text{Minimise } C = \sum_{i=1}^{m} \sum_{j=1}^{n} T_{ij} c_{ij} \qquad (9.3)$$

$$\text{subject to } \sum_{j=1}^{n} T_{ij} = O_i, \, i = 1, 2, \ldots m \qquad (9.4)$$

$$\sum_{i=1}^{m} T_{ij} = D_j, \, j = 1, 2, \ldots n \qquad (9.5)$$

$$\text{assuming } \quad T_{ij} \geqslant 0 \text{ for all } i, j \qquad (9.6)$$

where T_{ij} = predicted flow from zone i to zone j

$\quad\quad c_{ij}$ = cost of transport between i and j (in these results represented by distance, d_{ij})

$\quad\quad O_i$ = total actual flows originating in zone i

$\quad\quad D_j$ = total actual flows terminating in zone j

$\quad\quad$ m = number of originating zones

$\quad\quad$ n = number of terminating zones

The doubly-constrained gravity model with a power deterrence function may be written as:

$$T_{ij} = A_i\, O_i\, D_j\, d_{ij}^{-\beta} \tag{9.7}$$

$$\text{where } A_i = \left[\sum_{j=1}^{n} D_j\, B_j\, d_{ij}^{-\beta} \right]^{-1} \tag{9.8}$$

$$B_j = \left[\sum_{i=1}^{m} A_i\, O_i\, d_{ij}^{-\beta} \right]^{-1} \tag{9.9}$$

Calibrating these models on rail data (the calibration methods are described in Pitfield 1978a) yields the results of Table 9.6. This shows the goodness-of-fit achieved for some of the commodities suggested in section 9.2–1. The mean of the standardised root mean square statistics (R^*_{MS}) for the more efficient gravity model is 15.24, and this compares to a mean of 6.03 when the same model is used to predict flows of 28 commodities moving by road for the same year. Both sets of results are disappointing, but especially that for rail flows.

Table 9.6 Goodness-of-fit of transportation problem and gravity model predictions of selected commodities moved by rail

Commodity		Transportation problem R^*_{MS}	Gravity model ($d_{ij}^{-\beta}$) R^*_{MS}
Code	Description		
1	Coal plus coke	11.55	7.62
2	Steel	14.53	8.05
4	Ores	11.41	11.30
5	Lime	24.16	23.68
15	Earths plus stones	15.48	15.21
23	Fuel oil	17.49	10.33

In the case of road flows, experiment with alternative deterrence functions, such as the negative exponential $(\exp -\beta d_{ij})$ failed to produce superior results. If such a deterrence function is used for rail, then the results of Table 9.7 are obtained; to date, exponential function based gravity model results are only available for four commodities. Goodness-of-fit as indicated by R_{MS}^* is improved for coal and coke, earths and stones and fuel oil, but not for steel. In general this result might well be expected as a flatter decay of traffic over distance is more likely for rail than for road and besides, rail traffic data may be less likely to conflate the movement types discussed by Gordon and Pitfield (1981). However, the P_{EP} statistic which shows the percentage error in prediction off the matrix diagonal, is still large especially in the case of coal and coke and so a multistream model may be appropriate to correct this bias (see section 9.2−5).

Table 9.7   Goodness-of-fit indicators of gravity model (exponential deterrence) predictions of selected commodities moved by rail

Code	Commodity Description	R_{MS}^*	P_{EP}
1	Coal plus coke	7.53	17.20
2	Steel	9.71	6.46
15	Earths plus stones	13.99	−0.22
23	Fuel oil	9.51	−2.28

9.2−5 Distribution models: possible improvements

Poor goodness-of-fit and a high P_{EP} statistic indicate that a conventional single stream gravity model may be inappropriate to a data set on distribution. This is because such a model may be unable properly to account for the distributive and trade flows with their different susceptibility to distance impedance. In these cases, a model that recovers estimates of each stream and provides separate parameter estimates for each stream may improve overall fit and reduce bias.

For three of the four commodities dealt with in Table 9.7, Table 9.8 provides the results of a two-stream gravity model. This model takes the form:

$$T_{ij} = \sum_{s} A_i^s B_j^s O_i^s D_j^s \left[\exp(-\beta d_{ij}) \right]^s \tag{9.10}$$

where the elements of equation (9.10) are the conventional components of a doubly-constrained gravity model but where the summation is over the number of different streams of movement denoted by the superscripts s. In the application here, the two streams (trade and distribution) are distinguished by experimentally varying the cut-off distance and estimating for each cut-off, flows above the cut-off first, and then modelling the positive residuals of the whole flow matrix as the distributive stream. The calibration of such a model is discussed in Gordon and Pitfield (1981).

Table 9.8   Goodness-of-fit indicators and parameter estimates
for two-stream gravity model predictions of
selected commodities moved by rail

| Commodity | | | | Cut-off | Coefficients | | Flow | |
Code	Description	R^*_{MS}	P_{EP}	distance	β^T	β^D	Trade	Distrib.
1	Coal + coke	7.41	8.06	25 miles	0.035	0.96*	83721	33554
2	Steel	7.27	0.11	25 miles	0.012	0.96*	8748	2527
23	Fuel oil	10.76	0.62	13 miles	0.025	0.96*	22162	108

* This is the maximum allowable parameter value without causing underflow in the computer algorithm.

These results are illustrated for the empirically determined cut-off distance that minimises P_{EP}, although it is clear that in two of the three cases an improved overall fit over the previous best-fitting model is also obtained. A fuller discussion of these results would note the perversity of the parameter estimates for one of these commodities and the lack of stability in the others as cut-off distances are varied. However, at this preliminary stage it simply requires noting that these best models still compare unfavourably with the best estimates of road flows as far as fit is concerned. For 28 commodities moving by road the mean P_{EP} is 10.24 and R^*_{MS} is 4.43 and for the same three commodities examined here the figures are 10.19 and 3.83 respectively for road flows. Although the bias is less, the overall goodness-of-fit is appreciably worse.

What other improvements to these models are possible? Firstly, analagous to the road flows case, it may be that alternative deterrence functions need to be incorporated in the two stream model either side of the cut-off distance, for example a Tanner function, and that these functions should vary with value/weight ratios. Secondly, as previously noted, the distance data used in the model calibration is based on road freight flows and, as discussed elsewhere, is likely to be biased anyway. Thirdly, Q mode factor analysis at the generation stage might reduce the scale of the modelling exercise of zones and commodities to be studied. Global models for all commodities where only parameter values vary are not likely to provide the most efficient predictions.

However, whether such suggestions lead to improved models of rail freight or not, it is clear from an examination of the organisation of rail freight business in Britain that there is no substitute for better data. Such a plea has frequently been made in the cause of improving models and understanding of road freight; in the rail case, this plea is also appropriate and extends to an understanding of the way in which rail traffic comes to be and, as far as forecasting is concerned, what significant trends are discernible in the organisation of the rail freight business. Further, if judgements are ultimately to be made on infrastructure requirements, then the degree to which investment needs are freight specific needs to be determined, as does the likelihood of these changing over time. These topics are the focus of the next section.

9.3 Organisation of the rail freight business

Freight movements on British Rail have several notable characteristics. The first of these is that the rail freight business is dominated by large-scale regular movements of bulk materials, in a relatively small number of commodity groups. The second characteristic is that within most of these commodity groups a comparatively small number of well-defined origins and destinations account for a large proportion of rail traffic, which is typically provided by relatively few freight customers. For these customers, rail freight is normally used for movements of raw materials, or at an intermediate stage in the production or distribution process, rather than as a means of final delivery. Even though rail freight facilities exist to accommodate wagon-load or smaller consignments of containerised freight, most of the important users prefer to provide freight in train-load consignments. For such traffic, many users have made substantial private investments in rail freight infrastructure and equipment, for instance in sidings and rolling stock and this entails some form of commitment to rail with consequences for modal split. A final, related, consideration is that business between British Rail and · its major customers is normally subject to long-term contract, and relatively few rail freight consignments are arranged on an individual basis. These characteristics plainly have implications for any generation and distribution models of rail freight flows, and so need to be explored in greater detail.

Total rail freight tonnage has declined slowly in recent years, from 209 million tonnes in 1970 to around 170 million tonnes in 1979. The commodity composition of rail freight tonnage, however, varied remarkably little over this decade, as can be seen from Table 9.9. Throughout the period, the heavy bulk commodities of coal, coke, iron and steel have provided 70—75 per cent of all traffic, and other bulk traffic has accounted for most of the remainder.

Table 9.9   Commodity composition of rail freight traffic, (1970—79)

Commodity group	1970	1975	1979
		(% of tonnes)	
Coal and coke	54.7	55.6	55.2
Iron and steel	19.3	14.7	14.8
Agricultural, food and drink	1.8	1.0	0.8
Earths and stones	6.5	8.6	8.7
Building materials	2.1	2.9	2.7
Oil and petroleum	8.8	9.8	9.6
Chemicals and allied products	2.2	2.4	2.5
Motor vehicles and components	1.5	0.6	0.5
Miscellaneous and unallocable		0.5	0.7
Freightliners	3.1	3.8	4.5
	100	100	100

Source: Department of Transport, *Transport Statistics Great Britain 1970—1980*

One notable change which has taken place over this period is the steady increase in the proportion of rail freight tonnage that is moved in complete train-load consignments. In 1970 only 55 per cent of tonnage was moved in this way, but by 1980 the proportion had increased to 88 per cent. The decline in carryings of iron and steel relative to commodities such as earths and stones, oil and petroleum, chemicals and building materials may be expected to promote an increase in train-load traffic, but not to the extent actually experienced given the comparatively small changes in commodity mix. This trend must then be ascribed either to revised methods of railway operation for existing traffic, or to changes in the types of freight carried within each broad group of commodities. To disentangle these effects and to determine their relative importance it is necessary to look more deeply at the recent history of rail freight in each of these commodity groups.

Coal and coke remains the most important commodity group for rail freight, accounting for more than half the total tonnage and generating half the total rail freight revenue in 1979, despite having a short average length of haul when compared with other commodities (Table 9.10). There have been fundamental changes in the rail transport of coal, however. A sustained decline in wagon-load coal traffic, operated in the traditional manner with slow trunk hauls between large marshalling yards and local trip workings for collection and delivery, is associated with the reduced use of coal for industrial purposes and for household consumption. This reduction has been off-set by a substantial increase in the rail transport of coal from collieries to power stations. In 1978, British Rail delivered 61 million tonnes of coal to power stations, representing 65 per cent of all coal moved by rail. Traditionally, collieries have possessed extensive rail siding systems, but these were designed for wagon-load working. Accordingly, recent developments have been associated with modernisation, consolidation and rationalisation in the coalfields and in the electricity supply industry. Smaller pits and power stations have closed and have been replaced by a smaller number of much larger installations, capable of handling high volumes of train-load traffic. High rates of train utilisation can be achieved by application of the principles of 'merry-go-round' operation, whereby marshalling is unnecessary and trains need not stop even during loading and unloading. This train-load traffic is worked under long-term contract for the Central Electricity Generating Board, with British Rail providing rolling-stock as well as traction. The modernisation of rail transport of coal, which is clearly related to long-term trends in patterns of energy consumption, has radically altered the pattern of distribution in this commodity group. Flows are now larger, and operate between a limited number of distinct origins and destinations, but the pattern of distribution varies considerably even over short periods, due to changing patterns of imports and exports, stock-piling at power stations and other factors.

Coal is responsible for a significant proportion of the total change from wagon-load to train-load working, but similar trends can be seen in other commodity groups. In the case of iron and steel, for example, there has typically been a substantial amount of wagon-load rail movement of products. Recently, steel production has been concentrated on a small number of coastal locations, a factor which might be expected to reinforce this pattern of distribution, but wagon-load traffic (both traditional and modern 'Speedlink') still exists. Indeed, the introduction of modern, airbraked, high capacity wagons on a scheduled basis on a number of routes in 1976 and its marketing as 'Speed-

Table 9.10 British Rail: freight transport statistics, 1979

Commodity group	Million tonnes lifted	(%)	Million tonne-km moved	(%)	Average haul (km)	Revenue (£ m)	(%)
Coal and coke	93.5	55.2	6,788	34.1	73	218.0	50.5
Iron and steel	25.1	14.8	2,916	14.7	116	67.5	15.6
Agricultural, food and drink	1.3	0.8	546	2.7	427		
Earths and stones	14.8	8.7	2,142	10.8	145		
Building materials	4.5	2.7	740	3.7	163		
Oil and petroleum	16.2	9.6	2,633	13.2	161	125.6	29.1
Chemicals and allied products	4.5	2.5	1,004	5.1	235		
Motor vehicles and components	0.8	0.5	277	1.4	334		
Miscellaneous	1.1	0.7	280	1.4	265		
Freightliners and National Carriers	7.6	4.5	2,567	12.9	338	21.0	4.8
	169.3	100	19,893	100	117	432.1	100

Source: Department of Transport, *Transport Statistics Great Britain 1970–1980*

link' was a response to the realisation that an emphasis on train-load working could not be a success when traffic levels were inadequate. On the other hand, the policy change within the steel industry has created a small number of extremely large flows of iron-ore, transported in train-loads of privately-owned wagons. Another result of this rationalisation programme is that British Steel has maintained a number of finishing mills at inland locations. These depend on rail transport to maintain regular train-load deliveries of semi-finished iron and steel, to allow continual production whilst economising on stock-holding. British Steel is the largest rail freight customer in this commodity group, and its various traffics are subject to long-term contract. Both British Steel and private sector steel manufacturers have used government grants under Section 8 of the 1974 Railways Act to provide or improve rail freight facilities at their establishments.

Earths and stones commodities have provided good business for British Rail in recent years, but once again it is possible to identify trends that have changed the nature of rail traffic, leading to concentration of traffic on a few large customers and promoting the use of train-load working. A distinction can be made between commodities destined for use as industrial raw materials (salts, clays, industrial sands, limestone and gypsum for chemical and various other industrial uses) and materials used in the building and construction industries (stones and sands for macadam, hard-core and concrete aggregates). Traditionally, methods of railway operation for both types of materials have involved small consignments dispatched by wagon-load services, sometimes with road-rail trans-shipment at one end of the trip. In the case of materials for industrial processes, some of this wagon-load traffic still exists, though much has transferred to road transport. Train-load operations between privately owned terminals, using modern rolling-stock, have been introduced in comparatively few instances. On the other hand, rail movements of aggregate and roadstone have undergone radical transformation in recent years. Most of the old wagon-load traffic has now ended, but there has been strong growth in rail transport of stone and aggregates from large quarries to purpose-built distribution railheads. In the 1970s there were significant short-term flows connected with motorway projects and other major investments. More important is the considerable regular traffic on long-term contract which has justified substantial private investment in rail freight facilities, often with the aid of the 'Section 8' grant scheme. Rail facilities at quarries have been upgraded, company distribution depots have been established and high capacity high speed rolling stock has been obtained to permit operation of company trains. The high demand for aggregates in south-east England, and planning restrictions preventing extraction sufficient to meet this demand, have promoted longer hauls into the region, producing a substantial amount of extra traffic for rail. Thus, as for the commodity groups discussed already, there are relatively few rail flows of earths and stones, and these typically involve large tonnages between privately owned rail terminals. In this case, the pattern of distribution is relatively well-established, though tonnages tend to vary according to the state of the building and construction industries.

Cement is the most important commodity in the rail transport of building materials. Most of the relatively few producers of portland cement in Britain use rail freight for deliveries from factories to distribution depots or concrete batching plants, at least for part of their output, but the importance of rail depends on company production and distribution policies, and these range from concentration of production at a very few large plants serving wide areas to more localised production at smaller factories. The former policy creates the more favourable conditions for distribution by rail, because of the longer hauls involved. The efficient use of rail in this case depends on modern methods of company train operation, rapid loading and discharge of wagons being required to achieve satisfactory utilisation. Rail freight distribution patterns have changed slowly over time as company strategies have been affected, but as with earths and stones, tonnages can be affected by economic factors, and single large investment projects from time to time result in important rail flows outside the normal pattern of distribution.

Rail freight flows of oil and petroleum are similarly dominated by company train operation on long-term contract. Most of the major oil companies use rail for regular supplies from refineries to regional distribution centres, and some important customers such as oil-fired power stations also receive oil by rail. Oil companies were very early investors in privately owned rail freight facilities (both private terminals and rolling-stock), and the well-established distribution pattern for oil and petroleum is reflected in the long-term contracts under which their traffic is operated.

A substantial amount of rail freight transport of chemicals is train-load traffic, worked between privately owned terminals in company trains. The same is true of rail movements of motor vehicles and components. A characteristic of these commodities, however, is that they provide a substantial part of the freight carried on the network of 'Speedlink' scheduled express freight trains. This modern counterpart of the traditional wagon-load service also carries most of the rail freight in commodities in the agricultural, food and drink sector (such as grain) and in general merchandise. Some 'Speedlink' traffic is collected from and delivered to customers' private sidings at industrial premises and distribution depots, some is loaded and unloaded at the remaining

British Rail freight depots, and a considerable amount is international ferry traffic catered for by 'Speedlink' services to and from ports serving the Continent. 'Speedlink' provides a good standard of service to customers with insufficient freight to justify company train operation, as can be deduced from the sustained growth in traffic since its introduction. In 1976, 29 daily services carried just over 2 million tonnes of freight. The number of scheduled services has grown, reaching 38 in 1979, 58 in 1980 and 72 in 1981, and traffic has risen to 3.5 million tonnes per annum over this period. Some of this 'Speedlink' traffic is existing rail traffic, transferred from the rapidly-declining traditional wagon-load services, but British Rail has estimated that 25 per cent of the additional 'Speedlink' traffic was not previously carried by rail. Though still a small part of total 'Speedlink' traffic, one growth area in recent years has been in the carriage of general merchandise on contract for other operators — for example road haulage firms or national distribution companies. These companies have found that rail can offer economical trunk haulage over long distances between rail-connected distribution depots, from which local deliveries are made by road. 'Section 8' grants have been available to help provide these depots.

The 7.5 million tonnes of containerised freight carried annually by 'Freightliner' services comprises traffic in a very wide range of commodities, from bulk train-load traffic such as bricks to single consignments of manufactured goods, components, consumer goods and general merchandise. Rail transport of domestic containerised freight has grown only slowly since the 'Freightliner' system was established in the late 1960s, largely because most inland hauls are too short for economic rail transport, given that local distribution to and from container terminals is by road. On the other hand, 'Freightliner' has achieved notable growth in recent years in the rail transport of maritime container traffic, to the extent that port authorities have been willing to invest in rail container terminal facilities. Many 'Freightliner' services now connect ports with inland centres.

This discussion of the nature of rail freight transport shows that many factors must be considered when an attempt is made to forecast traffic in future years. Three conceptual stages can be identified in the forecasting procedure. Overall tonnages must be predicted, supplies and demands in different regions must be balanced in a procedure for distribution, and the resultant flows must be assigned to rail routes. Generally, it is likely that tonnages and distribution patterns will depend in part on trends in the national economy. However, as we have seen, train-load traffic is dominant for many of the commodities important in rail freight. Few companies are involved and there are relatively few traffic origins and destinations. Traffic patterns between these may or may not be stable. Specifically for this train-load traffic, distribution patterns are largely the result of the overall production, transport and distribution strategies of the firms in question. Consequently, there can be notable changes in the amount of rail traffic, and in the pattern of distribution, as company transport and distribution policies evolve. Examples have been cited in which restructuring of particular industries and changing patterns of demand have led to important changes in the use of rail transport. Moreover, even within a particular industry different firms can follow distinct alternative overall strategies and will have different rail freight requirements as a result. That is, mode choice decisions are being made in a broad framework in which production, transport and distribution costs are subject to simultaneous examination.

For particular organisations and commodities, it has been found that models can produce reasonably good results in matching modelled flows to observed, but even in this restricted use modelling procedures will not forecast possible changes over time in modal choice in the light of cost changes. Thus, long-term forecasting of train-load rail freight, depends not so much on modelling procedures or on any extrapolation of existing flows, as on detailed knowledge of the supply and demand for particular commodities and the relative costs of alternative methods of transport and distribution. In these circumstances forecasting must inevitably include qualitative analysis as well as quantification.

A further reason why conventional modelling procedures are unsuitable for forecasting the amount of rail freight traffic is connected with the method of pricing of rail services. The amount of traffic clearly depends on pricing policy. However, prices must be set with a view to inter-modal competition on the one hand and rail costs on the other hand. As a commercial service, rail freight traffic must generate revenue sufficient to cover the costs of rail-specific infrastructure as well as the direct costs of operation. Thus the price depends to some extent on the amount of infrastructure necessary to operate any specific traffic. In the long-run, however, the amount of infrastructure depends on the expected volume, which is a function of price. There is considerable two-way interaction, therefore, between pricing policy and the provision of infrastructure. One result of this is that if spare capacity exists in the short run, train-load traffic could be accepted at low rates to reflect low marginal cost, and 'Speedlink' traffic could be treated similarly if trains are running at less than full capacity. If these extra traffics are to prove worthwhile in the long run, however, any contract must be at a price that ensures that sufficient capacity can be maintained when reinvestment is required. A second result relates to traffic lost due to uncompetitive rail prices. Such losses will eventually lead to opportunities to reduce capacity on the routes affected, so that railway operating costs can be reduced. If train-load rates become uncompetitive, there will be discrete losses of large tonnages, which may by themselves produce notable excess capacity. They are most likely to occur when firms need to make renewed investments in order to continue to use rail. Rising relative prices on 'Speedlink' or 'Freightliner' services, on the other hand, will cause a more gradual and continuous reduction in traffic, but the possibilities for reduction of capacity will be discrete in this case as well. Train services will run until the revenue for the service in question falls below the threshold for economic operation, and only when the entire service has gone will it prove possible to reduce capacity; in the interim, operation of the remaining traffic will become increasingly unprofitable as it has to bear a higher proportion of track and signalling costs.

Finally, the interaction of freight and passenger traffic on infrastructure requirements needs to be considered. Typically, 'Speedlink' and 'Freightliner' are scheduled services for general freight, and the amount of traffic attracted to these services is likely to depend on general economic conditions and on the overall competitiveness of rail freight rather than on the decision-making processes of particular commercial customers. The distribution of this traffic is likely to be more diverse than that of the train-load traffic. However, the commercial remit of the rail freight business is such that the distribution pattern must be translated into an economically viable network of routes. The routes that generate traffic sufficient to consolidate into complete train-loads are likely to be the inter-city routes and the links between conurbations and the major ports, and thus the final network may not differ substantially from that of the inter-city passenger railway. As a result, a great deal of route mileage will be shared between passenger and freight services and a comparatively small amount of railway infrastructure will be freight-specific.

The decline of the traditional wagon-load freight service, partly as a result of the developments already mentioned, is another factor leading to the reduction in freight-specific infrastructure. Previously, extensive sorting and marshalling yards had to be maintained for the wagon-load services. Moreover, additional track capacity was necessary to cater for the large numbers of slow freight trains. With the reduction in the number of freight trains and the notable increase in average freight train speed it has been possible to economise in these provisions. In addition, many railway freight depots have been closed as freight traffic has become concentrated on privately owned sidings. Moreover, a significant proportion of freight trains operate at night which means that motive power can be shared with passenger trains. Thus, freight trains today, whether they be company trains, regular 'Speedlink' services or 'Freightliners', generally require less railway-provided terminal and marshalling infrastructure, and they share the tracks on the main trunk routes with each other and with inter-city and other passenger services.

In the long run, an attempt will be made to adjust track and signalling capacity on a route to the total traffic on that route, with the implication that the existence of freight traffic will call for some provision of capacity in the form of refuge sidings or additional signalling which would not be needed for passenger trains alone. Although these infrastructure requirements are due to freight, and hence their costs must be met out of freight revenue, the extent to which they are necessary is often dependent on the nature of the passenger services on the route as well as on the amount of freight traffic. In particular, high-speed passenger services produce major disparities in the running speeds of the various trains using a route, such that overtaking facilities are often required. Again, operation of freight at night, frequently desirable from a commercial point of view, will also have the advantage of reducing the amount of additional infrastructure required for freight. An apparently simple rule such as that freight revenue should cover its avoidable costs on a route is clearly not simple to practically implement, as Joy (1971) also showed.

9.4 Conclusions

It has been demonstrated that conventional models of freight generation and distribution are not very successful and, in fact, are unsuited for prediction of the demand for railway infrastructure. This is largely because tonnages and distribution patterns are heavily dependent on the policies of a comparatively small number of large rail freight users, meaning that tonnages on particular rail routes may be susceptible to discrete fluctuations over time, for instance when contracts require renewal. An appropriate methodology for forecasting future use of rail infrastructure on particular routes must first of all acknowledge the existence of the important user organisations. The nature of their transport requirements should be investigated in the light of their overall production, transport and distribution processes. Future changes in their modal choice policies can then be forecasted if it is possible to predict trends in the comparative costs of each transport mode. In this procedure, it is also important to consider the complex set of inter-relationships between the present amount of railway infrastructure, the preferred infrastructure to cater for the total traffic expected on the route (taking into account the types of traffic involved, including passenger traffic) and the need to include infrastructure charges in long-term contractual freight charges, thus affecting comparative charges by different modes and hence the balance of inter-modal competition. In short, better data is required if modelling strategies are to succeed and much of the relevant basic data may be inherently non-quantitative. A unique modelling strategy may be appropriate for each homogeneous category of flows. Further, even accurate traffic predictions and forecasts in themselves are not sufficient grounds on which to base decisions on infrastructure requirements; full knowledge of future passenger traffic is also usually required.

References

Benheddi, A. (1980), 'Multi-Regional Freight Generation Models', unpublished Ph.D. thesis, University of Loughborough.

British Rail (1975), *Freight Market Background Study Report*, mimeo, (British Rail, Strategic Planning Studies, London).

British Railways Board, *Annual Report and Accounts* (published annually) (British Railways, London).

Cliff, A.D. and Ord, J.K. (1973), *Spatial Autocorrelation* (Pion, London).

Department of Transport (1981), *Transport Statistics, Great Britain, 1970–1980* (HMSO, London).

Department of Transport (1982), *Transport Statistics, Great Britain, 1971–1981* (HMSO, London).

Economic Commission for Europe (1965), *Commodity Classification for Transport Statistics in Europe*, mimeo, (Inland Transport Committee, Economic Commission for Europe, Brussels).

Epperson, J.E. *et al.* (1980), 'Program planning with Tobit analysis — the U.S. food stamp case', *Socio-Economic Planning Sciences*, Vol.14, pp.91–5.

Goldberger, A.S. (1964), *Econometric Theory* (Wiley, New York).

Gordon, I.R. (1979), 'Freight distribution model predictions compared: a comment', *Environment and Planning A*, Vol.A, pp.219–21.

Gordon, I.R. and Pitfield, D.E. (1981), 'Separating trade and distributive flows in freight transportation models'. Paper presented to PTRC Summer Annual Meeting, University of Warwick, 13–16 July.

Joy, S. (1971), 'Pricing and investment in railway freight services', *Journal of Transport Economics and Policy*, Vol.5, pp.231–46.

Pike, J. and Gandham, B. (1980), *Review of the Commodity Flow Studies (1975–1979)*. University of Newcastle Transport Operations Research Group, Research Report no. 36.

Pike, J., Wallace, H. and Hughes, G.F. (1979), 'Inter-regional freight flow research: An appraisal of the commodity approach'. Paper presented at the 11th annual conference of the Universities Transport Studies Group, Southampton University, January 1979 (unpublished).

Pitfield, D.E. (1977), *The Freight Distribution Data*, mimeo, (Department of Transport Technology, University of Technology, Loughborough, Leicestershire).

Pitfield, D.E. (1978a), 'Freight distribution model predictions compared: a test of hypotheses', *Environment and Planning A*, Vol.10, pp.813–36.

Pitfield, D.E. (1978b), 'The volume of internal and external trade: Is Britain a closed economy?', *Regional Studies*, Vol.12, pp.665–82.

Pitfield, D.E. (1979), 'Freight distribution model predictions compared: some further evidence', *Environment and Planning A*, Vol.11, pp.223–26.

Pitfield, D.E. (1982), 'Modelling hierarchical freight flows'. Paper presented to Third European Colloquium on Theoretical and Quantitative Geography, Augsburg, 13–17 September.

Pryke, R.W.S. and Dodgson, J.S. (1975), *The Rail Problem* (Martin Robertson, London).

Whiteing, A.E. (1981), 'Freight subsidies and the environment', *Public Money*, Vol.1.

Whiteing, A.E. (1982), 'Testing the sensitivity of modal choice for bulk freight movements to a range of important variables'. Paper presented at the PTRC Summer Annual Meeting, University of Warwick, July 1982.

Part IV
Efficiency

.

10 European railway comparisons — what can we learn?

C. NASH

10.1 Introduction

Recent years have seen a renewed interest in comparisons of railway productivity in North America, inspired by the work of Caves, Christensen and Swanson (1980). Their elegant solution to the traditional problem of combining a variety of outputs and inputs in a single productivity measure avoids the full range of restrictive assumptions made in previous work on the subject (e.g. Deakin and Seward 1969) and thus leads to greatly increased confidence in the results.

In Western Europe, too, there has long been an interest in, and indeed fierce controversy over, comparisons of the performance of different rail systems (see, for instance, Munby 1962; Paul 1962; Glassborrow 1962; Pryke 1971). But here the fact that one is dealing with the rail systems of different countries, with different accounting conventions and different regulatory and competitive frameworks adds a lot of extra problems to those faced in any comparative study. In 1979, the current author was one of a joint team from British Rail and the University of Leeds which published a study of the subject follow-

* The work reported in this chapter draws heavily on work undertaken by a joint BR/Leeds University team, and on subsequent work financed by a grant by the Social Science Research Council. The author wishes to acknowledge his debt to fellow members of that team (Prof. K.M. Gwilliam and Mr K. Mason of Leeds University; Dr J.D.C.A. Prideaux, Mr P. Wicks, Mr P. Jacques and Mr F. Gunton of British Rail). He is also grateful to Mr. P. Jacques (BR) and to Mr H. Geehan (CIE) for comments on an earlier draft of this chapter. None is in any way responsible for the conclusions drawn here.

ing a direct data-gathering approach to the railways concerned (BR/ Leeds University 1979).

This chapter draws heavily on the results of that study, updated wherever possible using published statistics. Readers should be warned that the accuracy of such comparisons is always open to question due to definitional problems, and that responsibility for the interpretation of both original and new data in this chapter is solely that of the current author. Data for which no specific source is quoted has been collected direct from the railways concerned.

In the next section, we discuss the philosophy of railway cost causation underlying our interpretation of the data. Then we discuss problems in the measurement both of outputs and of inputs before presenting some labour productivity comparisons. Commercial performance in both passenger and freight sectors and overall financial performance are also considered in subsequent sections.

10.2 The structure of railway costs

The costs of operating a railway may be divided into four broad areas: (i) *train working costs*, which are the costs of provision of the train service itself (i.e. fuel, crew, maintenance and depreciation of rolling stock); (ii) *track and signalling* (operating, maintenance and depreciation); (iii) *terminals* (operating, maintenance and depreciation); and (iv) *administration*. A breakdown of costs in this form for British Rail and for the average of 10 Western European railways (Table 10.1) suggests that the first two items are dominant, accounting for respectively 44–45 per cent and 23–26 per cent of total costs, although the varying treatment of the calculation of depreciation may tend to distort the picture a little. (Most railways only depreciate at historic cost in their accounts, and the age and assumed lives of assets vary.)

Within train working costs, it is rolling stock maintenance and depreciation and train crew that are the largest items. The conventional wisdom within British Rail is that rolling stock costs are partly time and partly distance related; that is, total expenditure under this heading will depend both on the amount of rolling stock owned and on the distance it runs. (Similar results for US railroads were obtained by Meyer *et al.* 1959: Appendix B). Fuel costs clearly depend mainly on car-kilometres run for each type of vehicle, whilst train crew costs depend mainly on train kilometres run (for a given size of crew, which itself varies between types of traffic).

Turning to track and signalling costs, there is perhaps more room for debate. Clearly, one determinant of their volume is the length of route served, since this must all have a minimum of a single, low-quality track.

238

**Table 10.1   Cost structure of
Western European railways (%)**

Train Service Costs	Britain	Average of 10 European Railways[a]
Train crew	14	13
Fuel and power	4	4[b]
Traction and rolling stock maintenance	19	13
Traction and rolling stock depreciation	2	4[b]
Other train operating	5	11
Total	44	45
Track and Signalling		
Civil engineering	14	14
Signal operating	4	5[c]
Signal maintenance	4	4[d]
Electric traction equipment	1	3[e]
Total	23	26
Terminals	14	16
Administration	16	11[d]

Note: Totals do not add to 100 because of rounding.

[a] Namely Britain, West Germany, Denmark, Italy, Netherlands, Norway, Sweden, Belgium, France, Finland.

[b] Data not available for Denmark.

[c] In Denmark, Netherlands, Norway, Sweden, France and Finland signal operating is combined with terminals.

[d] Data not available for Finland.

[e] Data not available for Denmark or Finland.

Source: BR/University of Leeds (1979), p.64.

Above this minimum, the amount of track and signalling required will vary with the number of trains for which paths are required. But the relationship is not proportionate; for instance, a single track will rarely handle more than two trains each way per hour; an appropriately signalled double-track may handle up to 20–30, provided that they are operating at similar speeds. For a given amount of track, the maintenance costs and life of the track itself will also vary with the standards to which it is to be maintained (whether for passenger trains, and at what speeds) and the gross weight of trains passing over it (again, see Meyer *et al.* 1959, for US evidence).

Terminal expenses, of course, depend on the volume of traffic placed on and taken off the railway, and have long been recognised as a reason why costs do not rise proportionately with length of haul. They do, however, vary considerably with the type of traffic – e.g. bulk freight versus parcels – and long distance passengers are usually provided with more expensive facilities than short. General administration is a problem of greater proportions; it is clear that it does vary in some way with the overall size of the system being administered, but the precise nature of the relationship is difficult to specify.

Drawing together the threads of the last few paragraphs, then, we expect the total costs (TC) of running a railway to vary with the train km run (T), the car km run (C), the length of route served (R) and the number of tonnes of freight (F) and number of passengers handled (P). In each case, where there is a variation in the characteristics of the output measure concerned (types of train, car, route, freight and passengers) these need to be identified separately. Thus we may write our total cost function:

$$TC = f(T_1 \ldots T_i, C_1 \ldots C_j, R_1 \ldots R_k, F_1 \ldots F_l, P_1 \ldots P_m)$$

where the subscripts refer to the separate categories of each variable identified.

It would be useful to estimate this relationship directly. Unfortunately, it is very difficult to do so with European data. With either annual time-series data or cross-sectional data for comparable countries, one is very short of degrees of freedom. There is a lack of variability in time-series data for a single railway, whilst cross-sectional analysis is immediately confronted with the problems of differing currencies, and allowing for other external factors of topography and economic geography. In either case, factor prices have to be included as additional variables.

Given these difficulties, one is usually reduced to rather more simplistic productivity comparisons. Yet the existence of such an underlying cost function has implications for these comparisons, too.

If we make comparisons between railways, or for one railway over time, in terms of inputs per traffic unit (passenger kilometre and freight tonne kilometre, approximately weighted), what we are assuming is that there is (or should be) a proportionate relationship between the volume of traffic carried and the variables in the cost function (namely train km, car km, route km, freight tonnes and number of passengers). In other words, mean train loads, mean car loads, mean train density over the route system and mean trip length or length of haul are all assumed constant. For otherwise, cost differences would be partly explained by changes in these ratios, rather than in the underlying efficiency of the railways concerned. The issue to which we turn in the next two sections is whether, for a sample of Western European railways, constancy of these ratios is a reasonable assumption.

Before doing so, we should mention one way in which researchers have been able to mitigate the severity of this assumption. This is by an appropriate identification of different types of output within the passenger and freight sectors. Thus, for instance, mean trainloads and mean trip lengths vary much less within the suburban passenger sector than within passenger services as a whole. Similarly, a subdivision of freight traffic by commodity and by length of haul may go a long way towards solving the problem. That this is far from being a complete solution, particularly within the passenger sector, will be argued below.

10.3 The determination of mean train loads

The preceding section suggests that the mean train load achieved by a railway will be a major determinant of its unit costs. This is because firstly, track and signalling capacity requirements depend largely on the number of trains operated rather than on their size, and secondly, because some train operating costs (notably crew) are also generally invariant with train size.

Table 10.2 shows the mean loads of passenger and freight trains for twelve Western European railways for 1981 and 1971. It will be seen that the variations are enormous; in each case the largest load is more than twice the size of the smallest. Why do such differences occur?

Clearly, a major part of the explanation lies in the characteristics of the traffic handled by the various systems, and would be taken account of had we sufficient detail on the outputs produced. For instance, there is some evidence of a relationship between mean train load and average trip length or average length of haul, reflecting the fact that on longer distance services it is more worth accumulating traffic over time and for a variety of origin/destination pairs than in the case of short distances (Figures 10.1a and 10.1b). However, neither relationship is statistically significant at the 5 per cent level, and that for freight is much weaker than for passenger. (The correlation coefficients are respectively 0.61 and 0.44.) Especially in the freight sector, characteristics of particular bulk flows may make them suitable for handling in large train loads. The most extreme case of this is probably the Kiruna-Narvik iron ore trains of Swedish and Norwegian railways, which load up to 3000 tonnes, and contribute substantially to the high mean train loads of Swedish railways.

Table 10.2   Mean train loads of European railways*

	Mean Passenger Train Load (passengers)		Mean Freight Train Load (tonnes)	
	1981	1971	1981	1971
BR	91	90	217	196
CFF	136	140	251	214
CIE	120	109	136	132
DB	105	95	306	299
DSB	99	99	166	237
FS	177	167	318	267
NS	94	94	232	194
NSB	103	73	258	246
SJ	112	75	380	343
SNCB	95	132	338	310
SNCF	190	171	311	309
VR	129	90	418	307

* For key to railways in this and subsequent tables see p.269

Source: UIC, *International Railway Statistics, 1971 and 1981*

But it would be wrong to regard the explanation of differing train-loads as wholly geographical. For instance, the relatively low mean passenger train loads of Swedish railways, despite long trip lengths, arise from a conscious decision on commercial grounds to provide a regular hourly or two-hourly service in a country where the population, and hence traffic potential is low.

Similarly, service frequency is often an important part of the social obligation laid on Western European railways by their governments. This is particularly so in the high-density Netherlands, where a frequency (usually 1, 2 or 4 trains per hour) is stipulated for each type of service. It applies in vaguer terms in Britain, where British Rail is required to offer a passenger service 'comparable generally' with that provided in 1974. Moreover, mean train loads are heavily influenced by constraints on the complete closure of lightly used routes, which apply throughout Western Europe.

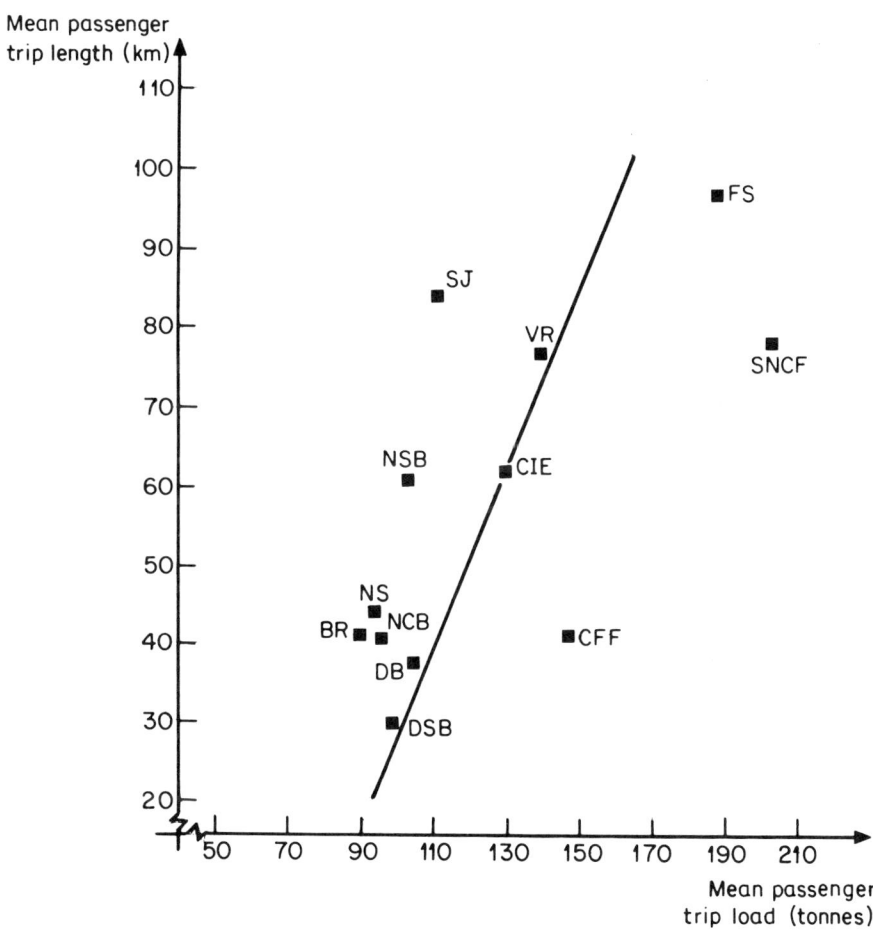

Figure 10.1a   Passenger train loads and trip length, 1981

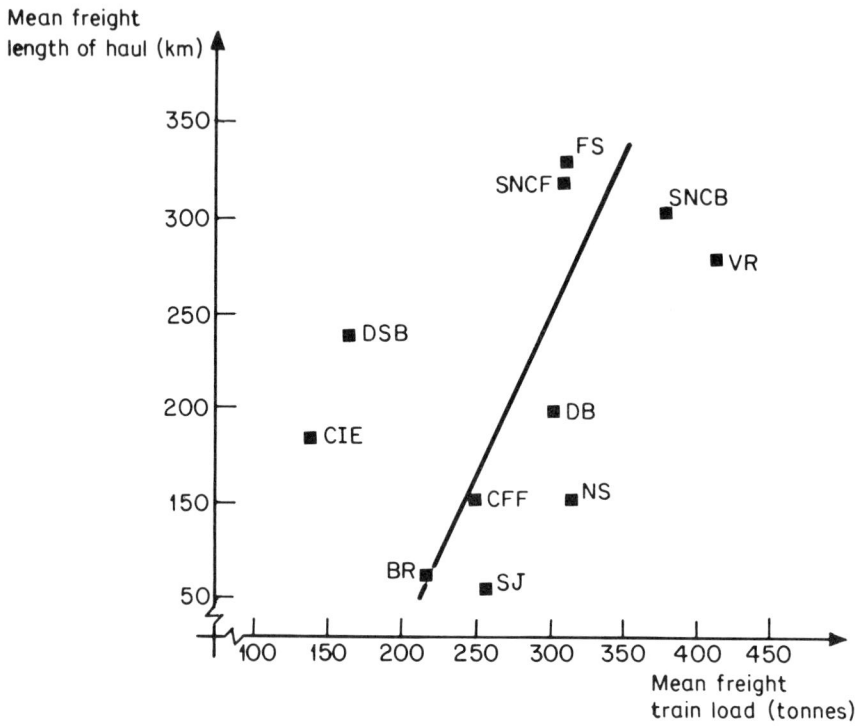

Figure 10.1b   Freight train loads and length of haul

Further evidence of the lack of a close relationship between traffic and service levels is provided by an examination of changes in traffic and in train kilometres over the decade from 1971 to 1981 (Figure 10.2a and Figure 10.2b). Experience in the passenger sector ranges from the case of Sweden, with a 69 per cent growth in passenger km for an increase of only 13 per cent in train km (this is partly the result of an explicit decision by the government to provide finance for a low off-peak fares scheme to make better use of capacity), to that of Belgium, where a 27 per cent rise in passenger train km has been accompanied by a 9 per cent loss of traffic. The correlation coefficient

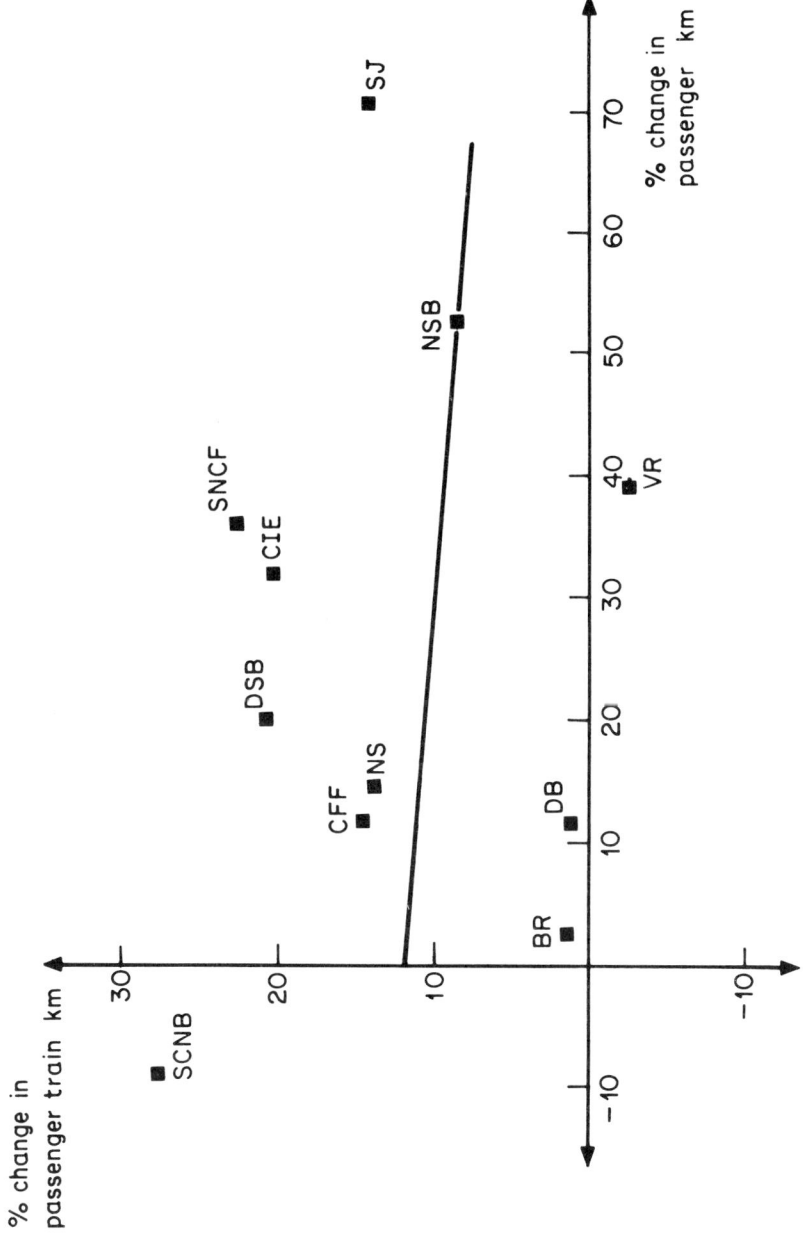

Figure 10.2a   Changes in passenger km and passenger train km, 1971−81
Source: UIC, *International Railway Staistics, 1971 and 1981*

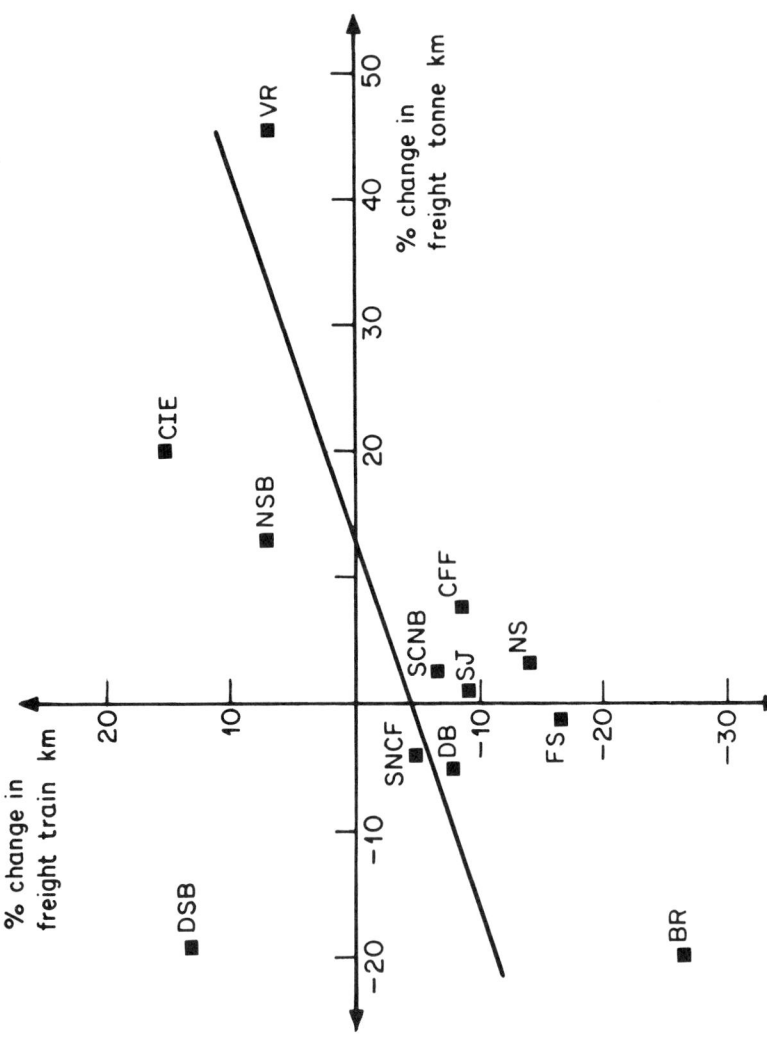

Figure 10.2b   Changes in freight tonne km and freight train km, 1971–81
Source: UIC, *International Railway Statistics, 1971 and 1981*

is in fact very small but negative, at −0.13. In the freight sector, the relationship is positive, but statistically insignificant, with a correlation coefficient of 0.44. Generally, there has been a modest increase in mean train loads over the period, but one major exception to the rule is that of Denmark. This may partly reflect changes in traffic composition but it is probably mainly the result of changes in operating practice, as smaller yards and depots are closed.

In short, then, particularly in the passenger sector, the service level provided depends on a host of geographical, commercial and social factors as well as on the amount of traffic on offer. No fixed relationship between service levels and traffic volumes can be assumed.

10.4 The measurement of railway output

The evidence of the previous section points to a large discrepancy between changes in sales of passenger km and freight tonne km and the amount of service provided. Yet we have argued previously that the service provided is the major determinant of costs. Thus we believe that it is best to judge the efficiency of railway management on the inputs used and costs incurred relative to the train service provided. Of course, the loads carried are important in measuring the commercial and social efficiency of the railway, but that is best examined as a separate issue, heavily influenced by the geographical and policy framework within which management is performing its role.

Having said this, we are left with a problem. Clearly train kilometres of different types cost different amounts to produce, and it is still to be expected that where trains are on average more heavily loaded, there the amount of rolling stock and terminal capacity, and thus staff and costs, will be higher. Should we adopt some form of weighting system, which would reflect the variation in costs by type of train kilometre?

We have some evidence on the specific (i.e. train services and terminals) staff required per train km for ten railways for a single year, 1977 (Table 10.3). In comparing passenger and freight train km there is a fair degree of consistency with freight train kilometres requiring from two to three times as many staff as passenger (the average figure is 2.2). Within the passenger sector, we only have a breakdown for three railways, and the results are less consistent (Table 10.4). For Britain, the only sector to differ significantly from the rest is the London inner suburban sector, which requires 58 per cent more staff than the sector with the highest productivity; in both France and Norway, inter-city trains require considerably more staff than other services, but the differences are nowhere near as great as those between

Table 10.3 Specific staff per million train km

	Freight and parcels	Passenger	Ratio
BR	464	189	2.45
CFF	618	158	3.91
CIE	566	260	2.18
DB	565	271	2.08
DSB		n.a.	
FS	733	330	2.22
NS	270	147	1.84
NSB	351	187	1.88
SJ		n.a.	
SNCB	548	219	2.50
SNCF	415	218	1.90
VR	588	207	2.84

Table 10.4 Specific staff[a] per million train km by type of service, 1977

	BR	SNCF	NSB
Inter-City passenger	189	269	223
Long distance commuter	165[b]	—	—
Shorter distance commuter	261[c] (194[d])	164[e]	163[f] (149[g])
Local passenger	172	156	152
Freight and parcels	464	415	351

Notes:
 [a] Train service and terminals staff as defined in Table 1.
 [b] London outer suburban services.
 [c] London inner suburban services.
 [d] Suburban services in other British conurbations.
 [e] Paris suburban services.
 [f] Oslo suburban services.
 [g] Other Norwegian commuter services.

passenger and freight. This is fortunate since published statistics give us only a simple two-way split of train kilometres. Nevertheless, we should remember that measuring passenger train service output in terms of train kilometres may work to the disadvantage of those railways – notably France and Italy – that operate a large proportion of long, heavily loaded trains. Within the freight sector, we only have evidence for Britain, but the conclusion is that the principal variable is method of working, train load working, requires much less staff than car or less than car load traffic. Again, comparisons in terms of train kilometres work to the disadvantage of railways such as Italy, with its high proportion of wagonload services.

From the small share of total cost accounted for by terminals, and the fact that in the passenger sector long-distance passengers are provided with more expensive terminal facilities than short, one would not expect length of trip or length of haul to be all that important in determining productivity. On the other hand, it may be argued that operating staff and rolling stock generally achieve higher utilisation on long distance work than on short. That this is not necessarily so is illustrated by the fact that the highest utilisation of train crew, electric locomotives, loco-hauled passenger coaches and electric and diesel multiple units in Western Europe are all achieved by Netherlands railways. It may of course be that this simply reflects an extremely high level of efficiency by the railway concerned but perhaps also a high density regular internal service lends itself even more to high productivity operation than do long-distance services.

Thus we might consider that in any productivity comparisons, the most important difference in services is accounted for if freight trains km bear from two to three times the weight of passenger train km. This may be an overstatement, however. To the extent that marginal costs for the two types of service include elements of track, signalling and administration cost, there is no guarantee that these bear the same relationship. Whilst the track capacity requirements and wear and tear imposed by heavy freight trains probably exceed those of local passenger trains, high-speed passenger trains also impose significant track and signalling costs and passenger services generally require more administration. In producing productivity indices we therefore tested the sensitivity of results to the weights adopted by calculating both unweighted train kilometres and weighted train kilometres with a weight of 0.45 applied to those in the passenger sector.

We argued in section 10.2 that as well as train kilometres, car kilometres, passengers and freight tonnes, the density of the traffic is an important characteristic which may influence the costs of carrying it. Important economies of scale in staff per train km are likely to arise from the density of train services over the route system. (Some

evidence of this in the US context was presented by Keeler 1974.)
Again, the density of service is obviously related to the geography of
the country concerned (Table 10.5), which varies from the extremely
high density of Switzerland and the Netherlands, down to the very low
densities of the Scandinavian countries and Ireland. The correlation
coefficient between train km per route km and population per square
kilometre is statistically significant at 0.81. But again, there are factors
involved other than geography. The obligation to provide high
frequency services in the Netherlands has already been mentioned,
whilst the train density of Swiss Federal Railways is raised by the fact
that many lightly used Swiss branch lines are separate organisations,
with a mixture of private and local government ownership.

Table 10.5   Train km per route km

	1981	1971	Population per sq km (1980)
BR	25.1	24.8	237
CFF	32.5	30.9	154
CIE	6.9	5.3	49
DB	21.2	20.9	248
DSB	24.5	17.7	119
FS	17.8	17.2	189
NS	38.1	32.9	347
NSB	8.5	7.6	13
SJ	8.9	8.4	18
SNCB	23.2	18.8	323
SNCF	14.6	12.4	98
VR	7.5	7.1	14

Source: Train km and route km − UIC:
*International Railway
Statistics, 1971 and 1981.*
Population per sq km −
*Transport Statistics Great
Britain, 1971–81.*

In terms of changes between 1971 and 1981, all railways have enjoyed some increases in train density, usually as a result both of growing train kilometrage and small reductions in network size. But in some cases, notably Denmark, Netherlands and Belgium, train density has increased markedly as a result of policies of improved passenger train frequencies.

Both the absolute differences in train density and the changes over time appear to be largely unassociated with overall traffic volumes and constitute a significant external factor to be borne in mind when comparing the performance of Western European railways even in terms of the inputs needed for the level of service provided.

In conclusion, then, we decided to measure railway output either as a simple level of train kilometres produced or as a weighted sum of passenger and freight train kilometres, where the weights are 0.45 and 1 respectively, but in examining results, the many provisos put forward in this section need to be borne in mind.

10.5 Measuring railway inputs

If there are problems involved in measuring railway outputs, these are as nothing compared with the problem of measuring inputs. The usual approach is to measure physical quantities of labour and fuel, and to add these to the value of materials and the value of the capital stock of the railway concerned, using as weights the share of each input in the costs of the railway. The justification for this procedure is that it is appropriate if one assumes cost minimisation, given the existence of a neoclassical production function, in which each of these four types of input may be substituted for each other.

At the outset, we may express our reservations about the appropriateness of this approach in principle. Certainly, some substitution possibilities do occur between all four of these inputs. For instance, one may substitute labour and capital for fuel and materials by running trains more slowly. There are many opportunities for labour-saving capital investment in rail operations. But, particularly in cross-sectional comparisons, it seems likely that these effects will be swamped by external differences and historical factors. A railway with a particularly high fuel consumption, or particularly high investment in infrastructure and rolling stock, is more likely to experience this because it is operating a different type of service or over difficult terrain rather than because it is substituting these inputs for others.

In any event, the practical difficulties of measuring capital stock made the approach infeasible for our study. Balance sheet valuations of capital are grossly distorted by differences in accounting conventions and in the average age of assets, whilst assembling consistent investment series proved equally daunting due to major differences in the definition of investment relative to operating expenditure. Moreover, the point must be made that much investment has not been applied in a cost-minimising fashion, because of management errors (e.g. failure to foresee shifts in the structure of demand), the desire to improve service quality and government interventions on social grounds (e.g. the massive investment in suburban rail systems in West Germany). It is hard to know what one would make of aggregate money values of capital stock of European railways even if one had them.

Thus we are thrown back on measuring the productivity of the single most important factor of production, labour. But again we must bear in mind that differences in labour productivity may reflect differences in labour-saving capital investment in previous years. In some of the most important areas where this could apply — electrification, powerbox signalling, automated level crossings — physical data can help us identify the extent of the investment.

A few other problems should be mentioned at this stage. Firstly, we do not have full information on hours of work. But in 1977, only two railways — British and Irish — were working substantial amounts of overtime. Thus it should be remembered that, when comparisons of productivity per man are made, these probably overstate productivity per man-hour for these two railways by 20—25 per cent. Secondly, railways undertake varying degrees of heavy maintenance and construction work in their workshops: we have simply excluded workshop staff from our totals. Thirdly, railways subcontract varying amounts of work to private firms. We have included all staff supplied to the railway by private companies in our totals, but this does not necessarily cover other forms of subcontracting.

10.6 Labour productivity in European railways

After this long list of provisos, let us turn to some comparative productivity statistics (Table 10.6). Clearly, one should ignore small differences, and look for explanations in terms of efficiency only where countries are believed to be reasonably comparable in other respects.

The broad conclusions are not sensitive to whether train kilometres are weighted or not, although the expected minor variations in position do occur. Britain, as a predominantly passenger railway, does best on the unweighted criteria, whilst France and Ireland appear noticeably better when train kilometres are weighted.

Table 10.6 Output, staff and productivity, 1971–81

	Unweighted train km per staff member			Weighted train km per staff member		
	1981	1971	% change	1981	1971	% change
BR	2.46	2.16	+13.9	1.36	1.27	+ 7.1
CFF	2.70	2.41	+12.0	1.66	1.54	+ 7.8
CIE	2.13	1.33	+60.2	1.40	0.88	+59.1
DB	1.99	1.66	+19.9	1.26	1.07	+17.8
DSB	2.97	2.43	+22.2	1.63	1.34	+21.6
FS	1.22	1.33	– 8.3	0.68	0.78	–12.8
NS	4.41	4.07	+ 8.4	2.29	2.19	+ 4.6
NSB	2.49	2.13	+16.9	1.55	1.33	+16.5
SJ	3.29	2.67	+23.2	2.18	1.84	+18.5
SNCB	1.67	1.63	+ 2.5	0.96	0.99	– 3.0
SNCF	2.34	1.69	+38.5	1.58	1.20	+31.7
VR	1.95	2.18	–10.6	1.29	1.49	–13.4

Note: Because BR also undertakes construction for itself and for third parties, it employs a bigger proportion of its staff in its workshops (which are operated by a subsidiary, BREL) than any other railway except CIE. For this reason, staff employed in main workshops have been excluded in this table, but there is still a risk of distortion if the balance of work between workshop and depots varies between railways.

Source: *International Railway Statistics, 1971 and 1981*

What then do we conclude?

The first point is obvious. Two railways, Netherlands and Sweden, stand out from the rest on labour productivity grounds in 1981. Interestingly, these railways are diametrically opposed in operating characteristics, the Netherlands enjoying high density operation over short distances and Sweden very low density operation over long. Switzerland and Denmark also clearly show above-average performance, whilst the worst performances are those of Belgium and Italy.

One of the major uses of productivity comparisons of this type is to enable railways to pinpoint their own areas of strength and weakness relative to current best practice. For instance, the 1979 study (BR/University of Leeds 1979) showed clearly that British and Italian railways lagged seriously behind other railways in freight train crew productivity, and that the principal reason for this is that both employ a minimum of two — and usually three — staff on a freight train, when elsewhere single-manning is common. By contrast, British and Netherlands railways had succeeded in rationalising their freight and parcels operations to the extent that marshalling and terminals staff requirements had been reduced substantially below those of other railways.

Equally interesting are the changes in productivity over time, which also reveal a very different picture from railway to railway. Most remarkable is the achievement of Irish railways, which has succeeded in climbing from its extremely poor performance of 1971 to a level ranking alongside such major neighbours as Britain and Germany. France, Denmark, Sweden, Norway and Germany have all achieved considerable advances in productivity in the decade. Progress in Norway, Switzerland, Britain and (from its very high base) the Netherlands has been slower, whilst in Belgium, productivity has stagnated and in Finland and Italy it has actually declined.

Why should there be this marked difference in performance over time? One important factor explaining differential rates of productivity growth in many sectors of the economy is the rate of growth of output in the sector concerned (e.g. Smith, Hitchens and Davies 1982). Fast growing output enables exploitation of economies of scale, minimises the problem of redundancy and requires an influx of new capital which itself may embody improved techniques.

Figure 10.3 shows that there probably is some correlation between productivity growth and output growth in our sample (at 0.48, the correlation coefficient is not quite significant at the 5 per cent level). Of course, the direction of causation could be the reverse to that suggested above, that high productivity growth leads to increased output, but given the institutional arrangements in this sector — which pose major barriers to the feedback from costs to output levels — this

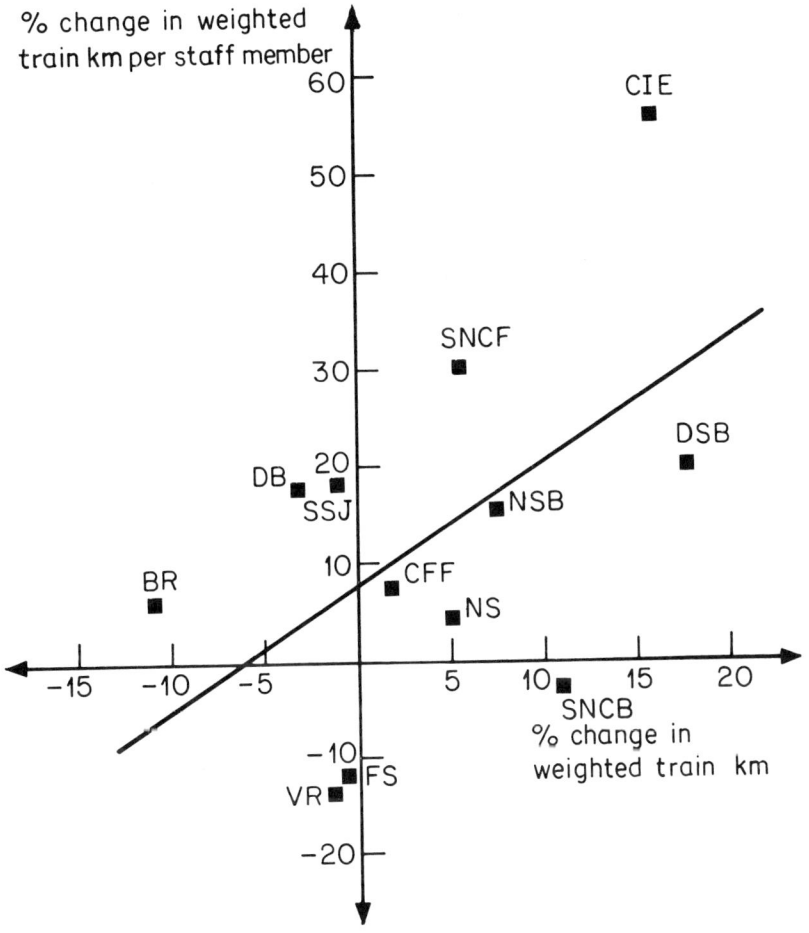

Source: UIC, International Railway Statistics, 1971 and 1981

Figure 10.3   Changes in labour productivity and output, 1971–81
Source: UIC, *International Railway Statistics, 1971 and 1981*

seems unlikely. In the light of this diagram, the productivity performance in particular of British Rail seems somewhat more creditable. It
has reduced staff almost as quickly as the high-productivity growth
railways, but given its abnormally large decline in output, this was
insufficient to raise productivity very fast. Clearly, part of the problem
of British Rail lies in the commercial sphere (see sections 10.7 and
10.8).

A second explanation might be sought in terms of differences in
capital stock. Despite the difficulties surrounding this area, we have
undertaken two simple tests of this hypothesis. The first is to compare
levels of investment spending for a single year, 1981, in the belief that
the differences do represent long-run differences in the climate for rail
investment in the various countries. The problem of an adequate
measure of output for such comparisons is very severe, since the
capital requirements of different types of service are very different,
but we decided to use simple unweighted train km. The results (Table
10.7) show relatively little variation, with Sweden and Britain somewhat low (and the cash flow difficulties of British Rail have since led
to further major reductions) and two countries — Belgium and Italy —
very high. Interestingly, far from revealing a positive relationship
between current investment and labour productivity, these railways
are currently the two least efficient! It should be noted, however, that
in Italy (as well as in the Netherlands, France and Germany), a significant proportion of the spending is on completely new routes, rather
than increased capitalisation of existing routes, whilst in Belgium, the
high spending is concentrated on track, signalling and electrification
rather than on rolling stock.

The second test is to look at the percentage of gross tonne kilometres
hauled that is handled by electric traction. There is evidence that traction and rolling stock maintenance requirements are reduced by at least
50 per cent by the use of electric traction, and this is a very significant
part of total operating cost. Table 10.7 reveals that four railways,
Britain, Denmark, Ireland and Finland, and also to a lesser extent
Belgium, suffer the disadvantage of low levels of electrification,
although this will not show up fully in our labour productivity figures
because of the exclusion of workshops staff. All the most efficient
railways are largely electrified, but so too is Italian railways!

It might also be thought that those railways with high productivity
in 1971 would have had less scope for productivity improvement in
the decade than those starting from a low base. The very slight growth
in productivity in the Netherlands from a high base, and the very fast
growth in productivity in Ireland from a low base, support this. But that this is not
the whole story is shown by the rapid growth in productivity in the
second most efficient 1971 railway, Sweden, and the fact that labour

productivity in the least efficient 1971 railway, Italy, has actually declined. Much again would seem to depend on the regime under which the railway operated. For instance, in Ireland there has been great concern at deteriorating financial performance leading to recruitment bans in a number of years, whereas in Italy the railway has actually been required to recruit unnecessary staff to relieve unemployment. Again, however, the regimes — tight budgeting control and a distinction between commercial and social activities — in Britain and Sweden have been similar for much of the decade with very different results. Of course, industrial productivity in Sweden is generally much higher than in Britain, but if this is the explanation then why is there little difference in railway productivity between Britain and West Germany? One can only conclude that a host of historical and institutional factors explain the differences; no simple explanation seems to fit.

Table 10.7   Investment and electrification

	Anticipated 1981 investment (£m at November 1980 exchange rates)	Investment per weighted train km (£)	% of gross tonne km hauled by electric traction
BR	516.9[a]	1.24	36.2
CFF	172.8	1.81	99.8
CIE	21.3	1.59	0
DB	917.9	1.53	85.0
DSB	67.0	1.35	20.4
FS	774.6	2.76	89.3
NS	191.5	1.70	81.8
NSB	n.a.	n.a.	n.a.
SJ	126.9	1.28	94.5
SNCB	346.3	3.58	56.7
SNCF	827.3	1.66	79.9
VR	73.3	1.61	35.3

Note: [a] This includes £105.7 million spending on continuous welded rail.

Source: Investment — survey of intention published in the *International Railway Journal*, January 1981. It is not known how closely this corresponds to the actual outturn.
All other data — UIC, *International Railway Statistics, 1981*

10.7 Commercial performance — the freight market

So far we have concerned ourselves solely with labour productivity in the production of train services. But the commercial performance of the railway — the amount of traffic it attracts and the price at which it attracts it — is clearly also important as a determinant of the value for money provided by the rail system. Moreover, we have suggested above that there is a correlation between commercial performance and labour productivity — a growing railway finds it easier to raise labour productivity than does a declining one. In this section, we consider commercial performance in the freight sector: then we turn to passenger traffic.

The popular image of the freight market is that of one in which there is a steady drift from rail to road in terms of market share. Of the seven Western European countries for which reasonably complete data is available, only in Western Germany does this picture hold good for the last decade (Table 10.8). True, in every other country except for Sweden, rail has lost market share, but so (marginally) has road. The only mode experiencing consistent growth (except for West Germany) is pipeline, and this is associated not just with capture of traffic from rail but also with the continuing conversion from coal to oil in the early part of the decade.

Despite this similarity in trends over time, there remain very major differences in the absolute mode split between countries, with a rail share varying from 3.3 per cent of tonnes in the Netherlands to 16.2 per cent in Switzerland.

What explains these differences?

It is generally accepted that rail is most suitable for two types of traffic. The first is concentrated movements of bulks, where it is possible to operate full train loads between private sidings. In this sphere, the strongest competition is usually from pipelines (if the product permits), inland waterway or coastal shipping. The second is long-distance movements, where the economy of the rail trunk haul offsets the cost of trans-shipment and marshalling involved in handling smaller consignments. Here, direct road haulage is the principal competitor. Thus it is natural to look for differences in commodity mix and length of haul as explanations of differences in market share.

Details of the commodities carried in domestic traffic by all modes have been obtained for six countries for a single year, 1975 (Table 10.9). Two points should be noted about this table. First, exclusion of international traffic has the effect of making the market shares of rail in Britain, West Germany, France and Belgium virtually equal at around 10 per cent, whilst Holland and Italy fall right back

Table 10.8   Freight market share (% of tonnes lifted)

	1970				1980			
	Road	Rail	Pipeline	Inland Waterway	Road	Rail	Pipeline	Inland Waterway
BR	86.4	11.2	2.1	0.0	85.1	9.5	5.1	0.0
CFF	77.8	18.5	0.1	2.8	77.7	16.2	3.5	2.7
CIE			n.a.				n.a.	
DB	74.9	13.7	3.1	8.3	79.2	11.1	2.3	7.4
DSB			n.a.				n.a.	
FSa	86.5	6.5	6.6	0.0				
NSb	51.3	4.6	3.5	40.6	49.8	3.3	6.9	40.1
NSB		n.a.			86.2	4.9	8.9	0.0
SJc	87.1	12.9	n.a.	0.0	86.8	13.2	n.a.	0.0
SNCBd	64.8	15.2	1.0	18.9	59.5	14.1	7.1	19.3
SNCF	77.7	12.9	3.9	5.5	76.3	12.6	6.0	5.1
VR			n.a.				n.a.	

Notes:
a Inland waterway data refer to 1969.
b Road data refer to 1970 and 1979; pipeline data to 1969 and 1978 for international traffic only.
c Percentages based on a total which excludes pipelines.
d Road data refer to 1970 and 1979.

Source: *Transport Statistics Great Britain, 1971–81*

to 1½ per cent. This is because rail is generally at an advantage in international traffic due to its longer average length of haul; its market share of domestic traffic is correspondingly smaller. This advantage in international traffic does not, of course, apply in Britain and Ireland, where there are no fixed links to other rail systems.

Table 10.9   Rail mode share (%) by commodity (tonnes) 1975 (domestic traffic only)

	GB	WG	F	H	B	I	Weighted mean
Agricultural products	0.78	16.00	6.47	1.38	2.43	3.43	5.54
Foodstuffs and animal fodder	0.36	2.67	6.72	0.16	0.57	1.85	2.33
Solid fuels	57.70	58.39	53.23	2.00	43.64	18.92	56.20
Petroleum products	11.11	11.78	8.26	5.21	3.39	0.30	7.93
Ores and metal waste	54.40	68.10	59.47	6.25	78.47	11.98	57.56
Metal products	10.41	50.67	43.69	1.35	38.89	9.05	26.94
Crude and manufactured minerals, building materials	4.31	1.75	3.15	0.11	1.06	0.44	2.13
Fertilisers	8.33	56.60	27.32	10.61	8.33	3.77	23.64
Chemicals	6.27	5.90	22.97	4.0	6.32	3.14	7.36
Machinery transport eq.	0.58	8.57	11.63	2.94	19.50	2.33	5.00
Total	9.99	10.08	9.78	1.44	9.48	1.66	8.26

Source: Derived from: European Communities, Statistical Year-books, Transport, Communications, Tourism, except Britain, where data from British Rail

Second, the rail share of the market differs enormously by commodity, from over 50 per cent for solid fuels, ores and metal waste — to under 5 per cent for foodstuffs, animal fodder, crude and manufactured minerals and building materials. This suggests that the commodity structure of transport demand may indeed be a major determinant of the rail share of the market.

So it turns out. If we look at the proportion of total transport demand accounted for by solid fuels, ores and metal waste we find it totals 11.6 per cent in Britain, 8.3 per cent in Belgium, 6.9 per cent in West Germany, 5.4 per cent in France, but only 1.8 per cent in Italy and 0.6 per cent in the Netherlands. But this gives rise to another question. If, of the first four countries listed above, Britain has by far the largest amount of bulk traffic suitable for rail transport and France the least, why are their market shares so similar? The answer emerges if the rail share by commodity is examined. France has a higher rail share of the market than Britain for seven of the ten commodities, and frequently much higher.

The reason for this difference in performance appears to lie partly in the second dimension of competitive position, length of haul, and partly in a third dimension, competitive position. Table 10.10 shows that France (and Italy) do have far longer lengths of haul than all the other countries examined. But it also reveals another very interesting difference. In all countries other than Britain and the Netherlands, the rail length of haul is on average some five times that for road (and in the Netherlands, most of the rail traffic is international, with a longer true length of haul).

In part, this picture is a natural corollary of the presence of a large amount of bulk traffic, mainly moving short distances, on Britain's railways. But it also reveals a greater road dominance of many commodities in Britain, and a greater road penetration of the longer distance end of the market. This is not altogether surprising. Both French and German railways enjoy protection by regulation from public road haulage for longer distance traffic (over 150 km). Moreover, both receive some, admittedly small, government subsidies for selective freight tariff restraint, whilst Italian railways operate freight traffic at a huge deficit. Only in Belgium does the competitive position approximate to that in Great Britain.

A final point should be made about the freight market in Western Europe. In all countries except Britain, the rail system still has an obligation to carry at maximum rates controlled and published by the government. Except in Italy, and to a lesser extent Germany, the railway is free to enter specific contracts with individual customers, and most traffic is carried at special rates of these kind. But only in Britain is there complete commercial freedom for the railway in setting freight tariffs and in selecting traffic.

Table 10.10   Mean length of haul (km) for freight, 1975

	Road	Rail	All modes
Great Britain	60	119	77
West Germany	37	189	62[a]
France	58	292	100[d]
Holland	47	154	58
Belgium	31	114	46
Italy	60[b]	345	94[c]

Notes: [a] Excludes coastal shipping (0.2% of tonnage)
          [b] 1973
          [c] Excludes inland waterways (0.3% of tonnage)
          [d] Excludes coastal shipping (3.1% of tonnage)

Source: As Table 10.9. Includes international rail traffic.

10.8 Commercial performance in the passenger sector

There are two passenger markets in which rail transport tends to dominate other modes in Western Europe. The first is commuter journeys into large congested cities, and the second is medium to long-distance inter-city trips. (For instance, British Rail and London Transport railways between them carry 70 per cent of commuters into central London, whilst British Rail has some 40–50 per cent of the total passenger transport market between London and Manchester, Liverpool, Newcastle and Glasgow.) Generally, those railways in Western Europe in which the average passenger trip length is long (Italy, Sweden, France, Finland) are dominated by traffic of the second type; those where it is short (Denmark, Belgium, Netherlands, Britain) have large amounts of commuter traffic. There are two clear exceptions to this rule — West Germany and Switzerland — where short trip lengths are associated with a large amount of short-to-medium distance traffic distributed over the system, rather than concentrated on commuter flows into a few main cities. In Switzerland, this traffic pattern is associated with the largest rail share for any Western European country.

Given the varying mix of these two types of traffic, it is hard to say which countries are the most favourable for rail traffic, although in terms of profitability, there is no doubt that a large proportion of inter-city traffic is an advantage. What is to be expected is that rail will be at a disadvantage in areas of low population density, unless that low density is associated with major concentrations into a few large cities. This might suggest low rail market shares in Ireland and in the Scandinavian countries, although in practice the latter do not look consistently low (Table 10.11).

As regards trends over time, the popular view of a general change in market shares towards private transport is broadly true. It should be stressed, however, that this general decline in public transport market share is quite consistent with absolute growth in a rapidly growing overall market. In fact, rail passenger traffic grew in all twelve countries with the single exception of Belgium, and in five of the twelve countries, the growth was more than 30 per cent (see Figure 10.2a above). Despite this growth, the subsidy requirements of rail passenger services have increased enormously in the past decade. This has not generally been the result of declining revenue − in most countries growth in traffic has been sustained with little or no reduction in real fares. (Italy is the most marked exception to this rule, in that fares have been allowed to drift steadily downwards. In both Ireland and Sweden there were deliberate fare cuts in specific years designed to improve utilisation of the rail system.) In general, the problem has been one of rising real costs.

In part, this has been the result of conscious decisions by governments to commit public funds to the improvement of rail services. Thus there have been enormous investments in expanding suburban rail systems in many German cities and in Paris (the former financed in part from a surcharge on petrol and the latter from the transport tax on employers in the area). Local services have been greatly improved in the Netherlands. In no way would a purely commercial organisation have undertaken these investments, but the relevant political authorities have judged them to be socially worthwhile.

The background to investment in long-distance passenger transport is more difficult to judge. The British high-speed train network, operating at 125 mph, was a purely commercial investment. On the other hand, the construction of new main lines in France, Italy and West Germany arose partly from a commercial desire for an infrastructure suitable for higher speeds and partly from acute congestion on the existing main lines. Thus these investments − even the passenger only

TGV line in France — were undertaken for the joint benefit of all sectors of the business operating on the routes in question.

Table 10.11 Passenger market share, 1970, 1980
(% of passenger kilometres)

	1970			1980		
	Car	Bus	Rail (inc metro)	Car	Bus	Rail (inc metro)
BR	78	13	9	85	8	7
CFF	82	3	15	85	3.	12
DB^a	81	11	8	81	12	7
DSB^b	81	10	9	n.a.	n.a.	n.a.
FS^c	76	11	13	76	15	9
NS^d	81	11	9	84	9	7
NSB^e	67	23	10	81	12	8
SJ^f	n.a.	n.a.	n.a.	88	7	5
SNCB	69	17	14	78	13	10
SNCF^g	n.a.	n.a.	n.a.	83	6	12
VR	74	19	7	76	17	7
CIE	n.a.	n.a.	n.a.	n.a.	n.a.	n.a.

Notes: a 1980 estimates are based on 1977 figures for car and 1979 for bus
b 1965 estimates
c 1980 estimates are based on 1979 figures for all modes, except metro which is 1977
d 1980 estimates are based on 1979 figures for car and bus, and 1977 for metro
e 1980 estimates are based on 1979 figures for bus and 1977 for metro
f 1975 estimates

Source: *Transport Statistics Great Britain, 1971—81 and 1966—76*

However, the real problem for rail passenger services has been a failure to achieve productivity growth at a sufficient pace to offset rising real staff, fuel and materials costs. Thus, even in the absence of expenditure on improved services, the economic performance of individual passenger services has generally declined. Indeed, recent studies in a number of countries have suggested that the profitable core of passenger services able to pay for the track on which they operate is very small. Only on a few busy trunk routes, and on some other routes where there is spare capacity on infrastructure needed for freight services, would a purely commercial passenger service survive.

The response of most Western European governments to this situation has been to stress the importance of maintaining a good quality rail passenger service wherever volumes are reasonably high, but to look to bus services — usually well integrated with rail services at regional centres — to take over in less densely populated areas. The system has worked well in a number of countries (e.g. Sweden, Netherlands, Belgium) but still arouses great hostility whenever withdrawal of a rail service is suggested. Thus passenger service withdrawals have been few in number. The major exception to this general approach is Britain, where the current government has to date adopted the rather curious policy of maintaining a largely unchanged network of subsidised rail passenger services, but of encouraging public and private sector bus and coach operators to compete with it for traffic, rather than to feed traffic into it.

In short, passenger services — which in most European railways account for a much greater share of train kilometres than does freight — must be seen predominantly as a social service, the nature and extent of which is determined by the political process rather than the market place. Correspondingly, models that assume profit-maximising or (for a given volume of traffic) cost-minimising behaviour by the railway will be unrealistic.

10.9 Overall financial performance

The overall financial performance of a railway is the product of the prices charged, traffic levels, mean train loads and the cost per train kilometre operated. We have discussed all these issues individually above, except that we have concentrated on a single determinant of the cost per train km, labour productivity. The other major determinant is the level of real wages, which differs enormously between Western European countries. In this section, we bring these factors together.

There is a number of problems involved in measuring financial performance. First, most Western European railways receive explicit subsidies for particular obligations regarding fares and service levels. In principle, these represent the cost of departing from purely commercial policies in the particular respect in question, but given that most of the European rail network — commercial and social traffic alike — would disappear in the absence of subsidies, such an explicit interpretation is often difficult. Second, most European railways have still been declaring for many years a loss after subsidy, which governments cover by grants or loans. In the latter event, of course, the interest on the loans adds to the deficit in subsequent years and contributes to an alarming growth in the apparent loss made by the railway. Other factors which may distort the true picture are varying historical obligations regarding pensions to past employees, and varying treatment of capital in the accounts from the charging of full replacement cost depreciation at one extreme to a failure to depreciate assets at all where these are financed by government grant.

In the face of all these difficulties, we have chosen to measure financial performance as a simple ratio of traffic receipts (excluding subsidies) to current and capital expenditure for the year in question except for any expenditure relating to wholly new lines (i.e. excluding depreciation and interest, but including investment). The results for 1977 are shown in Figure 10.4, which also demonstrates a clear relationship between financial performance and fares relative to wages (the correlation coefficient is significant at 0.65). It will be seen that the smallest subsidies are received by Swedish and British railways. Both of these in 1977 were high-fare railways, but the position of Sweden will have been changed by the 1979 fares reduction. It would appear that, in return for a very marginal reduction in the proportion of costs covered by revenue, real fares were reduced on average by some 30 per cent and traffic grew by over 25 per cent in the first year. Since this was mostly achieved by increased load factors, with some lengthening of trains, costs rose very little. This example clearly illustrates the social benefit arising from abandoning a purely commercial role for inter-city services to ensure that fares are set at a level which attracts good load factors.

10.10 Conclusion

One of the themes of this paper has been to stress the difficulties involved in comparing the efficiency of Western European railways. Nor is this simply due to the inadequacies of published data — a whole host of factors unique to the countries concerned in terms of economic geography, government intervention and the competitive position influence the performance of the railway concerned.

That being said, we do not believe that such factors go more than a little way towards explaining the very high labour productivity achieved by Sweden and the Netherlands. Each railway has some factors operating in its favour, but neither constitutes ideal railway operat-

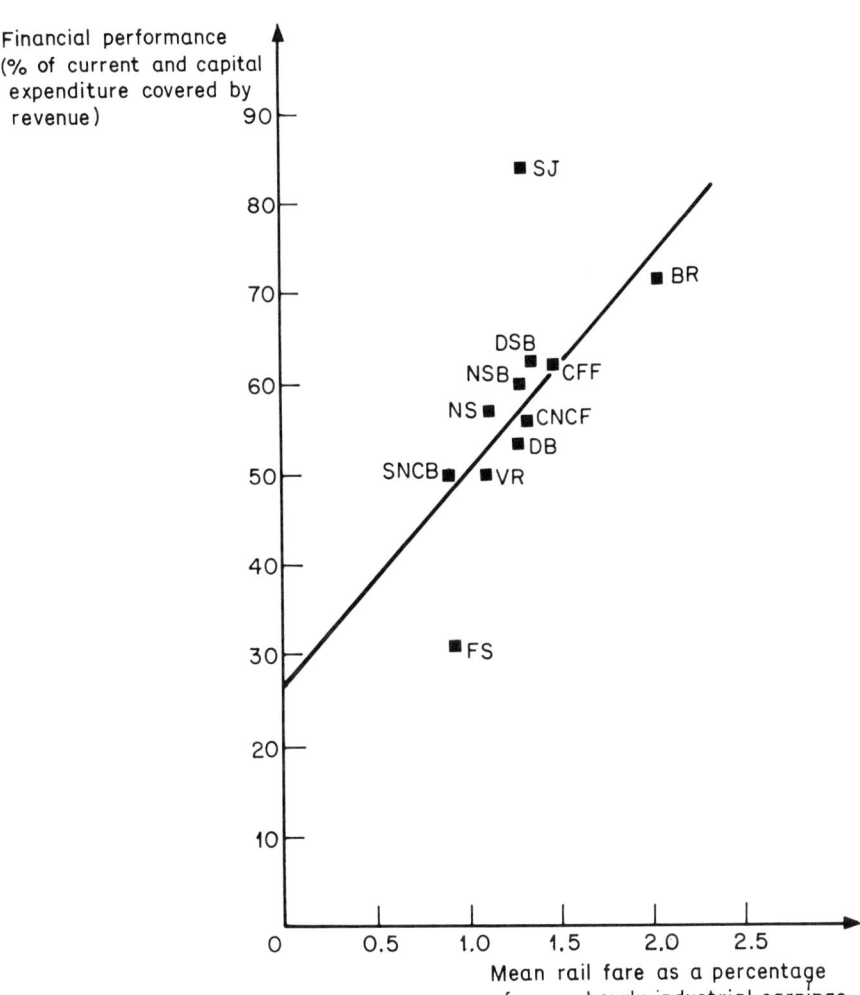

Figure 10.4   Financial performance and fares relative to wages, 1977

ing territory. Generally, their strong performance shows that most other Western European railways still have considerable room for productivity improvement, and in a practical sense it is the exploration of the scope for such improvements that provides the most valuable outcome of international comparisons.

There is evidence that such improvements are easier to achieve in a growing market. Some railways have been able to enter a virtuous circle of rising traffic, rising local factors, rising train kilometres run and rising labour productivity. Labour productivity improvements appear correspondingly more difficult to achieve when the external environment is hostile. This factor should be borne in mind by any government seeking simultaneously to cut services and improve productivity.

The value for money provided by a rail service depends not just on the efficiency with which the service is run but also on the volume of traffic carried. This is heavily influenced, particularly in the freight sector, by geographical considerations, whilst in the passenger sector, government policies are more influential. High service frequencies and an extensive low-density network tend to reduce mean train loads, and governments need to be careful to ensure that the benefits of such levels of service justify the costs. At the same time, if a certain level of service is required on social or commercial grounds, the benefits of the rail system are reduced by following a revenue-maximising pricing policy which causes serious reductions in the volume of traffic carried by, and corresponding user benefits produced by, the service, particularly if strong competition by bus and coach is permitted. The most extreme case of such a policy is the high average revenue per passenger kilometre charged in Britain, although its harmful effects are mitigated by extensive price discrimination. Obtaining a sensible mix of subsidies, fares and service levels on a socially oriented passenger railway remains the most serious problem in obtaining value for money from the rail systems of Western Europe. In this area, too, international comparisons provide good examples of what can be achieved; in particular, the combination of bus-rail integration and high peak but low off-peak fares now offered by Sweden merits close examination by other countries.

268

Appendix

Key to railways

BR	=	British Rail
CFF	=	Swiss Federal Railways
CIE	=	Irish Transport Company
DB	=	German Federal Railways
DSB	=	Danish State Railways
FS	=	Italian State Railways
NS	=	Netherlands Railways
NSB	=	Norwegian State Railways
SJ	=	Swedish Railways
SNCB	=	Belgium National Railways
SNCF	=	French National Railways
VR	=	Finnish Railways

References

British Rail/University of Leeds (1979), *A Comparative Study of European Rail Performance* (British Railways Board, London).

Caves, D.W., Christensen, L.R. and Swanson, J.A. (1980), 'Productivity in US railroads 1951–74', *Bell Journal of Economics*, Vol.11.

Deakin, B.M. and Seward, T. (1969), *Productivity in Transport* (Cambridge University Press, Cambridge).

Glassborrow, D.W. (1962), 'The comparison of partial productivity ratios for national railway systems', *Bulletin of Oxford University Institute of Economics and Statistics*, Vol.24.

Keeler, T.E. (1974), 'Railroad costs, returns to scale and excess capacity', *Review of Economics and Statistics*, Vol.56.

Meyer, J.R., Peck, M., Stenason, J. and Zweck, C. (1959), *The Economics of Competition in the Transport Industries* (Harvard University Press, Cambridge, Mass.).

Munby, D.L. (1962), 'The productivity of British railways', *Bulletin of the Oxford University Institute of Economics and Statistics*, Vol.24.

Paul, M.E. (1962), 'International productivity comparisons over time', *Bulletin of the Oxford University Institute of Economics and Statistics*, Vol.24.

Pryke, R. (1971), *Public Enterprise in Practice* (MacGibbon and Kee).

Smith, A.D., Hitchens, D.M.W.N. and Davies, S.W. (1982), *International Industrial Productivity: A Comparison of Britain, America and Germany*, National Institute of Economic and Social Research, Occasional Paper 34 (London).

11 Railways in rural areas

R. KILVINGTON

11.1 Introduction

This chapter concerns itself with the economic logic of maintaining railway services in areas of low population density. There are at the outset some definitional problems. What constitutes low density? How far can one generalise between a five-mile route to a small country terminus and a long distance inter-urban route which passes through a sparsely inhabited region? Fortunately, precision of definition is not an overriding consideration, since the examples quoted will be largely self-evident. For general clarification, however, it is helpful to focus upon the considerable route by route variations in total traffic flow which characterise the rail systems of almost all countries. Attention here is directed towards services at one extreme of the spectrum, namely those carrying the lowest volumes of traffic.

Common parlance ascribes to these routes names such as branch lines or secondary routes. In terms of function, Keen (1978) considers that Britain's rural railways fall into one of three categories:

(1) those which serve an area which it is impossible to serve adequately by other means, due to geographical location (e.g. Plymouth-Gunnislake);
(2) services to remote, thinly populated, but politically sensitive areas (e.g. Cambrian Coast and North of Scotland);
(3) services on routes of significance for other purposes such as

inter-urban (e.g. Nottingham-Lincoln) or with heavy seasonal traffic (e.g. Grantham-Skegness).

Unlike several other European countries, Britain's rural rail network has been subject to major curtailment, most notably under the Beeching era of the 1960s. Between 1963 and 1968 passenger route mileage was reduced by 25 per cent and the number of stations by 37 per cent. In both cases the greatest loss fell upon country areas. This is important to subsequent discussion because there is apparently great public sensitivity to the idea of railway closure in all countries, the feeling in Britain is perhaps more acute than most.

Data problems often complicate the debate. For aggregate statistical and sector management purposes, the remaining rural routes are grouped by British Rail (BR) under the broad heading of 'Provincial Services'. This differentiates such operations from two other types of passenger service — main-line 'Inter-City' and London and the South East — and also from freight and parcels operations. The provincial category thus also includes local services in the conurbations, other than Greater London, and several long distance inter-urban hauls such as Glasgow—Aberdeen, Birmingham—Norwich and Plymouth—Penzance. In fact, of 160 services operated, only 31 services are in areas where the largest settlement is of less than 25,000 inhabitants. The broadness of definition merely ameliorates the strength of comparison between the lowest density routes within this group and the other sectors, statistics for which are shown subsequently.

Two further points should be made about this data. It will be seen that almost all of the examples relate to routes which carry passenger services, primarily or exclusively. This is a function of both data availability and current accounting practice in several countries. To clarify the latter, it is the case that 'minor user' types of traffic (invariably freight on rural routes) are only debited against the avoidable (marginal?) costs which their operation necessitates. The major burden of infrastructure cost is borne by the prime user. This applies to both the British and Dutch examples cited, and the statistics should be seen in this context. Hence, withdrawal of a passenger service might not eliminate all of the costs allocated to it, if it is deemed expedient to maintain the line for freight.

Additionally, there is the problem of contributory revenue. Except where otherwise stated, income figures relate to the money earned on the length of line in question and ignore contributions to revenue elsewhere on the network. With regard to the scale of such income per se, Keen (1978) showed this to be extremely variable. On a random selection of eight rural lines on BR in 1975, for example, the ratio of contributory revenue to local earnings was between 0.03 and 6.26, with an average of 0.89. Unfortunately, very little is known about the effects of branch line closures on network revenue, although it seems generally accepted that some loss of railway business does take place.

11.2 The financial performance of rural railways

Passenger rail operations perform least successfully in rural areas because of the specific nature of both supply and demand conditions. These are discussed below. To gain a full appreciation of the issues involved, reference should be made to Tables 11.1 and 11.2. These show current performance on BR. It should be noted however, that the divisions employed are crude and relate to broad categories, albeit that Table 11.2 does separate PTE (conurbation) services from the remainder of the provincial category. We see, in particular, in Table 11.2 that only 1 per cent of provincial services cover direct operating costs, whereas the figures for inter-city are 91 per cent and London/South East 80 per cent.

If Table 11.2 is used to compare the extreme differences between the weakest and the strongest services, then it can be seen that 11 per cent of 'other' provincial services are at least eleven times weaker than the top 2 per cent of inter-city services when examining direct costs alone. (Given the greater proportion of indirect costs attributable to the lowest density routes this would seem a relatively favourable comparison.)

An even greater contrast can be seen in the following statistics from Norwegian State Railways (NSB). Norway is very thinly populated throughout but, nevertheless, a considerable rail network is maintained. Table 11.3 shows the three principal main lines compared with the three weakest rural branch lines (in terms of financial loss per unit of traffic).

Table 11.3 also introduces an additional financial contrast, namely between absolute and relative loss. Whilst the latter is admirably demonstrated by the loss/traffic unit column, one should note that 40 per cent of NSB losses were incurred on the three main lines shown. The comparable figure for the three branch lines was just 1.75 per cent.

If these conditions are general, then the elimination of the substantial operating deficits which typify most European railways would not automatically follow from major branch line surgery Indeed history already gives a clear example, in 'the Beeching era' of British Railways. The traffic surveys of April 1961, on which the Beeching Report was based, revealed that 33 per cent of route mileage carried just 1 per cent of all passenger miles. Moreover, 50 per cent of passenger stations contributed just 2 per cent of all passenger revenue. The financial pro-

Table 11.1 British Rail passenger services financial performance by sector, 1982

	Inter-City	London/South East	Provincial	All services
Share of route mileage (%)	24	23	53	
Income (£m)	350	447	136	933
Direct expenditure (£m)	280	386	272	938
Indirect expenditure (£m)	262	376	357	995
Total operating cost	542	762	629	1933
Operating cost per passenger mile (pence)	7.8	10.4	22.9	11.4
Financial loss per passenger mile (pence)	2.8	4.3	17.9	5.9
Income as a percentage of				
Direct expenditure	125	116	50	99
Total operating cost	65	59	22	48

Notes: Direct expenditure is mainly train service and terminal operations; indirect expenditure is mainly infrastructure (track and signalling etc.), administration and replacement allowance costs.
For clarity, the table excludes the minor items of 'other income' and 'interest' — a net additional total cost of £44 million.
Overall figures for 1982 severely affected by industrial action.

Source: Adapted from BR *Annual Report*, 1982

Table 11.2 BR passenger train miles operating ratio, 1982 budget

(percentage of each service type in each ratio category)

Revenue: direct costs	Inter-City	London/ South East	Provincial Passenger Transport Executives	Provincial 'Other' provincial services
0 − 0.25	—	1	7	11
0.25 − 0.50	1	3	14	47
0.50 − 0.75	2	7	39	31
0.75 − 1.00	6	9	40	10
1.00 − 1.25	18	19	—	1
1.25 − 1.50	22	9	—	—
1.50 − 1.75	17	37	—	—
1.75 − 2.00	16	8	—	—
2.00 − 2.25	11	4	—	—
2.25 − 2.50	5	3	—	—
2.50 − 2.75	—	<1	—	—
2.75 − 3.00	2	—	—	—
	100	100	100	100

Notes: System average ratio = 1.16
System average ratio covering all costs = 2.11

Source: Adapted from the Serpell Report; diagram of Operating Ratios. Department of Transport (1983)

Table 11.3 NSB financial results, 1981, for selected lines

	Units of traffic (millions)	Income (m kr)	Expenditure (m kr)	Loss (m kr)	Loss/ kilometre of railway (000 kr)	Loss/ traffic unit carried (øre)
Oslo–Bergen	773	308	384	–76	–163	–9.9
Oslo–Trondheim	1187	437	560	–123	–224	–10.4
Oslo–Stavanger	996	376	531	–155	–253	–15.5
Nelaug–Arendal	3.6	2.6	10	–7.4	–206	–204.3
Reinsvoll–Skreia (freight only)	0.3	0.5	1.7	–1.2	–57	–443.8
Voss–Granvin	1.1	0.9	7.6	–6.7	–248	–558.2

Notes: A traffic unit is 1 tonne of freight travelling 1 kilometre or 1 passenger travelling 1 kilometre.
100 øre = 1 kroner
12 kroner approx. = £1

Source: Ministry of Transport, Norway (1982)

gramme of substantial route and station closure which followed did not however eliminate the deficit as hoped for. (Although it must be admitted the cuts were not as rapid or severe as the Report advocated.) Due to inflationary pressures, the operating deficit was merely contained, albeit in monetary terms, at around £120–150 million between 1962 and 1970.

A more up-to-date illustration is provided by further reference to the Serpell Report (1983) on BR finances. Looking ahead to 1992, it tested several options to elicit the financial effects of reducing the size of the network. It concluded that deficit could not be eliminated unless the current route mileage of almost 11,000 miles were to be reduced below 2000. Even then, the result is subject to a considerable degree of uncertainty.

Table 11.4 analyses the three options from the Serpell Report which involve the lowest level of cutback. An implementation of option C3 would certainly close down all of the rural services which were categorised in the introduction. Particular attention should be paid to the percentage figures, showing the cost reductions which might be achieved. Option C1 shows a disproportionate fall in the deficit *vis-à-vis* route mileage and patronage. The route mileage figure in this option is somewhat misleading with regard to passenger services, since many mixed traffic routes would become freight only lines. Nevertheless, relative differences within each set of statistics become smaller as the progression is made through to option C3.

Having thus illustrated the relatively poor financial position of rural rail services, albeit that they are not unique in requiring subsidy, consideration can now be given to the reasons for such performance.

11.2–1 The supply side problem: high unit costs

The obvious characteristic of a railway is the ownership of a dedicated infrastructure. This may be seen as a major asset in terms of *modus operandi* but, equally, the uniqueness of the railway is a significant financial burden. Whilst there can be considerable variations in the extent and degree of sophistication to which the infrastructure is provided, such as signalling, track maintenance etc., these have a relatively limited bearing on total costs.

The infrastructure requirement thus imposes a high unit cost. Inevitably, this works to the considerable detriment of rural routes, where the level of train operation is usually at its lowest. Table 11.5 compares BR as a whole with the provincial sector and four lines in rural Wales. (The figures for the latter relate to 1972 and are calculated in a slightly different way, utilising the 'Cooper Brothers' costing formula adopted by BR following the 1968 Transport Act. This allowed line by line

Table 11.4 Serpell Committee options for BR network, 1992, at 1982 prices

	Reference case R1	Option C1		Option C2		Option C3	
		Actual	(%) reduction on R1	Actual	(%) reduction on R1	Actual	(%) reduction on R1
Total deficit (£ m)	982	817	17	667	32	534	46
Route mileage	10,070	9,990	1	8,310	17.5	6,120	39
Passenger mileage	18,000	17,200	4.5	16,400	9	15,300	17
Revenue			2		5		13
Cost			7		15		24

Source: Adapted from Department of Transport (1983)

Table 11.5 Cost structure of railway services (percentage of total costs)

	BR[a] (1982)	Provincial sector[a] (1982)	Whitland—Pembroke Dock	Rural Wales[b] Shrewsbury Llanelli	(1972) Cambrian Coast	Shrewsbury—Aberystwyth
Direct Expenditure						
Train services	42	33	40	36	24	23
Terminals	10	9	7	5	7	8
Miscellaneous	2	1	n.a.	n.a.	n.a.	n.a.
Sub total	54	43	47	41	31	31
Indirect Expenditure						
Infrastructure	25	34	47	51	64	65
Administration	18	20	6	8	5	4
Asset replacement provision	3	3	n.a.	n.a.	n.a.	n.a.
Sub total	46	57	53	59	69	69

Source: [a] BR *Annual Report*, 1982
[b] Rees and Wragg (1975)

accounting to be carried out. This practice ceased in 1974, following which publicly available statistics on a route basis have been few and far between.) Inconsistencies in the statistics are not, in any event, sufficient to alter the differences in the degrees of magnitude revealed.

11.2–2 The demand side problem: low utilisation of capacity

Whatever the precise method of operation, the existence of a fixed track and associated works creates a considerable potential carrying capacity. The objective of any rail system is usually seen in terms of maximising utilisation of that capability. The short-run marginal costs of achieving such a situation can be very low indeed. For example, to double the current average load factor of provincial services from 19 per cent (Serpell Report 1983, Table 2.6) to 38 per cent would be un-likely to incur significant costs, unless it is assumed that extra staff would be required for ticket issuing, general administration, etc. A recent review of the Inter-City sector, by Bleasdale (1983), shows that the long-term marginal costs of operating an extra railway coach (72 seats) can be as low as 0.4 pence per seat mile and even for an addition-al run by an Inter-City 125 train 1.3 pence. This compares with 1.4– 1.5 pence for an express (road) coach service. There are, however, two broad reasons why rural services find it difficult to maximise this potential.

Firstly, the level of travel demand in rural areas. By definition, such locations have low levels of population in absolute terms. Moreover, the distribution is of a dispersed nature. The four routes in rural Wales, cited in Table 11.5, each possess population catchment areas of only 50–90,000 (Rees and Wragg 1975). In this context, catchment is generously defined to include all persons within 30 minutes car driving time of a railway station on the line. By contrast, few Inter-City stations have similarly defined catchments below 100,000. Thus, whilst the provincial sector comprises 58 per cent of all BR passenger stations, it accounts for only 32 per cent of loaded train miles and just 16 per cent of passenger miles (Welsby 1983).

The second reason concerns the quality of service offered. There are several factors here. Average operating speeds are relatively low (20–40, cf 60–80 mph). This is so due to a variety of factors, many of them historical. For instance, the type of traction and rolling stock used is usually confined to low powered diesel railcars — whilst the original construction of the line often imposes limitations due to track layout, curvature, gradients, strength of bridges, etc. The generalised time taken to complete a journey is also normally compounded by the limit-ed frequency of service offered, poor interchange, and lengthy travel time to the railhead. This last point applies at both the macro and micro scale. Using rural Wales once again, it can be shown that rail services are provided to only 16 out of the 33 settlements in the area with populations over 1000 persons. Even then, at a local level, the precise location of the railway station is often sub-optimal for the majority of the populace served.

Low potential demand and relatively low levels of service are major drawbacks to rural rail operations. As such they can often combine to bring about one further aspect which will have an influence on demand. This can best be termed service neglect. Particularly where the operating environment is difficult and highly competitive, there has been a reluctance on the part of railway management to invest significant sums of money in services with the lowest potential earning capability. Thus, service quality tends to stagnate or, at times, decline. BR is currently a good (but by no means isolated) example with regard to, inter alia, its diesel multiple units. These units make up the majority of services provided by the provincial sector. Table 11.6 shows the age of the stock still operating during 1983. Given that the units were built with a life span of 15–20 years, the inference should be clear.

Table 11.6   BR diesel multiple units: numbers operating in 1983 compared to age of construction

1956–57	1200
1958–59	1300
1960–61	550
1962–63	125

Source: Welsby (1983)

11.3 Some comparative studies

The previous section has endeavoured to clarify the financial performance of railway services in rural areas. The examples have shown that operating losses are incurred on all routes. Moreover, such lines were seen to be the most heavily supported type of service in relation to the level of traffic conveyed.

Policy implications to be drawn from such analyses are not, however, self evident. For instance, within the operation of any multi-product firm there will always be certain parts of the enterprise which are stronger than others. Further, there are several activities, notably including public transport in general and public utility provision in rural areas, where the principle of cross-subsidy has long been established. In other words, profits from one area of operation are used to off-set expected financial losses in others.

To enable some judgement on the overall 'social worth' of loss making rural rail services it is necessary to look beyond current balance sheets. Three particular aspects are probed herein:

(1) What are the comparative costs of providing alternative means of transport to rail in rural areas?
(2) Are current rural rail services operated in the most cost effective way?
(3) What are the wider social costs and benefits arising from rural rail service provision?

11.3—1 Alternatives to rail

The option of replacing rural rail services by bus or coach operations has been much discussed and to some extent experimented with for many years. At a simplistic level, there is an obvious logic. Bus operations have extremely low unit costs, whilst the carrying capacity of individual units often covers the normal load found on many rural routes. Extra capacity can, in any event, generally be accommodated very flexibly. Rural rail services often display very low operating speeds (in rail terms). Whilst the road network in country areas can be equally inhibiting, the general lack of traffic congestion and the operational flexibility, for example penetration of local town centres can often lead to bus/rail journey times that hardly differ.

The concept of using buses to replace rural rail services gained greatest vogue in Great Britain during the Beeching years of the mid 1960s, albeit that this process had been ongoing for at least the previous 30 years. Beeching argued that the cost of providing replacement bus services for lightly used passenger lines (with flows of about 5000 passengers/week) was about six times less than that entailed in maintaining the rail service. Moreover, with such a passenger throughput, it was expected that the bus operator might make a modest profit, in contrast to significant railway operating losses.

The implementation of this theory has belied the forecast. Keen (1978) reviews the outcome of the many bus services which replaced routes closed by BR. Looking back only to 1968, he found that one third of all such services had themselves disappeared, whilst a further third had been 'substantially modified'. Why has this been so?

Much can be blamed upon the philosophy with which rail replacement services were instituted. There was, in the main, a slavish adherence to the route of the former railway, regardless of the pattern of travel demand — even to the extent of serving the inaccessible (closed) railway station rather than the actual village/town centre. Marketing was poor and little attempt was made to integrate the service into the rest of the bus network. Finally, if the new route failed to cover its costs, there was no guarantee of service retention after the first two years of operation. The fact that bus was replacing a far more expensive option was no security. Ironically therefore many bus services became victims of their own operational flexibility. As Michael Posner (1981) notes:

> When buses can't cover their costs, they tend just to stop running and you can do that straight away. On the other hand, railways are a service characterised by very high overheads ... you tend to go on operating ... until the overheads need renewing.

As losses on the provincial services of BR have continued to mount, and much of the above mentioned overheads approach life expiry (see Table 11.6 and the following section), the idea of further replacement of passenger rail services by a road based alternative is once again a topical issue. Such debate is, however, surrounded by enormous political sensitivity, fuelled by the above experience. In an attempt to overcome this, the option is now discussed in the context of luxury coaches (including toilets, refreshments, etc.), and full integration and marketing within the rail network (special liveries, timetabled connections, etc.) including coaches running into parallel 'platforms' at main line railway station interchanges.

The Serpell Report (1983) was particularly enamoured with such possibilities. It considered that the provincial sector represented 'poor value for money' given that *realistic alternatives* can be provided at far lower cost. In this context it considered bus operating costs could be as little as one quarter of rail. Even the House of Commons Transport Committee (1983), which was highly critical of much of Serpell, considered there to be a 'strong case for bus substitution'.

Table 11.7 does much to illustrate the reasons for the foregoing views. Carried out by the National Bus Company (NBC), it was based upon several items of system wide average costs and limited passenger surveys. As such, it has been heavily disputed by BR. Regardless of statistical imprecision, the difference in the comparative costs of the two modes are immense.

In this context it is perhaps not surprising that, in their evidence to the Serpell inquiry, NBC claimed that 75 per cent of all provincial services could be successfully taken over by coach alternatives, the remainder being debarred only because of high peak demand and/or inadequate road capacity.

Table 11.7   Comparisons of rail and coach costs, 1979 prices

Railway route	Number of coaches required (peak)	Annual cost (£thousand)		Cost ratio rail:coach
		Rail	Coach	
Grantham–Skegness	6	1662*	327	5.08
Darlington–Bishop Auckland	6	956	248	3.85
Westbury–Weymouth	7	1762	502	3.51
Newcastle–Carlisle	24	4292	1221	3.52
Oxford–Hereford	26	4183	1183	3.53

* Costs of all year round regular service

Source: Barrett and MacBriar (1982)

Further evidence on comparative costs can be found in Norway. A review of the entire network of Branch and secondary railway routes outside the Oslo commuter area was carried out by the Ministry of Transport (1977). The study is particularly interesting since it also takes into account the costs of providing replacement freight as well as passenger services (which the NBC study neglects). Based on 1974, the line by line cost ratio of rail *vis-à-vis* bus/lorry varies between 1.36 and 4.52 and thus bears reasonable comparison with the NBC research.

The two studies cited above concentrate on cost comparisons between existing rail services and direct replacement by alternative modes. Particularly in Great Britain, where early rail replacement schemes have been such a dismal failure, there is also scope for broader considerations.

As Keen (1978) notes:

> If the solution (integrated coach alternative) is appropriate for the country town which still has a rail service — perhaps more or less by historical accident of the closure process — is it also appropriate for the town which lost its service ten years' ago?

An example of how such a possibility might be developed was explored in a study of rural Wales (Kilvington and Wragg 1975). It has already been noted that only 16 of the 33 significant settlements in the area still enjoyed a passenger rail link by the early 1970s. All of the remainder had formerly possessed such a facility. Thus, the alternative coach network — to replace five rural rail routes — was devised so as to provide links to main line railheads for all of the 33 locations. The key results are given in Table 11.8.

Table 11.8   Rural Wales rail and coach
alternative comparisons

	Annual operating costs	Railway revenue	Accessibility index
Rail services (5 routes)	£2.04m	£0.30m	288.2mins
Coach alternative	£0.25m		269.9mins

Source: Kilvington and Wragg (1975)

The less comprehensive rail network (covering just 15 per cent of total costs) is seen to be eight times more expensive than the coach alternative. Of equal interest is the accessibility index. This is derived from taking average public transport journey time from each of the 33 settlements to four principal destination areas (i.e. London, Birmingham, Cardiff/Bristol and Liverpool/Manchester). This average time is weighted by the population of each settlement, thus permitting an index reflecting average journey times for the whole of rural Wales to be derived.

It can be seen from Table 11.8 that the coach alternative improves average journey times by almost 20 minutes, with much being attributable to the greater connectivity of the new system. It was also found, however, that, for 11 of the 16 rail connected settlements, there was an improvement in average journey times provided by the coach alternative. This provides an illustration of the point made at the beginning of this section. Quite simply, many rural rail services are slow, indirect and ill coordinated with main line services.

There is thus evidence to suggest that the cost effectiveness of many rural rail services is in doubt, when compared with alternative means of providing the service. Interestingly, however, all of the routes discussed in this section remain in operation today, little changed, if at all, from the time when the research was undertaken. It should be stressed that all of the examples quoted are 'desk studies', and re-emphasise that the empirical evidence of rail substitution by bus has a disastrous history. Nonetheless, it would seem that broader perspective is required to justify retention of most of the examples cited. Two possible areas of argument are now discussed.

11.3—2 *Loss minimisation*

Ministers of Transport and senior railway officials are often confronted with difficult choices. They are frequently faced with strong public opinion and established government policy which seeks to avoid railway closures at all costs. There are major pressures competing for the scarce amount of investment available, both to and between various sectors of the railway system. The resultant policy on rural railway services is almost inevitable. Since revenue is, invariably, a considerable way from covering direct operating costs, there is no possibility of returning the lines to profit. Given that closing the line is an unacceptable stance, the only solution is to adopt the famous posture of the ostrich and bury one's head in the sand. A 'make do and mend' policy becomes both logical and inevitable.

The above emphasises a crucial point. Whilst one should never imagine that the railway routes discussed here could ever return to financial viability (whilst current trends continue) there is good reason to assume the possibility that cost minimisation, and to a lesser extent revenue maximisation, have not been pursued to their fullest extent. This is especially so where investment is a necessary prerequisite to such optimisation. What then is the strength of such evidence?

Certainly, it would appear strong with regard to BR. Since the definition of the 'social railway', under the 1968 Transport Act, rural routes have suffered considerable neglect — or to be accurate — a do minimum situation. Thus, the 1983—88 Corporate Plan of British Rail can make the following statement about the area of operations which consumes over half of the total subsidy (Public Service Obligation grant):

> ... the provincial sector has no agreed objective set by Government.

In practice, BR have made significant economies in certain areas — examples have been the removal of station staff and the introduction of the conductor-guard joint function. The key deficiency has been an inability to *invest* in order to minimise losses. With regard to cost reductions (the major area of potential) there are two areas of justification for such investment.

These are, firstly, to simplify the method of operation, and secondly to replace obsolescence. It is only when faced with an acute problem relating to the latter that the government is now agreeing to a significant investment programme for rural routes. The first priority is the replacement of the aged diesel multiple unit (DMU) fleet (see Table 11.6). The financial burden of this particular obsolescence is such that, according to Welsby (1983), unit costs of operation will increase by 18 per cent between 1983 and 1984 due to escalating maintenance requirements. At the time of writing, consent has just been granted for the construction of 150 new lightweight units. These will be deployed on low density rural routes, supplementing the first 20 units which have just entered service. The cost of construction is around £350,000 per two-car unit. Built with a similar life expectancy to those units which will be replaced, the expected pay-off time, i.e. beyond which the capital investment has been subsumed by what would have been the net cost of keeping the old, is less than 10 years.

This is an example of justifiable expenditure to overcome obsolescence, regardless of any beneficial revenue impacts which the new and better product may stimulate. Albeit at a more subtle level, it is equally an illustration of investment to simplify and therefore reduce costs. The particular rolling stock in question is of a radical lightweight construction, based upon a modular bus bodywork design. Replacement by units of more conventional/heavyweight construction would each have been in the likely region of £6–700,000 and as such unlikely to have been justifiable to the government.

There are further aspects of investment based upon simplification with even faster potential pay-offs and hence greater long-run savings. Noteworthy here are the automation/unmanning of level crossings and the introduction of radio signalling. In both cases 2–3 years are cited as the break even time (Welsby 1983). Progress with radio signalling is well advanced on the north of Scotland lines, following which at least 12 other rural routes are expected to be similarly treated.

Much progress is therefore expected in the area of cost reductions on BR's rural network in the near future. The 1983–88 Corporate Plan envisages an investment of £200 million on all provincial services, following many years of virtual stagnation. This is a key element in reducing the annual operating cost by £50 million in real terms (Table 11.9). Most significantly, without the investment, i.e. do nothing, the PSO grant for 1988 would rise to £530 million at constant prices. (Welsby 1983.)

No doubt the cynic will argue that such savings remain to be proven. Certainly, many BR forecasts in their previous corporate plans have been somewhat optimistic. However, there should be no doubting that radical change in operating methods has enormous potential effects for BR. A desk study of the East Suffolk line (a 48-mile route in East Anglia) by Hodge (1981), suggests possible savings of £0.5 million per annum based on an initial outlay of £2 million. The reduction in the annual cost of each major element would be:

Track	30%	—	partial singling
Signalling	65%	—	adoption of radio control
Level crossings	85%	—	conversion to unmanned operation
Train maintenance	30%)	—	introduction of new light-
Train running	15%)		weight units

If all of the above were attainable, the proportion of revenue to total costs (excluding interest payments on the £2 million, and assuming no change to revenue) would increase from around 25 to 45 per cent. Moreover, even with a discount rate of 10 per cent, the investment costs would be 'paid back' in terms of reduced subsidy requirements within six years.

Table 11.9   BR provincial sector forecast,
1983—88 (1983 prices)

	1983	1984	1985	1986	1987	1988
Revenue	156	157	159	160	162	164
Working expenses	664	654	636	614	610	614
Interest incurred	6	6	9	12	15	18
Other receipts	12	13	14	15	16	17
PSO grant	502	489	472	451	447	451

Source: BRB Corporate Plan (1983b)

The situation described above appears far from unique to Britain. Although operating practices are highly simplified upon rural lines of the Norwegian State Railways, the problem of obsolescent rolling stock is a major issue of concern to railway management. Similar problems have been encountered by Danish State (DSB) and Netherlands (NS) railways. In both cases, however, new investment has been forthcoming in recent years. A brief elaboration on the NS situation is particularly illuminating.

A major investigation during the late 1970s was undertaken regarding the future of six rural lines in the northern part of the Netherlands, centred upon the cities of Groningen and Leeuwarden. (The findings have been documented elsewhere by Kilvington 1983, and Dare 1984, and as such only limited detail is given herein.) The key results of the research into alternative transport options for the lines are shown in Table 11.10.

The new railway included the introduction of new lightweight rolling stock; the construction of a locally based maintenance depot; erosion of traditional areas of labour demarcation, e.g. creation of driver/fitter and guard/carriage cleaner combi-function grades. Subsequently, a significant extra cost saving of about 4 million per year, arising from resignalling of two lines (from traditional block to simplified central traffic control) has been devised. (This figure does not appear in Table 11.10.)

Faced with the evidence of the study, the Dutch Government opted for the improvement of the railway. Whilst the bus option was clearly favoured in financial terms, there are other factors not included in the analysis which improve the railway case. Most important are the extra costs of road traffic congestion likely to arise in the two major settlements. Additional costs would also have to be borne by freight services continuing to use the railway in the event of passenger trains withdrawal (the freight services are currently charged on 'avoidable cost' principles). Since the decision in 1979, much has been achieved in bringing about the necessary changes. Those mentioned above have been implemented, although some more contentious aspects of the plan (including one-person operation of trains) have been blocked by union opposition. Moreover, off-peak patronage increases on the lines after 1977 resulted in the final order for new diesel units increasing from 71 to 81 (replacing the previous total of 88) making an accurate interpretation of the savings realised in practice difficult to assess. Undoubtedly however, significant progress has been made. Dare (1984) suggests savings of 4.3 million guilders per annum arising from full implementation of the 'amended' scheme.

The figures throughout this section lead toward two conclusions. Firstly, there appears to be potential for significant operating economies in rural rail operation. Secondly, such economies, if implemented, can radically alter the degree of difference between the comparative costs of rail and bus alternatives such as were illustrated in the previous section. Further research into such matters and the launching of 'demonstration programmes' are long overdue, particularly in Great Britain.

11.3—3 The social dimension

... of all the sectors, provincial is the one whose existence can only be justified in terms of non-financial objectives; it is the archetypal 'social' railway.

British Railways Board *Corporate Plan 1983—88*

Table 11.10   Alternatives for improving six railway routes in the Northern Netherlands

(1976 prices expressed in million Hfl)

	Do nothing	New railway	Replacement bus assuming	
			Low transfer	High transfer
Number of personnel	538	464.5	334	424
Annual operating costs	35.7	29.9	19.7	25
Annual revenue	27.9	27.9	20.1	27.3
of which, on line	17.5	17.5	13.1	16.9
contributory	10.4	10.4	7.0	10.4
Balance	−7.8	−2.0	+0.4	+2.3
Improvement on Do nothing	—	+5.8	+8.2	+10.1

Notes: 4.5 fl approx. = £1
The lines are Groningen—Leeuwarden/Groningen—Roodeschool/Groningen—Delfzijl/Groningen—
Nieuwe Schans/Leeuwarden—Harlingen/Leeuwarden—Stavoren

Source: Adapted from PEN Study (Nederlandse Spoorwegen 1977)

Notwithstanding the previous section, there can surely be little argument over the verity of this statement. The chapter therefore concludes by addressing itself to the nature and quantification of this social dimension.

One starting-point is to consider the widespread emotional attachment between the general public and railways. The precise rationale for this does not seem to have ever been accurately pinpointed. Suffice it to say that there is, apparently worldwide, deep felt public sensitivity to the idea of closing *any* railway route. An interesting study in this context was carried out by Hillman and Whalley (1980). They investigated the social consequences arising from the closure of 10, primarily rural, routes on BR since 1968. Although no attempt was made to quantify the effects in monetary terms, there were considerable ramifications arising in terms of trip opportunities. Approximately half of the local population had made a rail journey in the year before closure (itself a significant proportion), of whom 72 per cent had subsequently reduced or stopped making journeys to the same destination after service withdrawal. Moreover, within the latter group, 49 per cent had not reoriented such trips, i.e. the journey per se had been forgone.

These findings should be treated with some reservation, since it was also shown that travellers tended to use the line, in the main, for occasional trips only. Hence, the effect upon total trip making was presumably not great. Most significant, however, was the general attitude found to exist amongst the populace regarding the closure. Of users 51 per cent declared that they had been 'very upset' at the time of service withdrawal. By contrast, at the time of the surveys (2 to 9 years after closure) 36 per cent still echoed this feeling, with a further 30 per cent categorised as 'modestly upset'. Amongst non rail users 60 per cent regretted closure, with 20 per cent in the 'very upset' grouping. Of specific interest was the fact that attitudes were apparently unrelated to the length of time since the service had ceased. Public sentiments are thus seen to be both strong and enduring with regard to railways.

However, if there is to be an argument in welfare economic terms which can support retention of rural rail services, there must be more substantive evidence to suggest that their value in community benefit terms outweighs the accounting cost. Following the introduction of line by line costing for grant purposes on BR in 1969, there was much interest in the application of cost-benefit analysis to such a consideration. At the forefront was a special economic unit within the then Ministry of Transport, set up for this particular purpose. According to the Leitch Committee (Department of Transport 1977), 32 routes, 21 of which would fall into a broadly 'rural' categorisation, were examined between 1968 and 1974. Unfortunately, with the one exception discussed below, the appraisals have never been made publicly available.

The review of the Cambrian Coast line (Ministry of Transport 1969) examined a classic rural route of 54 miles length serving many small communities in mid Wales. Some of the results, based on the option of retaining the line for a limited period of 10 years only, are shown in Table 11.11. It can be deduced that the quantification of social benefit to passengers was, in itself, a relatively small item and that there was little apparent justification for retention of the route.

Table 11.11   Cost-benefit analysis of the Cambrian coast line

Ten-year life only Discount rate = 8%	£thousand
Costs	
1(a) Operating costs	1768
(b) LESS use of labour with no opportunity cost	534
Total cost	1234
Benefits	
1. Cost of additional travel time for passengers transferring to bus	37
2. Loss to passengers not transferring to bus	38
3. Road construction costs avoided	50
4. Bus operating costs avoided	413.5
Total benefit	538.5
Net cost of retention	695.5

Source: Ministry of Transport (1969)

The publication of the study immediately sparked an enormous controversy. Richards (1972), for example, 'recalculated' the Ministry of Transport study. His approach was based on patronage data over a number of years, which led him to produce some rather optimistic trend estimates of upward growth. Several other factors, including valuation of children's travel time, loss of revenue to public transport operators, and road accident costs, which had been ignored by the initial research, were also quantified. This brought about the claim that there were net *benefits* in retaining the line in the region of £374,000 to £1,011,000 for the 10-year limited life option enumerated in Table 11.11. Many others were also active in this field at the time (see for example Clayton and Rees 1967, Else and Howe 1969, Foot and Starkie 1970, Sugden 1972).

One study, after contrasting cost-benefit studies of six loss making rail services on BR, concluded:

> ... in addition to [several] conceptual problems, it has been clearly demonstrated that analysts have been inconsistent in their approaches.
>
> (Kilvington 1973)

Applying such methodological differences to a common route — the 30-mile line from Norwich to Sheringham — it was possible to arrive at conclusions which showed a net social benefit of plus *or* minus £700,000 over a 10-year time horizon for a route with a then total operating cost of £198,000 per annum.

To synthesise the above, one may conclude that cost-benefit analysis, at least in this area, is hardly a finite art. The potential imprecision inherent in this or any other yet devised method of assessing 'social need' in transport, is an important factor which cannot be overlooked by policy analyst and decision taker alike.

Having stated this, there are good grounds for suggesting that the level of social benefit established in the great majority of studies of rural rail services has rarely been sufficient to offset the financial shortcomings. To return to the Cambrian Coast example, a further reappraisal was carried out as part of the Welsh Council study (Rees and Wragg 1975). This incorporated the great majority of Richards' methodological objections to the Ministry's study, yet still found that the benefits of retention against a new, more imaginatively designed, bus network were only 28—49 per cent of the total costs. In fact, the great majority of cost-benefit studies of rural rail services have been unable to quantify social benefits which justify the provision of subsidy and hence retention of the lines.

The implications of this statement are well spelt out in both Pryke and Dodgson (1975) and Dodgson (1977). After 'normalising' several cost-benefit studies of rural and urban railways it was found that whilst cost per passenger mile was likely to vary enormously (inevitably being highest on rural routes for the reasons discussed in section 11.2), there was a considerable degree of conformity in the level of social benefit per passenger mile. Taking an average figure for the latter, the analysts applied this as a 'screening procedure' against some relatively crudely calculated costs on a route by route basis. The former study suggests that, even allowing zero opportunity cost for railway labour which would incur redundancy in the event of service withdrawal, 89 out of 192 grant aided routes on BR would appear unlikely to be justifiable on cost-benefit criteria. Dodgson (1977) considered that 52 routes (approximately 36 of which are rural by the categorisation of this chapter) would not be justified against specific costs alone, i.e. those costs which are exclusive to the route in question and have no element of common cost. At the time of writing, only one of these rural routes in its entirety and one, partially, have been closed, reducing the network by just 17 route miles. In his most recent review of the subject Dodgson (1983), in considering the Serpell report options (see Table 11.4), states:

> For many of the services considered in moving from network R1 through C1 and C2 to C3, it is extremely unlikely ... that the social benefits not captured in railway revenue would be sufficient to justify their continued operation.

So what are we to conclude? There appear to be two possible alternatives. Either cost-benefit analysis is wrong, or at best inadequate as an analytical tool in this sphere, *or* there is a refusal/unwillingness to accept its conclusion. It is true that at the present time cost-benefit analysis does not normally fully quantify all the ramifications of a particular policy decision. Most of the studies undertaken recognise this and list a number of intangible factors alongside the financial appraisal to aid the decision maker in his choice. For instance, most studies leave in unquantified form the issues of contributory revenue (see section 11.1); the benefits of the railway to regional economic development — industry, tourism, stemming depopulation etc.; environmental issues such as noise and pollution; and differences between comfort and convenience of alternative modes of transport. In all of these cases, it is generally asserted that the intangible is a benefit in favour of retaining rail. Equally though, they are usually considered to be relatively insignificant to the overall analysis.

Perhaps, most saliently, one might also add that the emotional/psychological well being of communities with respect to being 'rail connected' is never considered. Whether such a factor should, or indeed could feasibly, be added to the analysis must remain an open question.

Economic analysis, of course, should never be seen as more than an aid to decision making. It does however appear that the dice, in the broader political context, are loaded heavily in favour of rail.

References

Barrett, B.M.M. and MacBriar, I.D. (1982), 'In place of trains', PTRC Summer Annual Meeting (University of Warwick).

Bleasdale, C. (1983), 'Providing transport for a mobile society'. Paper to Chartered Institute of Transport (London).

British Railways Board (1983a), *Annual Report and Accounts 1982*.

British Railways Board (1983b), *Corporate Plan 1983—88*.

Clayton, G. and Rees, J.H. (1967), *Economic Problems of Rural Transport in Wales*, Welsh Economic Studies no. 5 (University of Wales Press, Cardiff).

Dare, A.D. (1984), 'Local rail services in the Netherlands', *Modern Railways*, March.

Department of Transport (1977), *Report of the Advisory Committee on Trunk Road Assessment* (Leitch Committee) (HMSO, London).

Department of Transport (1983), *Railway Finances: report of a committee chaired by Sir David Serpell* (HMSO, London).

Dodgson, J.S. (1977), 'Cost-benefit analysis, Government Policy and the British Railway Network', *Transportation*, Vol.6, pp.149—70.

Dodgson, J.S. (1983), 'British Rail after Serpell', *The Three Banks Review*, No. 140, pp.22—37.

Else, P.K. and Howe, M. (1969), 'Cost-benefit analysis and the withdrawal of railway services', *Journal of Transport Economics and Policy*, Vol.3, pp.178—94.

Foot, D.H.S. and Starkie, D.N.M. (1970), *Ashford—Hastings Railway Line Cost Benefit Appraisal*, University of Reading, Geographical Papers no. 3.

Hillman, M. and Walley, A. (1980), *The Social Consequences of Rail Closures* (Policy Studies Institute, London).

Hodge, P.R. (1981), 'Low-cost rural railways and the BR Leyland railbus', Polytechnic of Central London seminar on rural transport.

House of Commons Transport Committee (1983), *The Serpell Committee Report on the Review of Railway Finances*, Second Report, Session 1982—83 (HMSO, London).

Keen, P.A. (1978), 'Rural railways', in R. Cresswell (ed.), *Rural Transport and Country Planning* (Leonard Hill, Glasgow).

Kilvington, R.P. (1973), 'Cost benefit analysis & railway services', Unpublished MA thesis (Department of Town and Regional Planning, University of Sheffield).

Kilvington, R.P. (1983), *Public Transport in Denmark and the Netherlands*, Department of Transport Technology report No. TT8204 (University of Technology, Loughborough).

Kilvington, R.P. and Wragg, R.F.W. (1975), 'External trip making in rural Wales', Polytechnic of Central London seminar on rural transport. Also available in P.R. White (ed.), *Rural Public Transport* (Polytechnic of Central London).

Ministry of Transport, Norway (1977), *Jernbanenett og jernbanetransport, NOU 30B*, Universitetsforlaget, Oslo.

Ministry of Transport, Norway (1982), *Budget Papers for 1983; St.prp.nr.1* (MoT, Oslo).

Ministry of Transport, UK (1969), *The Cambrian Coast Line* (HMSO, London).

Nederlandse Spoorwegen (1977), *Projekt Exploitatie Nevenlijnen (PEN)*, Internal report (NS, Utrecht).

Posner, M. (1981), 'The future of rural railways'. Introductory address to a conference of the same title (Policy Studies Institute, London).

Pryke, R.W.S. and Dodgson, J.S. (1975), *The Rail Problem* (Martin Robertson, London).

Rees, G.L. and Wragg, R.F.W. (1975), *A Study of the Passenger Transport Needs of Rural Wales* (Welsh Council, Cardiff).

Richards, K. (1972), 'Economics of the Cambrian coast line', *Journal of Transport Economics and Policy*, Vol.6, pp.308–20.

Sugden, R. (1972), 'Cost benefit analysis and the withdrawal of railway services', *Bulletin of Economic Research*, Vol.24, pp.23–32.

Welsby, J. (1983), 'Provincial services, subsidies and Serpell'. Lecture to the East Midlands Section, Chartered Institute of Transport, Derby.

12 Efficiency of railway transportation: the Indian experience

T. V. S. RAMAMOHAN RAO AND S. SRIRAMAN

12.1 The railway network in India

The intercity transportation network in India is multi-modal as in most other countries. Roads, railways, and airlines cater to the demand for transportation services in varying degrees. Though there is a reasonably well-developed air network its overall share remained low because of its relative cost disadvantage. As such, both passenger and freight movements are primarily restricted to railways and highways. However, there are significant diseconomies in operating vehicles on the highways over long distances. Hence, much of the long-haul traffic, passenger as well as freight, depends on the railway network. Thus, the railways constitute an important ingredient of the transportation system.

The railway network consists of approximately 65,000 kilometres of running track. This track capacity is divided about equally between the broad gauge and metre gauge sections. The former has double lines and approximately one-third of it has been brought under electric traction. Despite this composition of track capacity, the broad gauge routes carry as much as 75 per cent of passenger traffic and nearly 85 per cent of freight traffic. Even within the broad gauge section the lines connecting Bombay, Calcutta, Delhi and Madras have the highest route densities. They account for as much as 55 per cent of passenger

* The research leading to this chapter was financed by the Indian Council of Social Science Research, New Delhi.

and 75 per cent of freight moving on the broad gauge section.

There was a four-fold increase in freight movements on railways over the past 30 years. Bulk commodities such as coal, iron ore, food-grains, cement and fertilisers constitute the major share of the freight traffic. High-valued manufactured goods generally move by trucks. However, the geographic concentration of industrial production necessitates substantial length of haul. Consequently, railways are the efficient mode even for long-haul movements of manufactured goods. The management of the railways has been encouraging these flows by priority wagon allocation essentially due to their revenue earning potential.

The long distance (more than 300 km) passenger traffic nearly doubled over the past decade. Most of this traffic originates and term-inates at the four major cities mentioned earlier. The significantly large intercity passenger movements have been a source of phenominally high congestion in cities like Bombay and Calcutta.

The planning process of the railways should be viewed against this backdrop. At the beginning of the first five-year plan in 1950—51 the railways had a total running track of 59 thousand kilometres and a wagon stock of approximately 1.5 lakhs. Only about 7,000 kilometres of track was added over the past 30 years. But the wagon stock in-creased to 4.2 lakhs during the same time. Similarly the locomotive fleet was nearly doubled. The system sought to augment supply of services primarily by better utilisation of existing capacity. Capacity expansion was taken up as and when possible.

This approach to management was a result of the none too favour-able financial position. The railways do not have an adequate surplus to finance the necessary capital formation. To an extent this is a result of the low tariff rates for priority movements arising from the develop-mental objectives. However, the successive tariff enquiry committees did not accept the idea that the railways should raise finances for capital accumulation from their own sources. The value of service tariff structure has been a major source of problems in short-term operational execution and long-term capital formation.

The other source of revenues is the budgetary allocation from the central exchequer. Usually these revenues are provided in consonance with the services rendered to the government. There is not much of an excess over this to provide for capital formation to the extent desirable.

Consequently it appears that no major shift in long-term strategies is envisaged for the railways. Only some incremental improvements may be possible to augment supply in the short-run. It is therefore necessary to examine the short-run economic processes which give rise to the demand for and supply of services. Such an exercise alone has the prospect of offering at least a partial solution to the disequilibrium experienced on the system.

12.2 Dynamics of movement

The infrastructure provided by the railway system was historically one of the most important factors responsible for sustaining a growing and diversified economy. Movements of individuals, raw materials, as well as finished goods, made possible by the availability of the railway network, facilitated efficient utilisation of resources over both space and time.[1]

During any given span of time the demand for services has been basically dependent on the stage of economic development. The functioning of the railway network was generally of the following nature:

(1) As in most of the other less developed countries, exports of primary products account for one of the major demands on the system. For instance, iron ore forms an important share of the exports. These movements generally entail long hauls from the interior to the ports.

(2) There was a necessity for major imports of petroleum products and fertilisers. Their distribution to consumption centres also represented long-haul movements though in the other direction.

(3) Opening up of new areas and opportunities of economic activity, especially in the industrial sector, gave rise to major changes in the patterns of demand for manufactured goods. Concomitantly there were changes in the patterns of population settlements, location and growth of urban centres, and rural-urban migration. This gave rise to movements of passengers across regions in addition to freight flows.

(4) Prosperity in certain regions (mostly agricultural) also generated passenger movements quite unrelated to production and work. Thus the transport requirements, both in terms of passenger movements and freight flows, increased at a faster rate than industrial and agricultural outputs as well as the degree of urbanisation.[2]

The provision of railway services should be evaluated from this vantage point. Viewed from this perspective, and over a relatively long time horizon, the evolution of the railways exhibited one of the most dynamic economic processes. The ability of the railway system to provide the desired services was instrumental in bringing about changes in the patterns of production, location and relocation of consumption centres, as well as the development of the railway system itself. Each one of the three components of the process — namely, production, markets, and services rendered — was adaptive to variations in the others and often in rather complex ways.

12.3 Patterns of demand

Transport demand consists of passenger movements as well as freight flows as the basic components. Each of these aspects, in turn, has two dimensions. The first relates to the number of persons to be moved or the tons of freight carried. The second dimension is the average length of haul.

Table 12.1 represents the relative position of the railways in the provision of transport services. During the year 1950—51 the railways accounted for 74 per cent of total passenger traffic and 89 per cent of the freight traffic. The relative shares declined to 40 per cent and 67 per cent by the year 1975—76 and have been hovering around these limits thereafter. Despite this reduction in the relative position the burden of transport on the railways has been heavy in absolute terms. For, during the time period under consideration, there was a threefold increase in passenger movements and even greater augmentation in freight traffic. The figures for the average length of haul indicate that while there were no major changes in the passenger movements there were substantial increases in the case of freight flows.

Table 12.1   Passenger and freight movements

Year	PKM (billions)			ALHP (kms)	TKM (billions)			ALHF (kms)
	Rail	Road	% Rail	Rail	Rail	Road	% Rail	Rail
1960—61	78	57	57.78	48.7	87.7	35.0	71.48	561
1965—66	96	95	50.26	46.3	116.9	55.0	68.00	576
1970—71	118	169	41.12	48.6	127.4	66.0	65.35	648
1975—76	149	225	40.00	50.5	148.3	73.0	67.00	664
1979—80	177[a]	250	41.45	n.a.	148.7	82.2	64.54	749

Notes: PKM = passenger kilometres; ALHP = average length of haul of passenger movements; TKM = ton kilometres; ALHF = average length of haul of freight carried
[a] The figures for passenger movements are for the year 1978—79 only.

Sources: NTPC (1980: 17—18); *Eastern Economist*, annual number, 1979.

Rail traffic of high valued commodities, for which freight rates are generally higher than the rates charged by road haulers, exhibited a declining trend. But the proportion of bulk commodities, which have comparatively low unit values and for which rail freight rates are relatively low, was on the increase.

In addition, the demand patterns, both in relation to passengers and freight, exhibit significant seasonal effects over the year. For instance, the peak of the freight flows is generally recorded between October and March. Roughly a 20 per cent increase over the annual average is recorded during the peak season.

Though the demand for rail freight services was so far described in terms of originating tonnage and length of haul it does not manifest itself in that form in any practical setting. Instead, a shipper who has a demand for freight services expresses it in the form of a specific number of wagons to be made available at a predefined destination and well-defined point of time. There was a substantial increase in the demand for freight services even from this perspective.

12.4 Supply of services

In general, there are several choices open to the railways in their attempt to cater to the demands on the network. The railways provide different quantities and qualities of service for different users, depending on the nature of movements, origin and destination, and the time profile. Stated in somewhat greater detail, the railways can be considered as choosing a combination of the following in their search for a supply procedure: (i) creating additional track capacity and adding to rolling stock; (ii) improving the scheduling and routing so as to reduce delays in transit; and (iii) rationing out the available supply among competing users by appropriate freight rate choices and other priority specifications.

Table 12.2 represents a profile of the supply of services on the railway network. The following trends are discernible:

(1) In contrast to the growth in the demand for services there was no commensurate investment in rolling stock or line haul capacity. However, the assumption that supply can be augmented only by investments is deeply entrenched in policy level arguments. Hence, analytical exercises to identify demand patterns and drawing up investment requirements is quite common. However, it appears that even good investment plans could never be fully implemented due to paucity of financial resources. In general, it may be concluded that there has been an inadequate effort at resource mobilis-

ation and implementation of investment plans.

(2) Passenger services appear to have suffered relative to freight traffic whenever transport capacity was inadequate to meet the needs of both. Historically, as well as in the era of planned economic development, the railways were able to operate selectively to sustain major production oriented freight movements. The provision of passenger services was always of secondary importance.

(3) Though an overall improvement can be discerned in the available wagon stock and its actual usage, the turnaround time as well as the empty wagon movements have been on the increase. The most disturbing feature is the downward trend in the actual number of wagons loaded over the past few years. As a result, despite the overall increase in ton-kilometrage and the revenue-earning freight traffic, it appears that the supply of freight services is reduced significantly.

(4) While there has been a need for greater speed of freight trains to handle bulk movements of coal, steel, and foodgrains the speed differential between freight and passenger trains remains high. It is of the order of 40 kms per hour and has been one of the factors accounting for the increased turnaround time.

Table 12.2   Supply of railway services

Year	PC (thousands)	W (lakhs)	WL (millions)	SP	TAT	E
1960—61	20.06	3.08	6.48	16.7	11.2	30.4
1965—66	22.72	3.70	8.71	16.4	11.8	31.5
1970—71	24.59	3.84	9.38	17.9	13.3	30.3
1975—76	26.23	3.95	10.41	13.5	13.5	31.7
1979—80	27.41	4.00	10.56	19.5	15.1	29.8

Notes: PC = passenger coaches in use (thousands); W = wagons in use for freight movements (lakhs); WL = wagon loadings (millions); SP = speed of freight trains in train kilometres per engine hour; TAT = turnaround time of wagons in days; and E = empty wagon movements (percentage of empty wagon kilometres to total wagon kilometres)

From these observations it appears that the disequilibrium in the supply of freight services has been persistent and cannot be considered as a purely transitory problem. Certain features of the demand for services as well as the management process may have a bearing on the observed phenomenon.

12.5 Organisational aspects[3]

The transportation system and its functioning is quite complex. Efficient performance was attempted by broad delegation of authority. At the national level, the coordination of the different components of the transport system was entrusted to the planning commission. This group coordinates inter-modal investment decisions. Price policies on each of the modes was delegated to separate organisations. Similarly there are many other decision-makers at the operational policy level for each mode.

Within the railway system the railway board is at the apex of the decision-making process. It coordinates the policy-making as well as the executive functions. In addition, the hierarchical process consists of both horizontal and vertical dimensions of control. The horizontal division is generally by functional areas such as investments in tracks and rolling stock, price policy, and operations and maintenance. The vertical control divides some of these functions at the level of the central and zonal responsibilities.

Different managerial groups control the choices at the level of each of the subsystems. The manager of each subsystem organises and controls the particular set of resources available to the subsystem. In making these choices they follow certain overall guidelines and constraints defined at a higher hierarchical level. But the primary objective has been the performance of their own subsystems measured in terms of costs and revenues. In other words, the basic services on the transport network, such as the volume, the length of haul, and speed, are determined according to some minimally acceptable schedule. These service-quality criteria are set up on a system-wide basis and for a fairly long plan horizon. The zonal managers, who are primarily responsible for day-to-day execution, will then determine the train lengths and assembly policies, the number of hours of movement of a freight train per day, empty wagon movements and so on. Such a hierarchical decision-making system is expected to be more efficient simply because the decision-makers at each level would be responsive to the managerial needs at that level of organisation.

However, there have been two common observations: (i) the burden on each of the decision-making levels is disproportionate to the resources available with them to function efficiently. For instance, it was pointed out that the executive functions take a disproportionate amount of time of the railway board and that policy aspects of a long-

term nature do not get sustained attention at the requisite intensity.
(ii) The responsiveness of any level of managers to maintaining efficiency is proportional to the demands on the system. Since the railways have been a virtual monopoly and there is no other effective competitive mode the performance does not correspond to the highest possible level; or, for that matter, even to a level which caters efficiently to the existing demands on the system.

12.6 Disequilibrium dynamics

The disequilibrium in the market for railway services can be created in the following major ways: (i) changes in the demand for services which are normally external to the railway network, and (ii) decisions of the railway management with respect to the supply of services. In particular, the ability of the railways to efficiently cater to a given demand for wagons depends on the stock of wagons in use as well as the efficiency of their utilisation.

Any initial excess demand may lead to forces tending to decrease it as well as increase it. Prominent among the first category are the following: (i) as a result of the congestion and delays experienced on the railways there was a significant diversion of freight traffic to the truck mode; (ii) the development of a regional distribution system for foodgrains through the Food Corporation of India had the effect of reducing the pressure on the railway network by appropriate scheduling during slack times; and (iii) the management of the railways occasionally increased freight rates to discourage certain marginal users. On the other hand, as the turnaround time of the wagons increases and there are delays in obtaining wagons, there would be a tendency on the part of the shippers to increase the demand for wagons in the hope that their genuine requirements will be satisfied.

On the supply side, it was generally acknowledged that the rate of growth of demand was in excess of the growth in the capacity of the system to cater to it. For, the rolling stock of the railways remained more or less static. Annual acquisitions of the wagon stock were more by way of replacements rather than net additions. However, it may be possible to choose wagon allocation and other operating policies so as to reduce the shortage of supply. But, an initial deterioration of services may manifest itself in further reductions of supply. Consider, for instance, an initial increase in the turnaround time of wagons. Given the unidirectional movement of many commodities, the haulage of empty wagons will also go up. Both these factors have the effect of reducing the capacity of the system stated in terms of the availability of wagons.

On the whole, there are factors on the demand side as well as the supply perspective which account for the observed disequilibrium in the supply of freight services on the railway network. Further, it may be noted that an initial disequilibrium in the system has a tendency to augment itself rather than generate corrective counteraction.

These considerations indicate that in order to approach the problem of adequately providing the medium-term requirements of freight movements it is necessary to identify (i) the factors determining the length of haul and its relationship with the quantum of movement; (ii) the effect of these changes on the increase in the demand for wagons; (iii) the operational decisions leading to an observed supply of services; (iv) the causes of the reduction in the supply of wagons; and (v) the alternative mechanisms available for equilibrating the system of freight movements either by augmenting the carrying capacity of the railway network and/or reducing the demand for freight services.

It is against this backdrop that we have been attempting to set up models of short-term operations of the railway system in order to disentangle the major sources of disequilibrium and to identify possible corrective policy that can be initiated. A few highlights of this work will be presented in the following sections.

12.7 Modelling passenger services

There is a perplexing variety of modelling frameworks for an analysis of passenger movements as well as freight services. The complexity of the models is determined by the detailed level of explanation sought and the availability of the data base. Increasingly it has also been recognised that the demand patterns are sensitive to policy parameters chosen by the railway management. As such the behavioural models, in almost all their variants, are based on microeconomic theoretical considerations. They have been able to offer the most convincing insights from an empirical perspective as well.[4] Hence, this was chosen as the basic analytical framework.

The problem may be approached as follows: initially note that passenger kilometres of movement in a year = number of persons moving X average frequency of movement of each passenger X average length of haul.

The product of the later two components represents the average length of haul per passenger moving on the railways. Studying the two dimensions — namely, the total number of passengers and the average length of haul — should provide adequate information regarding the supply characteristics of the railway services as well.

Conceptually, passenger traffic is directly influenced by the growth

in income, urbanisation, etc. Further, it was observed that the agricultural and other incomes have had differential effects on passenger movements. In addition, certain service characteristics, such as the speed of
trains, can be expected to have a bearing on the demand for both the
dimensions of service under consideration. The demand model was
structured in such a way as to accommodate these possibilities.

The supply of services can be considered in a similar neoclassical
fashion. For, the costs to the railways depend upon the levels of
various services provided and the available infrastructural facilities.
Hence, the level of service provided by the railway system depends
upon the prevailing tariff rate and the capacity of the system. Supply
models were specified along these lines.

However, the supply literature, as it has been evolving in recent
years,[5] emphasises the possibility that the railway system may be
responsive to passenger demands. Within the framework chosen for
analysis it was necessary to examine the possibility that supply of
services is responsive to either or both the dimensions. The actual outcome depends upon the physical limits set up by the productive capacity of the system. It is even possible that the railway management finds
it uneconomical to cater to both. This aspect was also tested.

From an analytical viewpoint, each of the above models has the
structure of Zellner's seemingly unrelated regressions. They were estimated accordingly. The goodness of fit and test statistics adopted were
those defined by McElroy (1977) and Buse (1979).[6]

The following results were obtained from annual timeseries between
1960–61 and 1979–80.

(a) Demand for passenger movements

$$NP = -4.04 + 0.34 AGP + 0.74 INP \qquad (12.1a)$$
$$(1.78) \qquad (7.44)$$

$$ALHP = 2.83 + 0.24 AGP \qquad (12.1b)$$
$$(4.12)$$

$$R^2 \text{ McElroy} = 0.92$$

where

NP   = number of passengers moving by railways (millions);
ALHP = average length of haul of passenger movements
          (kilometres);
AGP   = index of agricultural production;
INP   = index of industrial production;

and all the variables are expressed in logarithmic form.
Similarly, the numbers in the brackets are the t-values of the

corresponding coefficients.

From these estimates it is evident that both the increases in industrial and agricultural incomes were a source of movement of greater number of passengers. But the movements from agricultural areas were the primary source of lengthening the average haul. Neither the tariff charged from the passengers nor the other service characteristics appeared to have had any major influence on the patterns of demand.

(b) *Supply of passenger services*

$$NP = -3.55 + 1.23PC + 0.56TRP$$
$$(2.02) \quad (2.40)$$

$$ALHP = 3.76 + 0.15TRP \qquad (12.2)$$
$$(4.52)$$

$$R^2 \text{ McElroy} = 0.87$$

where, in addition to the variables defined earlier, we have

PC = number of passenger coaches in use (thousands);
TRP = tariff charged per passenger kilometre (paise);

and all the variables are again expressed in logarithmic form.

The following observations are pertinent: (i) both NP and ALHP are sensitive to TRP and as such both are active decisions. (ii) However, it appears that the number of passengers moved might have been constrained by the available passenger coaches in use.

If the capacity constraint was effective it would indicate the presence of an excess demand from the number of passengers who wish to move. In order to ascertain this more definitively an attempt was made to estimate the percentage of excess demand on the tracks, at the prevailing tariff rates, with respect to both the number of passengers and the average length of haul.[7]

It can be observed from Figure 12.1 that over most of the sample period there was a persistent excess demand for ALHP and there were many years when the system exhibited an excess supply of NP. Hence, though an increase in PC appears to enable the railways to provide greater volume of services it was not an effective constraint on the capacity of the system to augment supply. The excess demand for length of haul should not be construed as representing the unwillingness to provide the ALHP demand by any passenger per trip. Instead, it indicates that there was a lower frequency of service because of managerial inefficiency. This phenomenon was only too evident on the railway system and explains the observed congestion on the passenger trains.

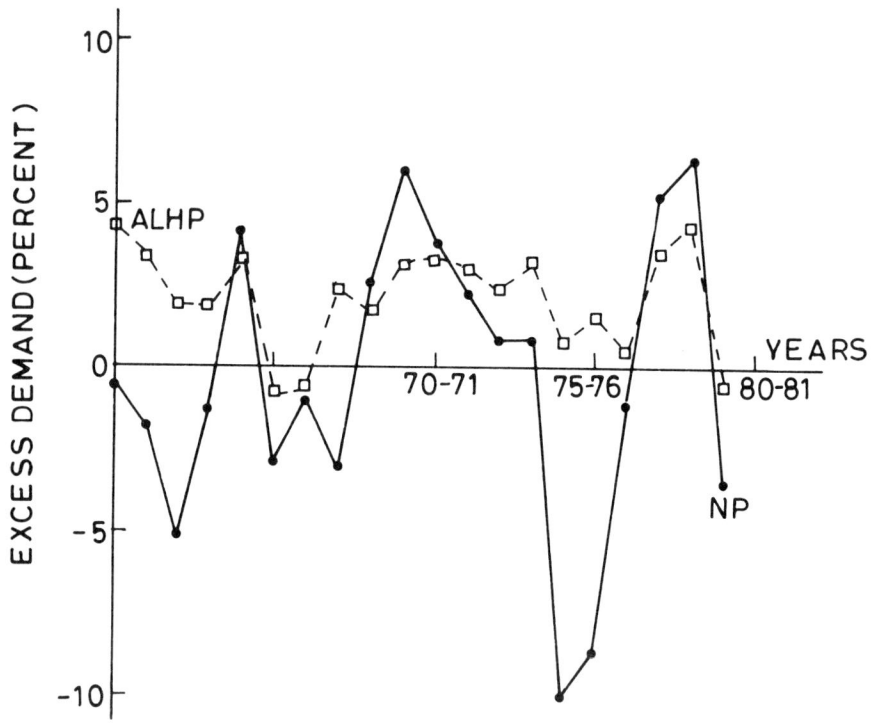

Figure 12.1 Disequilibrium in passenger services

(c) Demand responsive supply

The credibility of the above result can also be demonstrated by examining the responsiveness of railway management to the demand for the number of passengers moving and the average length of haul. The estimated equations, for the more significant of the two possible demand responsive models of supply, were as follows:

$$NP \qquad = -4.02 + 0.33AGP + 0.75INP \qquad (12.3a)$$
$$(1.73) \qquad (7.48)$$

$$ALHP \qquad = 3.76 + 0.15TRP \qquad (12.3b)$$
$$(4.52)$$

$$R^2 \text{ McElroy } = 0.92$$

From this it can be readily concluded that the management is responsive to the demand for NP while the choice of ALHP remains an active decision.

On the whole, it may be concluded that except for the recessionary years,[8] such as 1965—66 and 1966—67 and the more recent experience of 1979—80, there was no overall excess supply of passenger services. And since the capacity constraint does not appear to be limitative it can only be concluded that the management of passenger services was inefficient.

12.8 Freight flows and operating policy

Though the literature on freight movements has been quite extensive only a few behavioural models of freight movements have any micro-theoretic basis. The more commonly used gravity models have not performed satisfactorily and are not, in general, policy sensitive. The currently available behavioural models vary considerably in their content and depth of specification. However, most of these were inadequate for the analytical requirements of the present study.

The basic problem was the following: though the tariff rate for almost all commodity groups exhibit rate tapering it was felt that the quantity discounts are far more than those for increases in length of haul. Hence, the railway management, which has been conscious of revenue maximisation, considered longer hauls as an easier solution. Further, the railway system preferred longer hauls for the convenience of the management. But this policy has had the effect of reducing the volume of services supplied. Firstly, there was an increase in the turn-around time of wagons. Secondly, given the unidirectional movement of many commodities, the haulage of empty wagons has also gone up. Both these factors have had the effect of reducing the capacity of the system stated in terms of the availability of wagons. Hence, modelling the length of haul component of the demand for and supply of freight services was pertinent.

However, the consideration of the length of haul was conspicuous by its absence in most of the existing behavioural models. Such models, which take this dimension into account explicitly, had to be developed from fundamentals.

To begin with, it may be noted that

Ten kilometres of freight movement in a year = volume shipped each time X number of such shipments in a year X average length of haul per shipment.

The product of the first two factors constitutes the total demand from shippers for tons of freight moved. Hence, the quantum hauled and the length of haul will have to be considered as the major decision variables.[9] Such models of shipper decisions were reported in Rao, Sriraman and Swamy (1981 a,b). The framework is quite flexible and can take into account the effect of service quality on the demand for services as well.

These models were estimated extensively.[10] Only the aggregate results will be reported here. As in the previous section the models correspond to Zellner's SUR formulation. The estimated equations were as follows:

$$\text{LAGG} = 4.50 + 0.35 \text{QAGG} \qquad\qquad (12.4a)$$
$$(10.90)$$

$$\text{SAGG} = 1.99 + 0.57 \text{QAGG} \qquad\qquad (12.4b)$$
$$(11.82)$$

$$R^2 \text{ McElroy} = 0.93$$

where

LAGG = average length of haul in the aggregate (kms)
QAGG = index of aggregate output (obtained by dividing the nominal value of output of the mining, industrial and agricultural sectors by the unit price index)

and all the variables are expressed in logarithmic form.

The most significant observation is that the demand for rail freight services is inelastic with respect to both the tariff rate as well as the quality of service variables.[11]

The existing behavioural theories of the supply of freight services were far more inadequate. The literature is of a very recent origin and has not yet reached any steady state primarily due to the conceptual difficulties inherent in the problem specification and formulation. The major problem has been the definition of multi-service production and cost functions in the context of a transportation system.

In a recent paper Rao (1982) made an attempt to specify plausible

310

cost functions for multi-service systems and developed the theoretical implications for freight supply procedures. It was also recognised that certain constraints on the transportation network may not have any bearing on the cost structures but may nevertheless influence supply procedures. A few intuitively plausible specifications of such constraints have also been developed. These analytical formulations defined the supply procedures more firmly.

These models were estimated with rather encouraging results.[12] Only the results on the aggregate data are presented in this section.

Before proceeding further note that the major dimensions of supply which require attention are:

LAGG = average length of haul of freight movements (kms);
SAGG = originating tonnage (in million tons);
SP = average speed of freight trains (train kms per engine hour);
TL = average train load (thousand tons);
WK = wagon kilometres per wagon day;
E = empty wagon movements (percentage of empty wagon kms to total wagon kms).

Secondly, it was observed that the railway board generally sets up aggregate targets for SAGG, LAGG, and SP while leaving the other operating decisions to the zonal managers. Accordingly, the first three and the later three variables were grouped separately as simultaneous decisions of independent decision-makers. Each of the models can then be estimated by Zellner's SURE.

The estimated models of supply procedures are as follows:[13]

(a) LAGG $= 5.53 + 0.251$TAGG (12.5a)
(12.21)

SAGG $= 2.85 + 0.15$TAGG $+ 1.31$W (12.5b)
(3.65) (7.12)

SP $= 2.13 + 0.21$TAGG (12.5c)
(9.90)

R^2 McElroy $= 0.93$

(b) TL $= -1.34 + 0.37$D $+ 0.23$TAT (12.6a)
(6.66) (2.75)

WK $= 5.56 + 0.21$TAGG $- 0.78$TAT (12.6b)
(8.66) (8.61)

E $= 4.23 + 0.10$TAGG $- 0.46$TAT (12.6c)
(3.29) (3.97)

R^2 McElroy $= 0.89$

where, in addition to the variables defined earlier,

TAGG = average tariff rate per ton (Rs);
W = wagon stock in use (lakhs numbers);
D = density of freight traffic (net million ton km per route km);
TAT = turnaround time (in days).

The following salient features may now be noted: (i) both SAGG and LAGG are sensitive to TAGG and are active decisions as such. (ii) However, the tonnage moved was, to an extent, constrained by the availability of wagon stock. (iii) The railways appear to respond to increased turnaround time and congestion (represented by D as well) by increasing the train lengths. But this may be reducing empty wagon movements at the expense of the number of hours a train is on the wheels during a day. The effect of these factors and decisions on the supply potential is uncertain without further analysis.

Observe that if the capacity constraint was effective it should mean that there was generally an excess demand for the tonnage to be handled. In order to obtain a better insight an attempt was made to estimate the percentage of excess demand on the tracks, at the prevailing tariff rates, with respect to tonnage hauled and the average length of haul.

Figure 12.2 portrays the major trends. From this the following observations emerge:

(1) Consider the years during which there was an excess supply of SAGG. It was well-established by Shetty (1978) and others that around 1965 the economy experienced a substantial retrogression. As a result there was a reduction in demand which manifested itself in the form of excess supply. Hence, the excess supply from 1965 to 1970 cannot be attributed to an improvement in supply as a result of the response from the railway system. Similarly, the year 1974 recorded a quantum jump in freight rates and consequently a sharp reduction in the demand for freight services before the shippers could adequately adjust to the exogenous change. It may consequently be claimed that there was an excess demand for the quantum hauled throughout the time period under study. Hence, though an increase in wagon stock appears to enable the railways to provide greater volume of services there was a limit on the system due to managerial inefficiency.

(2) On the contrary significant excess demand for LAGG was not allowed to accumulate. Even relatively minor excess demands were corrected by adjusting the supply procedures. The excess supply of the length of haul should be interpreted as indicating a high frequency of freight train schedules.

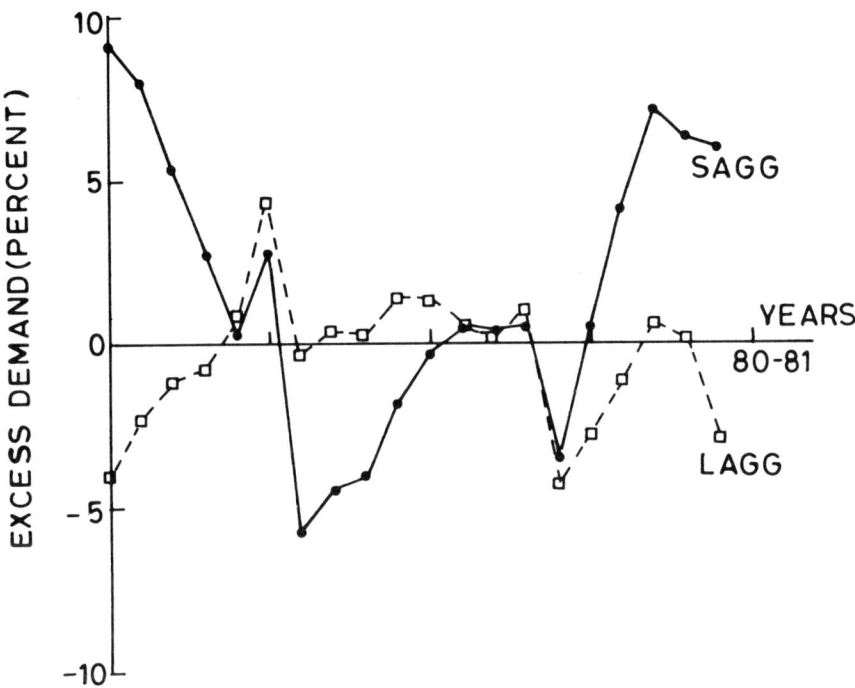

Figure 12.2   Disequilibrium in freight services

The upshot of this behaviour pattern with respect to the supply of freight services was an increase in the empty wagon movements, increased turnaround times and a reduction in the tonnage carried.

This inference would be substantially credible if it can be shown that the system was responsive to the demand for length of haul and that the quantum moved either remained responsive to the tariff rate or was constrained by the available wagon stock. Estimates of the demand responsive supply model had in fact substantiated this viewpoint. The best estimated equations were as follows:

$$LAGG = 4.52 + 0.35QAGG \qquad (12.7a)$$
$$(10.93)$$

$$SAGG = 2.97 + 0.20TAGG + 1.09W \qquad (12.7b)$$
$$(5.14) \qquad (6.28)$$

$$SP = 2.14 + 0.20TAGG \qquad (12.7c)$$
$$(9.83) \qquad (12.7)$$

R^2 McElroy $= 0.94$

On the whole, it may be concluded that though the volume of freight handled was somewhat constrained by the available wagon stock it remained an active decision. This indicates that the shortage of supply was predominantly a result of the inefficiency of the management in handling freight services. The decisions with respect to the length of haul reinforces this observation.

It was noted earlier that the demand for freight services generally manifests itself in the form of demand for wagons. Wagon demand as well as supply are a result of the choices with respect to the quantum hauled and the length of haul. As such it would be useful to provide corroborative evidence by estimating the demand for and supply of wagons. The estimated equations were:

Demand for wagons:

$$WLAGG = -1.81 + 0.99SAGG - 0.25WK, \quad \overline{R}^2 = 0.98 \qquad (12.8)$$
$$(29.66) \qquad (2.25)$$

Supply of wagons:

$$WLAGG = 0.053 + 2.17W - 0.28TAT, \quad \overline{R}^2 = 0.93 \qquad (12.9)$$
$$(10.54) \qquad (1.67)$$

where

WLAGG = wagons loaded on the aggregate (millions)

The implications of these equations for the excess demand for wagons is exhibited in Figure 12.3. Referring back to Figure 12.2 it may be noted that the years where there was an excess supply of WLAGG were exactly those for which there was an excess supply of SAGG. Excess demand for wagons has been building up since about 1975–76.

One further observation appears to be of paramount importance.

314

Throughout the estimation of the supply procedures an exogenously determined TAT was shown as the major cause of the reductions in the supply of services. This appears to occur despite the fact that both SP and WK were choices of the railways. Essentially it may be inferred that the detention times, loading and unloading policies, and so on, have been largely uncontrolled and excessive causing increased turn-around times to some extent.

Needless to say this exercise also leads us to conclude that the short run policies of the railways were inefficient.

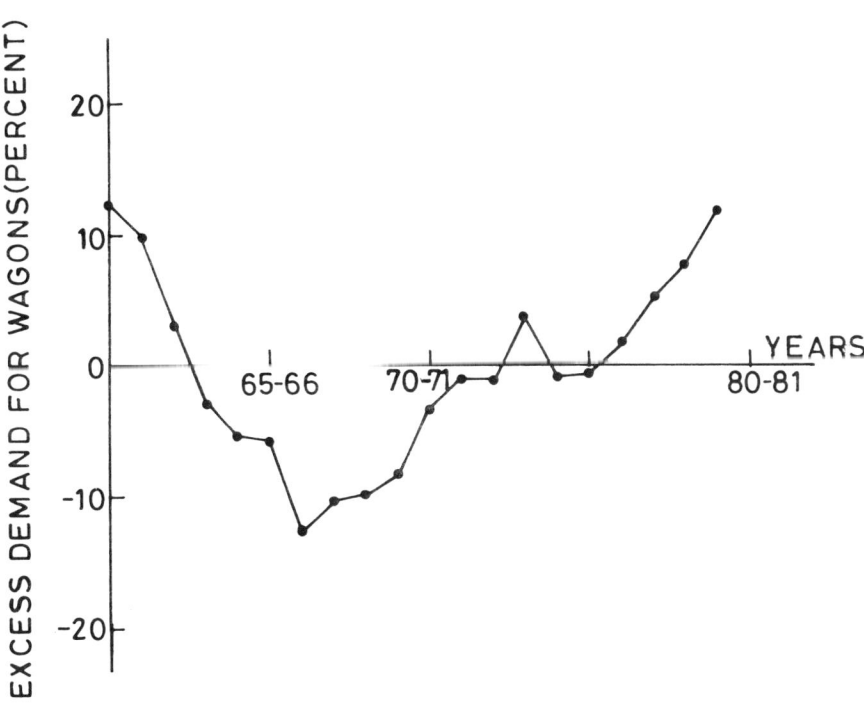

Figure 12.3   Excess demand for wagons

12.9 Efficiency of services

In the capitalist economies the forces of competition are such that supply has to be quite adaptive to the requirements. Hence, the managers of the transportation system continuously assess the major changes in the emerging demand patterns and adjust their policies accordingly. For, failure to appreciate it on time can lead to a financial disaster.

In the Indian case, the railways have a virtual monopoly for the class of services they provide. But since they maintain the character of a regulated public carrier they do have an obligation to cater to the changing demand patterns. The two basic premises from which they appear to proceed with their supply planning are (i) rail capacities, to the extent they can be utilised to increase the flow of services in the short run, are capable of generating the requisite services at lower marginal cost; and (ii) that consequently the augmentation of capacity by appropriate investments constitutes an important asset for the economy. It is therefore felt that good demand forecasts are a necessary condition to plan appropriate investments. Substantial effort has gone into demand forecasting. However, as observed earlier, none of this has any behavioural basis, and much of it has been at such an aggregate level that the real problem of identifying the bottleneck sections has not been done well.[14] Even when good investment plans have been drawn up, policy-makers at a different level did not find it possible to mobilise adequate resources to undertake capacity expansion. The upshot of this line of thinking has been the observed inadequacy of the infrastructural facilities to cater to the existing and growing demands with the currently prevailing managerial efficiency in the utilisation of facilities.

The NTPC (1980: 121) noted that 'coordination of transport policy cannot be achieved through coordinating investment and pricing decisions alone. It also requires coordination at the operational level'. They acknowledged that maintenance and improvement of operational efficiency of existing facilities can bring about an improvement in the supply of services and revenue for the railways. However, it appears that a systematic evaluation of the supply potential inherent in better management of existing facilities has not been taken up properly.

Primarily, there is no motivation from within the organisation, nor is there any external demand pressure on the managers of the system to function more efficiently. Setting up standards of performance at each level and providing adequate incentives to function efficiently has not been attempted on a systematic basis.

Even the fragmentary empirical evidence provided in this study confirms the existence of this problem. Consequently, it would be much more pertinent to concentrate on supply models and develop efficient operating policies to augment the short-run supply potential. When this is accomplished evaluation of the efficiency of possible alternative investment and operating strategies can be considered.

Developing such a demand responsive system of management may generate a possibility of the demand patterns rearranging themselves to the change in the supply position. An iterative movement toward efficiency may then be possible.

However, there are major conceptual difficulties which need analysis before this task can be taken up successfully. Firstly, the literature on supply procedures is still in its infancy. Some major conceptual developments to arrive at temporally dependent supply procedures on rather complex networks would be necessary to proceed further. Secondly, even if this is accomplished it is not altogether obvious that there can be a clear notion of what constitutes an efficient operational decision in a multi-service system. The problem is especially complex because the decisions of many of the managers at the day-to-day operational levels are not exposed to any competitive evaluation.

Needless to say the data requirements for any effective implementation of emerging conceptual refinements have to keep pace.

However essential these aspects may appear, each of them is a formidable task at the present stage of analytical development. This may be the primary source of the observed inadequacy in the management of the railway network.

Notes

1. The railway system was very well-developed during the British days. It proved useful for post-independence economic development. See, for instance, Khosla (1972).
2. Both NCAER (1964) and Lefeber and Dattachaudhari (1964) noted this. However, the railway administration did not pay attention to this in their planning process.
3. The material for this section was adapted from Poulose (1980) and NTPC (1980).
4. For a detailed review of behavioural models see Rao and Sriraman (1983).
5. Here, again, the best sources of references are Rao (1982) and Rao and Sriraman (1983).
6. Though the above description portrays the general emphasis the empirical work on passenger movements, reported in this section, is extremely limited. It will be clear from the sequel that we have been primarily working with models of freight movements.

7. Obviously the approach was to do *ex post* estimation from the available demand and supply equations.
8. See Shetty (1978) for a documentation of the structural retrogression experienced after the mid-sixties.
9. A similar interpretation is available when the supply of freight services is considered. Since the results are parallel to those of passenger movement they are not repeated in the sequel.
10. Refer to Rao and Sriraman (1983) for details.
11. This is not true for most of the commodity groups studied. Almost invariably it was observed that wagon kilometres per wagon day and turnaround time are the most important measures of the reliability of service.
12. See Rao (1983) for the empirical work on US Class I railroads and Rao and Sriraman (1983) for disaggregate commodities level estimation of freight movements on Indian Railways.
13. The results for different commodity groups exhibit diverse patterns. However, the broad trends of analysis that follow appear to carry over with minor modifications.
14. In fact, even attempts to set up disaggregate data have been very recent. The Rail India Technical and Economic Services (RITES) prepared a one-year cross-section study at the request of the NTPC recently.

References

Buse, A. (1979), 'Goodness of fit in the seemingly unrelated regression model', *Journal of Econometrics*, Vol.13, pp.108–13.
Government of India (1980), *Report of the National Transport Policy Committee*, May.
Khosla, G.S. (1972), *Railway Management in India* (Thacker, Bombay).
Lefeber, L. and Dattachaudhari, M. (1964), 'Transport policy in India', in P.N. Rosenstein-Rodan (ed.), *Pricing and Fiscal Policies* (MIT Press, Cambridge).
McElroy, M.B. (1977), 'Goodness of fit for seemingly unrelated regressions', *Journal of Econometrics*, Vol.11, pp.381–7.
NCAER (1964), *Transport Requirements of the Iron and Steel Belt* (NCAER, New Delhi).
Poulose, A.V. (1980), 'Challenges in railway administration in the coming years', *Indian Journal of Public Administration*, pp.684–96.
Rao, T.V.S.R. (1982), 'Supply of freight services on a railway network', *International Journal of Transport Economics*, Vol.9, pp.171–92.
Rao, T.V.S.R. (1983), 'Supply procedures for freight services on US class I railroads', *International Journal of Transport Economics*,

Vol. 10.

Rao, T.V.S.R. and Sriraman, S. (1983), 'Disequilibrium supply of freight services on a railway network', mimeo.

Rao, T.V.S.R., Sriraman, S. and Swamy, S.P.P. (1981a), 'Length of haul in rail freight movements', *International Journal of Transport Economics*, Vol.8, pp.89—100.

Rao, T.V.S.R., Sriraman, S. and Swamy, S.P.P. (1981b), 'A note on the length of haul in freight movements', *International Journal of Transport Economics*, Vol.8, pp.247—52.

Shetty, S.L. (1978), 'Structural retrogression in the Indian economy since mid-sixties', *Economic and Political Weekly*, pp.185—294.

Name index

Subject index

Subject Index